sexual abuse in america:
epidemic
of the 21st century

by Robert E. Freeman-Longo
and Geral T. Blanchard

Safer Society Press

© 1998 The Safer Society Press
PO Box 340 • Brandon, Vermont 05733-0340
(802) 247-3132

Editors: Janet Fabyankovic, Euan Bear

Design: Holly McGovern

ISBN: 1-448888-45-8

Library of Congress Catalog Card # 97-092306

Order # WP058

Price $20.00

Safer Society Press
PO Box 340
Brandon, Vermont 05733
United States of America

• ACKNOWLEDGMENTS •

We would like to remember, honor and thank the late Fay Honey Knopp who inspired in us the need to view all persons with a humanistic eye, and who encouraged us to be social activists for peace and the prevention of violence, and advocated our beliefs.

We would like to thank Fran Henry who as an individual, a survivor of sexual abuse, and founder of STOP IT NOW!, has also championed the idea of sexual abuse as a public health issue. Fran challenged our field to produce a book that addresses many of the issues in *Sexual Abuse In America,* and we thank her for that challenge.

We would also like to thank Joe Acinapura, Marilyn Kaskell, Chris McCarthy, Donna Reback, and the staff of the Safer Society Foundation for initial feedback on concepts and ideas for this book.

Finally, we would like to thank the following persons for reading this book and providing comments and suggestions before its publication: Dr. Fred Berlin, Stacey Edmunds, Kim English, Fran Henry, Connie Isaac, Elizabeth Karnes, Gail Ryan, Dr. Barbara Schwartz, and Joan Tabachnick.

Personal acknowledgments:

This book is dedicated to my loving wife, Pat, who has stood beside me throughout the course of my career in this field. She has offered me encouragement and support without question, while enduring many personal hardships and sacrifices to help me advance my career. This book is also dedicated to J & S, our foster children whom we hope to adopt. I hope this book will contribute to America being a safer place for them and all children in America.

I would also like to thank my family members, Earl, Shirley, Lori, Gene, & Helen, who have always shown an interest in my work, supported my work, and have always been there for me. There is nothing better than family.

I am most grateful to Dr. A. Nicholas Groth, my first mentor in this field, for his guidance and wisdom. I would also like to thank the many people who have shared their experience and knowledge with me. It is impossible to name them all in this small acknowledgment. Their willingness to share has enhanced my knowledge and ability to work in this field.

Additionally, I would like to thank the many people who have taken the time to listen to me talk about my ideas for this book and have made suggestions as well as given their opinions and support.

Finally, a heartfelt thank you to Estelle Kimberly Conner Caldwell, who always supported my work and especially encouraged my writing. Kim was a friend, colleague, co-therapist, and a writer, poet, and singer. Kim taught me a lot about her Native American heritage, respect for others regardless of their past, and respect for life. She was a powerful woman who was ever-present and ever-giving. I have done much of my writing while living on the Oregon coast where Kim and I worked together for several years. Kim passed away unexpectedly on August 11, 1997. Her presence was felt as I put some of the finishing touches on this book in Depoe Bay, Oregon, on the Oregon coast prior to attending her memorial service. Thank you Kim. You will always be remembered.

Rob Freeman-Longo

A very sincere thank you is sent to Rupert Ross, Assistant Crown Attorney for the District of Kenora, Ontario. It was Rupert who introduced me to the healing traditions being used with sexual abusers and victims in Aboriginal communities of Canada. It was also Rupert who encouraged me to "bust paradigms" and provoke healthy dialogue within the criminal justice system.

Deep appreciation and immense respect is extended to the Hollow Water First Nation of Manitoba, Canada — especially Burma Bushie — who so modestly offered their very humane approach for treating the sexual abuse epidemic. Megwetch!

Geral Blanchard

• CONTENTS •

• FOREWORD •

This book probably will frustrate many of its readers; some, undoubtedly, will find it infuriating. The authors begin by presenting a well-documented description of the contemporary spectrum of rampant sexual abuse occurring within all segments of American society. No effort has been made to sugar-coat or sanitize the information. Instead, the disturbing and discouraging facts are boldly presented. Even those desensitized by professional familiarity with this horrifying problem are likely to react by feeling disgusted or depressed.

Undaunted readers next will discover that this book is politically incorrect. For years, political activists have attempted to raise public awareness about sexual abuse and spur our legal justice system to react more stringently to sexual crimes. But now, two respected and well-credentialed professionals with decades of experience in the field of sexual offender treatment assert that our current application of the above remedies is not working. Indeed, Rob Freeman-Longo and Geral Blanchard take the position that the everyday practice of saturation media coverage and sensationalization of sexual abuse is counter-productive. They point out that playing up the horrific details of notorious cases goes far beyond informing the public, it actually panders to prurient interest. Likewise, whipping up widespread fear and outrage about highly publicized cases satisfies a voracious public appetite for excitement while simultaneously justifying ever more punitive criminal justice responses.

Widespread revulsion. Greater stigma. More rules. Stricter laws. Harsher punishments. Increased public spending to label and incarcerate known offenders. Minimal funding for community-based treatment for sexual offense behavior. Little or no support for effective public education about sexual abuse or meaningful prevention efforts. Enduring resistance to universal instruction of children and adolescents on the topics of normal human sexuality and the interpersonal skills necessary for safe and satisfying intimate relationships. Tolerance of a barrage of primetime media advertising that exploits and cheapens human sexuality for the purpose of selling an incredible array of consumer products. Official proscriptions against child pornography and commercial sexual exploitation of children within a national and international milieu of permissiveness. The authors mercilessly document all of the above and draw four unpalatable conclusions. First, our approaches to curb sexual abuse in the United States are not working. Second, our immature and hypocritical attitudes about human sexuality are contributing to the problem. Third, simple and rapid solutions are not likely to be forthcoming in the first part of the next millennium. Fourth, effective prevention of sexual abuse will require painful and unpopular changes.

What, then, are the alternatives? The authors have paid us the wry compliment of assuming that we can digest and assimilate provocative ideas as well as disturbing and sometimes contradictory information. They have taken a lead from Richard Krugman, M.D., editor of the <u>International Journal of Child Abuse and Neglect,</u> who recently suggested that physical and sexual abuse be addressed primarily as public health problems, rather than as criminal justice problems. Public health approaches include an emphasis on education and prevention, vigorous casefinding, comprehensive treatment of identified cases, and quarantining of affected individuals (abusers) who have not yet been treated or, in some cases, fail to respond to treatment and present a serious risk to the community.

The authors agree that a public health approach to sexual abuse should be tried and present detailed suggestions for primary prevention with heavy emphasis on effective public education about sexual abuse and enlightened citizen action. Further, they boldly assert that our current retributive justice approaches to sexual abuse have failed. Retributive justice emphasizes blame, shame, punishment and isolation of the offender from society. Instead, this book presents the concept of secondary prevention through restorative justice with an emphasis on accountability, treatment, making amends, and, when possible, reconciliation and reintegration of the offender into society. While acknowledging that adjustments to the paradigm will be required for its application to sexual abuse, the authors present convincing arguments for implementing a public health approach. Moreover, in the final chapter of the book, they present several examples of its application in a few North American communities.

My prediction is that this book will evoke howls of protest from those members of the professional and lay public who believe sincerely that retributive approaches to sexual abuse are the only answer. And those who are less committed to punitive and isolating responses may fear retribution from militant colleagues. I suspect that the authors and the ideas they present will be attacked and denounced. If so, that is predictable and understandable. Change itself is anxiety-provoking and labor-intensive. Changemakers always risk denouncement and retribution, especially when new ideas first are introduced. And yet, we live in a socio-cultural milieu in which significant changes have taken place in attitudes and behaviors involving formerly taboo topics. AIDS prevention can be discussed today with a greater degree of freedom than any other sexually transmitted disease throughout the course of history. In 1997, tobacco companies have acknowledged a direct association between smoking and cancer and were queuing up to pay billion dollar settlements to reimburse state governments for the cost of treating the medical sequelae. As this book is going to press, the tragic accidental death of Diana, Princess of Wales, focused the world's attention on her last crusade to raise public awareness about the savage inhumanity of the widespread use of land mines. All of these changes were unimaginable just a decade ago and inspire hope.

This is not to underestimate the magnitude of barriers to implementing the ideas in this book. Change requires hard work and dedication and all change-makers risk unpopularity. I did not particularly enjoy reading this book and put it aside several times before finishing. Parts of it, especially the chapters describing the scope of the problem of sexual abuse and current remedial approaches, are replete with mind-numbing and unpalatable information, some of which I would prefer not to know about. In the end, I found it well worth reading because it challenged me to think differently about prevention of sexual abuse and restorative justice. Now I feel stimulated to learn more and apply that knowledge in my own professional practice and as a citizen, as Rob and Geral have suggested.

I leave you with the following thoughts. Change is possible. Hope is warranted. I believe that readers who are ready to tackle a complex subject will find this book provocative, enlightening and helpful. I salute the authors for their courage in challenging societal and professional complacency and daring to suggest different approaches. Good luck to them, to their professional and lay readers, to all victims of sexual abuse, to abusers who are willing and able to change and to a society with the realizable potential of being enriched by the contributions of a greater proportion of its citizens in the 21st century!

Suzanne M. Sgroi, M.D.

Suzanne M. Sgroi, M.D. is Executive Director of New England Clinical Associates, a private office devoted to treatment, education and research for problems associated with child sexual abuse. She also is the director of the Saint Joseph College Institute for Child Sexual Abuse Intervention, the oldest continuously-operating educational program of its kind in the United States. Dr. Sgroi probably is best known as the editor and principal author of *Handbook of Clinical Intervention in Child Abuse,* Lexington Books, 1982. This award winning volume has been used widely as a textbook and practice manual for child sexual abuse intervention by clinicians, child protective services staff, law enforcement and court personnel, and educators. An eagerly awaited revised edition of the *Handbook* will appear in 1998.

• INTRODUCTION •

There are hundreds or even thousands of books, professional journals, and training events offered throughout the United States and abroad that provide accurate and usually well researched information for professionals who 1) work in the sexual abuse field, 2) want to learn about criminal sexual abuse or sexual behavior problems, and/or 3) are interested in learning about sexual abusers and the victims of sexual abuse.

The citizens of America, however, rely almost exclusively on the news and "infotainment" media to inform them about current issues and provide informed perspectives. While some of the material presented by these media regarding sexual abuse is accurate and informative, more often than not the popular media's focus on sexual abuse is 1) on a horrific case which is <u>not</u> typical but gives an impression that it <u>is</u> typical, 2) biased toward one side or another of a particular issue (for example, punishment versus treatment of sexual offenders), 3) lacking in detail and explanations that educate, and 4) not representative of the state-of-the-art knowledge. Therefore, the information does not adequately or accurately educate readers, listeners, and viewers about this serious social epidemic.

In addition to the problem of criminal sexual abuse, there are aspects of our culture that we believe contribute to the sexual abuse problem and unhealthy sexual attitudes in America. As authors we believe, and many of our colleagues concur, that there are aspects of the American culture and lifestyle that perpetuate or sustain the very problem that most Americans want to resolve. These sustaining factors include the media, the sex-for-sale industry, trends in sexual behavior, and the sexual attitudes and interests that support the abuse of human sexuality. As a result of these sustainers, sexual abuse continues to be a growing problem in the United States and it has now been labeled as a "silent epidemic" by the American Medical Association.

As we wrote this book, we were repeatedly shocked and appalled at the information we were finding. In addition to the issues related to sexual abuse, we learned about the destructive and unhealthy ways that the media and the sex-for-sale industries were influencing and/or altering Americans' views and understanding of human sexuality. We were equally as shocked at the narrow responses by the criminal justice system and political policy and decision makers to seek increasing degrees of punishment. We believe these systems are actually driving the sexual abuse problem "underground" in the name of prevention and community safety.

Human sexual behavior plays a critical role in our lives. It is normal and natural to have sexual feelings and desires. Healthy human sexual behavior is a benevolent act, a gift of intimate expression that perpetuates our species. When sexual behavior is hurtful, destructive, or has a serious negative emotional or physical impact on others or ourselves, a sexual behavior problem is apparent. In the extreme, sexual behavior problems become abusive, sometimes dangerous to oneself or others and, at the far end of the continuum, potentially lethal.

Sexual abuse is a complex problem for which there are no simple solutions. Criminal sexual abuse cannot be wished away by denial or legislated away. With criminal sexual abuse cases growing in number each year, it is evident that the punishment model in current and predominant use is not an effective deterrent to criminal sexual behavior.

In this book we begin to discuss the sex-for-sale industry's deviations from what most people consider to be healthy human sexual behavior. We explore the way our culture is abusing human sexuality. To help current and future generations develop healthy beliefs, attitudes, morals, and behaviors regarding human sexuality and human sexual behavior, we must develop appropriate channels through which we can educate the public about unhealthy and healthy sexual behavior. This book is one effort to begin that dialogue.

Sexual Abuse In America explores the problem of criminal sexual abuse in terms of those aspects of our culture and society that continuously perpetuate the misuse of human sexuality and sexual behavior problems (including sexual crimes). Our book also examines how we believe Americans tend to misuse and abuse human sexuality. We describe some of America's sexual obsessions, attitudes, and "sexploitations," and explain how these contribute to the sexual abuse epidemic. *Sexual Abuse In America* provides a candid and documented look at sexual abuse, explores some reasons for its prevalence, and proposes solutions for the twenty-first century to an epidemic social problem.

Finally, *Sexual Abuse In America* encourages a paradigm shift in addressing the sexual abuse problem. We describe how leading national organizations and agencies have begun to look beyond the criminal aspects of sexual abuse and are now addressing sexual abuse as a public health issue. We believe embracing a public health perspective today is the best way to prevent sexual abuse tomorrow.

Rob Freeman-Longo
Brandon, Vermont

Geral Blanchard
Sheridan, Wyoming

Identifying violence as a public health issue is a relatively new idea. Traditionally, when confronted by the circumstances of violence, the health professionals have deferred to the criminal justice system. Over the years we've tacitly and, I believe, mistakenly agreed that violence was the exclusive province of the police, the courts, and the penal system. To be sure, those agents of public safety and justice have served us well. But when we ask them to concentrate more on the prevention of violence and to provide additional services for victims, we may begin to burden the criminal justice system beyond reason. At that point, the professionals of medicine, nursing, and the health-related social services must come forward and recognize violence as their issue, also, one which profoundly affects the public health ... Henry David Thoreau in his book, "Walden," wrote: "It is characteristic of wisdom not to do desperate things." I think we have worked with patience and wisdom. And hopefully the time of desperation is over.

– C. Everett Koop, MD, ScD
  Surgeon General, 1985

Opening Statements

Throughout our lives we are confronted with information that challenges our conventional ways of thinking. For example, our changing attitudes about "second-hand smoke" have changed public policy regarding smoking in public places. Public education has also helped Americans understand that AIDS is not a "homosexual disease," but one that can infect anyone through a variety of sexual behaviors, intravenous drug use, and accidental exposure.

Hardly a week goes by without hearing a newscast about a sensational sex crime and the sexual abuse problem in America. The public reads, sees, and hears about high profile, sensationalized sex crimes, but seldom hears about the sexual abuse happening daily in every community in America. While some people are tired of hearing about it, others are frustrated with this problem and want to see it remedied. Some people are looking for simple answers and quick fixes for the sexual abuse problem like public notification and chemical castration, but few are willing to take a different approach to preventing this silent epidemic. Most Americans want to see the sexual abuse problem remedied, but don't know what to do to change the problem. Although many Americans are tired of turning to government to solve society's ails, they continue resorting to punishment - the cornerstone of the criminal justice model - as a solution, instead of prevention, which is the foundation of a public health model.

Legislators and the public continue to repeatedly turn to the criminal justice system to solve the violence problem in America. However, the series of tougher laws passed each year to address violence and to guide the criminal justice system do not address the underlying cause(s) of violence and, in particular, sexual abuse. The criminal justice system's responsibility is to punish illegal behavior, not to prevent the problem in the first place. The high incidence of sexual abuse suggests that a criminal justice model alone has not prevented sexual abuse from occurring.

The key to preventing sexual abuse is to shift paradigms. In addition to viewing sexual abuse as a criminal justice issue, we must also view it as a serious public health problem and a preventable social problem.

American institutions often turn to scare tactics, such as the enactment of tougher laws with more severe penalties in order to prevent people from behaving in a particular fashion, or to deter criminal behavior. Kim, McLeod, and Shantzis state that the education information movement of the 1960's and the scare tactics of the early 1970's slowly evolved to more humanistic and effective efforts that dominated the mid- to late-1970's.[1] In the 1980's and

---

[1] Kim, S., McLeod, J. and Shantzis, C. "An outcome evaluation of refusal skills as a drug abuse prevention strategy." Journal of Drug Education 19 (1989): 363-371.

1990's, we have turned back to developing laws with harsh sanctions and punishing criminals to prevent and reduce crime. So popular is new legislation around the country to build more prisons, that if "incarceration rates remain the same, an estimated one out of every 20 persons will serve time in a prison during his or her lifetime," according to a study by the Bureau of Justice Statistics.[2] However, the demand for more prisons tells us crime must be increasing. Therefore, it seems obvious that scare tactics, laws aimed at severely punishing criminals, and threats of incarceration, do not work at deterring crime or violent criminal behavior.

Unfortunately, we have never heard an American president talk about sexual abuse as a serious health or social problem in America. We believe this is because there is a level of denial in society concerning sexual abuse. The American culture has not accepted that sexual abuse and the abuse of sexuality are extensive and pervasive problems of our modern American lifestyle.

In the chapters that follow, we will discuss why we believe Americans, the media, and politicians have not been ready to look at sexual abuse from a different perspective, and why as concerned citizens the public has not been ready to shift paradigms (how we think about this issue). We believe that historically Americans have maintained a puritanical perspective regarding human sexuality, and therefore, the American culture has held a narrow perspective regarding sexual abuse.[3] This perspective has been slowly countered by a growing number of people who are willing to alter traditional sexual values in ways that may be damaging to the concept of what is healthy human sexuality. These and other issues related to how America addresses human sexuality may be preventing public and political opinion from making a necessary change in how we address sexual abuse.

The Complexities of Sexual Abuse

Sexual abuse is more than just a criminal justice issue. It is a social issue, a religious issue, an economic issue, an emotional issue, a political issue, a spiritual issue, a health issue, an educational issue, a racial issue, a gender issue, and more. In general, human sexuality is no different. Human sexuality and sexual behavior are complex aspects of human behavior. Therefore, we must

---

[2] "1 out of 20 persons expected to serve prison time." Criminal Justice Newsletter. March 1997, 28(6), p. 2.

[3] America was built upon the "King's Law" and puritanical justice. In present day legislative and judicial processes, legislative bodies and American courts still maintain a puritanical environment. The founders of our jurisprudence came from a country where the state and the church were one and the same, and while our constitution established a separation, the attitudes and customs of a church-allied state prevailed when laws were made.

address sexual abuse as a multifaceted problem for which there is no singular or simple solution. Preventing sexual abuse is virtually impossible if we view it narrowly and exclusively as a criminal justice issue.

The typical response of tougher laws with stiffer sanctions has failed to stem the tide of sexual abuse.[4,5] In fact some of these laws are driving the sexual abuse problem underground. Extremely punitive measures cause children to hesitate to report, or later to recant reports, because "Daddy" or "Uncle Joe" would go to jail for a very long time. Abusers who agonize over what they are doing are much less likely to report themselves to get help or confess when confronted when they know they are facing years in prison, in many cases without treatment, with many years on parole and perhaps with their names and faces posted all over any neighborhood where they might find a place to live. The result of this underground existence is a false statistic that sex crimes are decreasing.[6] In quelling our fears, we have not taken the time to recognize that the increasing numbers of sexual crimes is suggesting that our laws have not worked, nor have more stringent penalties served as a deterrent.

In order to prevent sexual abuse, we believe America must approach this serious social issue as a public health problem requiring responsible decision making and solutions. The nation's response should be based upon the most current data and research available. Addressing sexual abuse solely as a criminal justice issue may not be effective or the most responsible approach, because punishment alone does not reduce the incidence of sexual abuse and other forms of violence. There is a vast amount of sexual abuse in the American culture because sexual abuse reaches well beyond the criminal sexual behaviors we hear about most often. Criminal sexual abuse is illegal; however, there are aspects of our culture, our lifestyle, and our sexual interests and behaviors that are abusive of human sexuality. Yet in many instances these factors contribute to the sexual abuse problem, although they are perfectly legal.

Americans place a high value on sexuality. They glamorize a variety of sexual behavior through books, special newscasts, movies, and magazines. Entertainment media including books, major motion pictures, and made-for-television specials have focused on sexual themes ranging from the criminally violent (The Stranger Beside Me [Theodore Bundy], The Adam Walsh Story),

---

[4] Recent crime statistics suggest a decrease in reported rapes; however, researchers suggest that this decrease is a reflection of the aging of the baby boom population and not necessarily a decrease in overall incidence of rape. Butterfield, F. "Reports of Rape Decrease Sharply." The Rutland [VT] Daily Herald, 3 Feb. 1997: 1.

[5] Effective management of sex offenders in the community. Offender Programs Report. 1 (1) May/June, 1997: 1.

[6] Kerry Hinkle from the Governor's office in South Carolina states that there has been an increase in plea bargaining of juvenile sexual offenses to lessor crimes (nonsexual crimes), to avoid being labeled as sexual offenders, and to avoid mandates of public notification laws. Personal communication February 18, 1997.

to the bizarre (the Bobbit case), to the sex-for-sale industries (Pretty Woman, Striptease, The Mayflower Madam). We find it alarming that on the one hand people are appalled by sexual abuse and sexual violence, but on the other they spend billions of dollars on entertainment that is often abusive and distorts traditional values regarding human sexuality.

People use sex and sexual terms in a variety of ways. They tell sexual jokes; they use sex in advertisements to sell products; they describe inanimate objects (i.e., cars) as "sexy." They use sexual terms to swear and put others down. They describe children with sexual messages (e.g., "He's gonna be a ladies' man," or the National Tiny Miss Beauty Contests[7]). They use children in sexual poses to sell products and clothing. Sex is used as a theme in greeting cards, to describe individual appearance ("sexy hairdos," "sexy clothes"), and in the media, and especially television, as entertainment. References to sex are everywhere.

Many television programs make at least one reference to sex during each episode. From daytime soap operas to prime-time evening programs and sitcoms, sexual comments and behaviors flourish on television to the point that many people are now criticizing this emphasis on sex. A recent study by the Kaiser Family Foundation reported that during prime time television (8 to 9 pm), most programs have sexual content, and that more children watch TV during this time period than on Saturday morning or weekday afternoons.[8] The study reports that:

On any given evening, nearly six million children between the ages of 2 and 11 watch ABC, CBS, NBC or FOX during the so-called "family hour."

- TV can influence children's attitudes and behavior.
- 3 of 4 family-hour programs on TV contain some sexual content; 61% contain sexual behavior, averaging 8.5 sexual interactions per hour, of which 1/3 include talk about sex, and 2/3 involve physical behavior.
- Much of the sexual content on the air does not "go over their [the children's] heads," including jokes and innuendo.
- Overall, the vast majority of sexual content in family hour is not accompanied by any messages about sexual risks or responsibilities.
- The average child watches 3-4 hours of television per day.

---

[7] Associated Press. "Family's expert: Parents didn't kill girl." Rutland [VT] Daily Herald, 29 Jan. 1997: 14. The story of JonBenet Ramsey is a classic example of how Americans often place children in roles and positions that sexualize them by dressing them up as sensual adults for entertainment purposes.

[8] News Release. New study finds increase in sexual content on TV's family hour. Sex, Kids, and the Family Hour: A Three Part Study. The Kaiser Family Foundation. 11 Dec 1996.

Recently, the TV-industry developed a rating system for television programs. There are many critics of this new system, some who believe that the system is inadequate because it does not specify or flag excessive violence, sexual content, or language that may be of concern to parents or others who are caretakers of children.[9] Vicky Rideout, a director of Children Now in Oakland, California notes:

> An age-based system doesn't tell you why a program is appropriate or inappropriate for an age group ... There are hundreds and thousands of unplanned pregnancies and millions of cases of sexually transmitted diseases occurring among teenagers every year ... With statistics like these, all of us need to pay attention to the messages we're sending to kids about sex.[10]

According to the American Academy of Pediatrics, "By age 18, the average teen is estimated to have spent more time in front of the tube than in front of a classroom teacher. That same teen will see an estimated 14,000 sexual references and innuendoes per year on television, yet only 150 references to sexual responsibility, abstinence, or contraception."[11]

When viewers', listeners', and readers' sexual behavior and outlets are healthy and not problematic, the continuous sexual titillation and subsequent sexual awareness may have little negative impact. However, when one's sexual behavior and outlets are problematic, abusive, or criminal, the impact may support and increase sexual problems. To the victims of sexual abuse, unpleasant memories may be triggered by continuous exposure to sexual materials. For children who are learning about their own sexuality, constant exposure may be confusing or troubling.

Is the Media Really the Message?

The media plays a critical role in the lives of Americans. The media keeps us in touch with the world and updates us on important issues. In a word, it educates us. Unfortunately, the public is growing increasingly disenchanted with the news media. Americans rely on the news to keep informed. However, according to a national survey conducted by the Roper Center in conjunction with the Newseum, Americans have concerns about who presents the news, and question whether what we hear is inaccurate, biased, superficial, and

---

[9] "TV rating system panned by critics." Rutland [VT] Daily Herald, 20 Dec. 1996: 13.

[10] Sneers, outrage hit new TV rating system Youth Today: The Newspaper on Youth Work, 6(1) Jan/Feb. 1997: 39.

[11] Pediatricians say TV ratings should label content, not viewers' age. The Brown University Child and Adolescent Behavior Letter, 13(3), March 1997:5.

sensationalized.[12] The January 1997 survey of 1500 individuals from across the United States found the following:

- 64% think the news is too sensationalized.

- 64% think reporters spend too much time offering their own opinions.

- 60% think reporters too often quote sources whose names are not given in news stories.

- 52% think the news is biased.

Judith Valente, who reports on the survey in Parade Magazine,[13] notes,

> While 34% of those surveyed said that 'freedom of the press should be protected under all circumstances,' 65% agreed that 'there are times when the press should not be allowed to publish or broadcast certain things.' ... At the same time, 80% said that the press meaning newspapers, magazines, TV and radio was crucial to the functioning of a free society. And 71% said the news was useful in helping them make practical decisions in their lives, in such matters as investing, voting, health and education.

Disagreement exists about who influences whom and the source of public opinion. The media would have Americans believe they simply report the views of the public, and that they often gear their news toward representing mainstream public views and opinions. The other side of this argument is that the media strongly sways, shapes, and influences public opinion. This is especially true with issues about which the public has little knowledge or first hand experience. Sexual abuse is one of these issues.

Several organizations and foundations collectively published a report, MEDIA MATTERS: The Institute on News and Social Problems.[14] The report cites several books and articles written about the media and its influence on the public. In Media Matters, a book called News That Matters is reviewed and summarized. In the review, the authors of News are quoted as follows:

> By attending to some problems and ignoring others, television news shapes the American public's political priorities. ... News argues that television not only 'strengthen(s) or reinforce(s) the

---

[12] Valente, J. (1997, March 2). "Do you believe what news people tell you?" Parade Magazine. 2 Mar. 1997: 4-6.

[13] Ibid.

[14] News That Matters: Television and American Opinion by Shanto Iyengar and Donald Kinder (University of Chicago Press, 1987). Reviewed in Media Matters: The Institute on News and Social Problems. Sponsored by W. K. Kellogg Foundation, Benton Foundation, Advocacy Institute, Berkeley Media Studies Group, and Brandeis University. This paper was prepared for an institute titled Media Matters: The Institute on News and Social Problems held at Brandeis University September 29 and 30, 1995.

public's existing beliefs and opinions,' but is also 'stunningly successful in telling Americans what to think about.'

Responsible, credible sexual abuse information and education are potentially disseminated in one of four ways. First is written information. However, if you go into any bookstore, you will find few books written for the average citizen about sexual abuse. Most publications regarding sexual abuse are self-help books written for victims of sexual abuse, or treatment-oriented publications written for professional therapists and clinicians, and academicians/researchers. Journals and academic publications are also directed at professionals. Legislators, policy makers, reporters, and the general public are not likely to keep up with the professional literature.

The second source of good information on sexual abuse includes professional training events, seminars, workshops, or educational systems. These educational formats are also primarily directed at and accessible to professionals rather than the layperson. Legislators, policy makers, reporters, and the general public seldom attend such training events.

The third source includes self-help groups, advocacy organizations, public education workshops (most of which are for children), and other grassroots efforts.

The fourth potential source of accurate, credible sexual abuse information - the various forms of media, including television, radio, newspapers, and magazines - is the most likely to influence the thinking and knowledge of the public and legislators. Yet the electronic news media's method of reporting often requires reporters to reduce information to "sound bytes," brief, highly charged statements about the issue being investigated. Too often there is little effort or ability with sound bytes in a three-minute news clip, or even in a one-hour documentary, to accurately educate and inform viewers and listeners about the vastness and complexity of the sexual abuse problem in America. There is simply too much information to tell in too little time, often resulting in polarized answers (right vs. wrong) being given for easy understanding. These simplistic newscasts often lose the complexity of the issue being addressed. In fact, some research has concluded that:

> ... [s]ince the nightly news is too brief to treat fully the complexity of modern politics, too visual to present effectively most events, and too entertainment-minded to tell viewers much worth knowing, most network newscasts are neither very educational nor very powerful communicators.[15]

[15] Ibid.

While written forms of media can provide more information, space limitations and the need to sell papers via sensationalized headlines that satisfy advertisers determine what information is printed and how detailed the news item will be. When the story "needs to get out" to create a scoop, or even just to keep up with competitors, there's greater potential for mistakes and individual bias.

The media hurls statistics about sexual abuse at the American public on a regular basis. However, for most people, understanding statistics like the familiar "one in five children risk sexual abuse before they reach eighteen years of age," is difficult. For many, it is inconceivable that one in three women risks being raped or sexually abused during her lifetime.[16] The fact that there are 234,000 people in the United States correctional system charged with sexual crimes[17] creates public panic, not understanding. The public's antipathy toward crime and its hatred of criminals distracts us from hearing that more than 350,000 men are raped or sexually abused in American jails and prisons each year.[18] These data and statistics are more likely to instill fear and confusion, not knowledge, in the minds of Americans.

Because we typically view sexual abuse in the context of crime and the criminal justice system, people get angry, become fearful, and react quickly and harshly to the problem by enacting new and more stringent laws. As a result, once the criminal justice system has taken action, citizens put the information on the back burner of their mind — out of sight, out of mind. Consequently, this fear and anger, not factual information, shapes how we react to sexual abuse as a social issue.

As long as the media addresses sexual abuse from a criminal justice perspective, sensational headlines about a notorious sex offender will continue to instill fear and anger in the American public regarding sexual abuse. These horrific, emotionally charged headlines often leave people with a sense of hopelessness and helplessness in addressing the problem. It is no wonder that citizens feel the need to punish the criminal; while at the same time we are reluctant to learn the more complex facts that would give us a more complete picture about the nature of sexual abuse prevention and treatment.

---

[16] Martinez, Jeri. Vermont Coalition Against Domestic Violence. Montpelier, Vermont. Personal communication January 21, 1997.

[17] Laurie Robinson, Assistant Attorney General, U.S. Department of Justice. Keynote Address. National Summit: Promoting Public Safety Through the Effective Management of Sex Offenders in the Community. Department of Justice. Washington, D.C. (1996, November 24-26).

[18] Struckman-Johnson, C., Struckman-Johnson, D., Rucker, L., Bumby, K., and Donaldson, S. "Sexual coercion reported by men and women in prison." The Journal of Sex Research, 33(1), (1996): 67-76.

Paving the Way for a Paradigm Shift

The Centers for Disease Control and Prevention (CDC), the federal agency in the United States responsible for the prevention of health problems, has been working on violence prevention for more than 12 years. The CDC's focus has been on changing the way people think about preventing violence.[19] The CDC's effort to address violence in America has led to violence being recognized as a public health problem.

The World Health Assembly (WHA) also considers violence and its prevention as a public health priority. WHA has declared that violence is a leading worldwide public health problem, and "requests the Director-General, within available resources, to initiate public health activities to address the problem of violence that will ... promote activities to tackle this problem at both international and country levels including steps to promote greater intersectoral involvement in the prevention and management of violence and promote research on violence as a priority for public health research."[20]

The American Psychological Association (APA) has also declared violence to be a serious societal problem and recognizes the need for addressing the violence problem from a different perspective. The APA notes:

> "Societal attitudes and practices regarding violence also have an influence on the risk of family violence ... Research has shown that heavy viewing of violence on TV by children increases aggressive behaviors, and those behaviors persist into adulthood ... There is general agreement that prevention efforts are needed to address the society conditions that contribute to family violence ... and to change the environment that promotes the use of violence."[21]

Since 1992 Fran Henry, founder and president of STOP IT NOW!, has consistently encouraged the public and professionals working in the sexual abuse field to look at sexual abuse as a public health issue. STOP IT NOW! argues that the widespread incidence of abuse and abusive behavior calls for a public health response.[22] (Her innovative approach to sexual abuse prevention, a media and outreach campaign to abusers and those who know them, is discussed in Chapter Eleven).

---

[19] Friday, J. C. "Violence Prevention and Public Health: The CDC Approach." Atlanta Medicine, 68(2), Spring 1994: 41-44.

[20] Forty-Ninth World Health Assembly, Sixth plenary meeting. Agenda item 30.2. Prevention of Violence: Public Health Priority. May 25, 1996.

[21] American Psychological Association. Violence and the Family: Report of the American Psychological Association Presidential Task-Force on Violence and the Family (1996): v-viii. Washington, DC.

[22] Henry, F. Public Health, Public Policy, and Sexual Abuse. [Keynote Address] 15th Annual Research & Treatment Conference. Association for the Treatment of Sexual Abusers. Chicago. (1996, November 16).

On November 6, 1995, the American Medical Association (AMA) prepared a statement regarding violence and sexual assault in America.[23] The AMA, calling sexual assault a public health problem, labeled sexual assault as a "silent-violent epidemic in the United States today."

The AMA's recent announcement is a small but significant breakthrough for America because for the first time a credible, well-recognized, professional organization has labeled sexual abuse as something other than a crime. This determination, unbeknownst to many Americans, has opened the door to reducing sexual abuse in America. If Americans are serious about preventing sexual abuse, they must challenge traditional thinking about sexual abuse and question conventional wisdom and legislative solutions.

The AMA states, "Society as a whole must become better informed about the problems and realities of sexual assault. Special attention must be directed to correcting misconceptions and myths about rape and sexual assault ... Now is the time for us to begin changing the way we think about sexual abuse."[24] The effort by the AMA to address violence and sexual abuse as public health problems are a wake-up call to America. They are paving the way for America to turn the corner in preventing violence, and specifically sexual abuse and sexual violence. As James A. Mercy and his colleagues wrote:

> "A new vision for how Americans can work together to prevent the epidemic of violence now raging in our society has emerged from the public health community ... Public health seeks to empower people and their communities to see violence not as an inevitable consequence of modern life but as a problem that can be understood and changed."[25]

The Need for Accurate Information and Public Education

The authors' combined professional experience of forty-five years working in the sexual abuse field as clinicians, consultants, trainers, and authors, in addition to our extensive work with the media in relation to these issues, prompted us to write this book. We have found that outside of very few exceptional newspaper and magazine articles, and radio and television shows, there is little written information directed to the American public regarding this social issue. The little bits and pieces of information given to the public

---

[23] American Medical Association. Sexual assault in America. [Press release]. (1995, November 6).

[24] Ibid.

[25] Mercy, J. A., Rosenberg, M. L., Powell, K. E., Broome, C. V., and Roper, W. L. Public health policy for preventing violence. Winter 1993. Health Affairs Special Issue: Violence and the public's health. Published quarterly by Project Hope. Bethesda, MD. Winter 1993 12(4): .7-30.

about sexual abuse often provide an incomplete and inaccurate focus on a particular position or a single heinous case. They lack information about what action individuals should take to help prevent sexual abuse.

Most important, the cases that make national news and headlines do not represent the average sexual abuse case in America. The sexual abuse that happens each day in America is not considered sensational or newsworthy. It does not merit a front page story. Therefore, the public's image of what sexual abuse is and who is a sexual abuser is usually based upon extreme cases that account for less than one half of 1% of sexual abuse crimes in America. Unfortunately, these unique cases are often the misguided catalyst for developing new legislation to address sexual abuse, that result in changing public policy.[26] Changing public opinion when the sources of information for public education are not comprehensive and/or representative of the problem is difficult. Misinformation compromises our ability to create laws that will be effective in reducing sexual abuse.

We agree with the CDC, the AMA, the WHA, and the APA. To address the sexual abuse problem in America, and prevent sexual abuse in the future, Americans must change the way they think about sexual abuse. For years our profession has been talking about sexual abuse as a serious public health issue and refers to sexual abuse as an epidemic. Unfortunately, calling sexual abuse a public health problem is an approach that is seldom recognized, explored or perceived as anything but rhetoric by the media.[27] Yet, the media strongly influences the political climate and public opinion of our country.

Sexual abuse affects the lives of many people. Some have been victims of sexual abuse or attempted acts of sexual abuse. Others know someone who has been sexually abused. If you are a woman, you may have concerns regarding your sexual safety. If you are a parent, you are probably more concerned today about your child's safety than at any other time. In the absence of accurate information, what we hear about sexual abuse can seem overwhelming.

We wrote *Sexual Abuse in America* to inform readers about one of the most serious social issues of our time. *Sexual Abuse in America* provides information that addresses critical issues regarding sexual abuse and the abuses of human sexuality, and new ways of thinking about how Americans can prevent this abuse. We believe that if we stimulate new ways of thinking about how Americans can prevent sexual abuse, innovative prevention efforts can result.[28]

---

[26] Megan's Law, a federal law requiring states to use public notification of sexual offender release into the community, is an example of how a single tragic incident can change public policy.

[27] Our experience with the written media has been such that the use of terms such as "epidemic" and "public health problem" are seldom used in the published article or as quotations, regardless of how many times we mention these phrases during media interviews.

[28] The authors are grateful to STOP IT NOW!, for insight and references on the link between sexual abuse and public health.

Knowledge is power. We firmly believe that Americans can make proactive, prosocial decisions regarding sexual abuse prevention when the media and other sources give them accurate information. Accurate and complete information is the best building block for knowledge. It is the road to change. It is the foundation for building public policy, especially on an issue this complex and multifaceted.

About This Book

In *Sexual Abuse in America,* we invite you to look at sexual abuse from a new perspective. This new cultural point of view suggests that Americans abuse human sexuality. In a sense we are obsessed with its consumption - in much the same way many Americans abuse alcohol, over-the-counter medications, prescription medications, and illegal drugs. We believe that many Americans abuse sexuality to the point it becomes an unhealthy lifestyle or an addiction. In its extreme, the abuse of sexuality takes form in the sexual abuse of others, including children. For some people, the sexual attraction to children can be due to qualitative differences in their sexual makeup.

Sexual abuse is defined differently depending upon the source. Legal definitions often differ from clinical, medical, mental health, or personal definitions. In Chapter Two, we define sexual abuse from a public health perspective and describe the various types of criminal sexual abuse. We discuss the more common forms of sexual abuse including child sexual abuse, rape, marital rape, date rape, and the paraphilias, and we review the typologies of sexual abusers. Since men perpetrate most sexual abuse, we refer to the abuser with terms that reflect the male gender. However, we acknowledge that there is a growing number of teen and adult females who perpetrate sexual abuse.

In Chapter Three, we examine the theories about sexual abuse, and the small but growing body of scientific knowledge regarding its cause and development. We review the current thinking about why people sexually abuse others, and the aspects of our culture that we believe sustain sexual abuse in the American lifestyle. One part of the discussion explains sexual addiction and the cycle of sexual abuse. In this chapter we also address America's interest in, and in some cases obsession with, sex and how that obsession contributes to illegal sexual abuse and other forms of potentially damaging and traumatic sexual behavior. We review why we believe the public's obsession with human sexuality has an impact on criminal sexual abuse and human sexuality.

Among various aspects of our culture that support and encourage sexual abuse in America are organizations that promote sex between children and adults, and trends that may well be challenging traditional views and opinions about what constitutes "traditional and healthy" sexual behavior. In Chapter

Four, we discuss these organizations and trends that may be broadening the repertoire of behaviors we consider acceptable sexual practices between consenting adults. Some of these trends have begun to "distort" human sexuality. In the extreme, some trends self-described as "consenting adult sexual relations" mimic criminal sexual behavior. Others have accidentally taken the lives of individuals who have attempted to heighten their sexual experiences.

In Chapter Five, we will address the extent of criminal sexual abuse and sexual behavior problems within certain cultural subgroups. The clergy, the military, treatment professionals, and others are increasingly becoming the focus of national news stories that are challenging the stereotype image of sexual abusers. In Chapter Five, we also look at the issue of sexual harassment, sexual misconduct by persons in professional positions of power, and how sexual abuse has become pervasive and widespread in our society.

Chapter Six contains a review of the "sex for sale" industry. We discuss its role in contributing to sexual abuse. Pornography, prostitution, sex in the cinema, adult entertainment and sex shows, cyberporn, and 900 telephone numbers all contribute to a multi-billion dollar sex entertainment industry. Although many people claim to be repulsed by such material, a significant portion of our society is continuously consuming the products of this industry, therefore keeping it alive.

Sexual abuse has become a political football. Chapter Seven examines the legal system and the current legislation being considered to stop sexual abuse. While legislation to punish sexual offenders has been and remains trendy, the politics of sexual abuse prevention are appalling. In the name of prevention, state and federal politicians are passing laws that are untested and expensive. We discuss why we believe these laws may ultimately fail and in some cases contribute to making the problem worse.

In Chapter Eight, we look at the role of the media and how the various forms of media attempt to educate, but more often may misinform the public about sexual abuse. Sensationalized stories shape public opinion and influence attitudes, leaving people without the tools necessary to best address the sexual abuse problem we are experiencing. Because the media is such a powerful force in society, it can influence the public's view about what is and is not important.

References to human sexuality and sexual abuse in daily life, especially in the media, have become so commonplace that many of us have little awareness that our sexuality may be being negatively affected on a regular basis. This continuous influence on our sexuality keeps people sexually charged, our sexual awareness heightened, and sometimes stimulated to the point that human sexuality has become a focal point of our lifestyle. Does the media reflect the interests of America in regard to human sexual behavior, or does the media direct America's sexual interests? These issues and others impacted by the media are discussed and solutions proposed.

Sexual abuse occurs at tremendous personal and public costs to Americans. Besides the obvious direct impact areas, possible trauma, and costs associated with treating the victims of sexual crimes, there are many other costs not often taken into account when looking at the impact of this social problem. In Chapter Nine, we discuss the numerous and often extensive costs of sexual abuse to individuals and society. This chapter outlines the impact of sexual abuse on both child and adult direct victims, and on secondary and tertiary victims such as family, friends, and employers.

In Chapter Ten, we review some of the current efforts being used to control and prevent sexual abuse and explain why they are not enough to prevent the problem in the future. While experts identify three levels of sexual abuse prevention in America, we have generally relied only upon secondary and tertiary prevention methods, ignoring primary prevention. In this chapter we discuss the research conducted in sexual offender treatment programs which has provided the bulk of knowledge and information available to us today regarding the causes of sexual abuse.[29]

Chapter Eleven looks at the future of sexual abuse prevention and, specifically, primary prevention efforts for reducing sexual abuse. We review and propose some of the best methods for sexual abuse prevention and suggest it is possible to reduce sexual abuse to the point that it is no longer considered epidemic. Primary prevention means stopping sexual abuse before it occurs. It is not a reaction to crime that has already occurred.

Finally, we invite your thoughts. "It's not my problem" is an attitude that breeds apathy and discontent. Sexual abuse may be someone else's problem today, but that does not preclude any of us from being affected by sexual abuse tomorrow. Our goal is stopping sexual abuse now.

---

[29] Sex Offender Treatment: Research Results Inconclusive about What Works to Reduce Recidivism. GAO report #GAO/GGD-96-137. United States General Accounting; Washington, D.C. 20548-0001. June 21, 1996.

CHAPTER TWO

Understanding Sexual Abuse and the Abusers

Sexual abuse covers a wide range of events, behaviors, and activities. Because human sexual behavior is so intricately woven into so many different aspects of American culture, it is difficult to use a single definition that would be acceptable to everyone. Sexual abuse can be an act committed by one person upon another, by multiple persons against another, or self abusive. Therefore sexual abuse is not exclusively a legal concern. Human sexual behavior, including sexually abusive behavior, transcends the American culture and its laws. It involves a variety of behaviors and practices that are both legal and illegal.

We also believe that sexual abuse is, in part, the result of an attitude. What we chose to do in our lives regarding our sexual interests and practices, as well as what we believe we have the right to say and/or promote publicly shapes and expresses that attitude. In extreme cases, some individuals believe it is perfectly okay to endorse, make light of, and poke fun at sexual abuse.[1] With accurate knowledge and information, people are better equipped to decide what behaviors they will engage in and which ones they will avoid, and which behaviors are healthy or which behaviors may cause harm to others or oneself.

---

[1] The television show Life Without Shame airs on public access television in Rochester, NY, and makes statements that either endorse, promote, and or make light of child sexual abuse, rape of female children and adults, gang rape, domestic violence and wife battering, sadistic and violent sexual acts against women, sexual torture of women and children, and hate crimes. Personal communication Maureen Murphy, Family Service of Rochester. April 14, 1997.

We believe that many people engage in sexually abusive behaviors because they are willing to exploit others for personal gain, or in some cases because they don't know how to change their behavior.

In other instances, some individuals do not recognize that what they are doing is wrong, or hurtful to others. For example, the consumer who buys adult pornography probably assumes that the models and actors making pornographic films and pictures are of legal age and do so of their own free choice. Further, the consumer probably considers pornography to be non-abusive because he or she believes that the "porn stars" have entered into a contractual agreement for which they are paid.[2]

When porn star Traci Lords made adult films as a teenager, the filming constituted child sexual abuse. Would the consumer of pornography feel or believe any differently if he or she knew that some porn stars were victimized in making the pornography or had a history of being sexually abused as children? Would the consumer still make the purchase, or forgo the purchase knowing the personal histories of the pornography stars? Each person's answer to these questions is a facet of the American sexual attitude.

A variety of definitions have been used to describe the acts we regard as sexual abuse. From a legal standpoint, the laws and definitions are more similar than different from state to state. Defining sexual abuse is a difficult task regardless of whether legal or general definitions are considered. According to Webster's Tenth New Collegiate Dictionary[3] the words "sexual" and "abuse" are defined as follows:

sexual - (adj) 1: of, relating to, or associated with sex or the sexes 2: having or involving sex.

abuse - (n) 1: a corrupt practice or custom 2: improper or excessive use or treatment: MISUSE 3: a deceitful act: DECEPTION 4: language that condemns or vilifies usu. unjustly, intemperately, and angrily 5: physical maltreatment. (vt) 1: to put to a wrong or improper use 2: obs: DECEIVE 3: to attack in words: REVILE.

A combined definition might read as follows.

sexual abuse - deceitful, improper, corrupt, or improper treatment of oneself or another involving sex or sexuality.

---

[2] Traci Lords, an actress and previously a "porn star," began making adult movies at age 15, and completed over 80 by age 18. She made only one film legally, and then retired from the business. Biographical information for Traci Lords came from the Internet website: Http://us.imdb.com/M/person-biography?Lords,%20Traci. 4/23/97.

[3] Webster's Tenth New Collegiate Dictionary. Merriam-Webster, Inc. Springfield, MA. 1996.

For the purposes of this book, we propose a comprehensive definition of sexual abuse as follows:

sexual abuse: 1. the maltreatment of one or more people by one or more individuals involving sexual behavior, sexual practices, or sexual harassment; 2. any unwanted or uninvited sexual act; 3. sexual involvement or contact with a person under the age of legal consent by an older person;[4] 4. non-consenting sexual behavior between two or more persons; 5. deceptive sexual acts or practices; 6. sexual contact between two or more people which is determined to be injurious or harmful to one or more of the individuals involved; 7. sexual behavior, contact, or experiences an individual encounters which are determined to be harmful or destructive to his or her physical and/or psychological well being.

Since we believe that sexual abuse can include illegal or legal activities, events, or behaviors, that definition of sexual abuse can be amended as follows:

illegal sexual abuse - The act of engaging in sexual behaviors, activities, or events that are abusive and prohibited by state and/or federal laws.

legal sexual abuse - The act of engaging in sexual behaviors, activities, or events that are not violations of state and/or federal laws, but which are determined to be hurtful and/or harmful to an individual resulting in the person being victimized.

Consent

Consent is a complex issue, especially when it involves sexual behavior. When one thinks about human sexual behavior, the issue of consent is often a cornerstone of acceptable behavior or practice. There is a belief that whatever sexual behavior occurs between people in the privacy of their home, dwelling, or environment should not be of concern to others. While this basic provision of individual freedom makes perfectly good sense to most of us, there are concerns about what may result in abusive outcomes, regardless of individual rights, freedoms, and legal behaviors.

Our society is concerned about people who engage in self-destructive or injurious acts. We attempt to prohibit and prevent self-inflicted injury, suicide attempts and similar acts that pose potential harm or threat to an individual's

---

[4] Due to the range of laws, especially between states and other countries, the term "minor" has to be defined by the age of legal consent. In the United States those definitions of consent vary between states from as young as 15 years of age to as old as 18 years of age.

well being; we try to offer help and treatment to those who engage in such acts. However, we seldom if ever use this approach to human sexual behaviors outside the realm of illegal sexual behaviors, or sex crimes. On the one hand we attempt to engage self-destructive individuals in therapy, and on the other, the media airs television programs that demonstrate people engaging in sexual behaviors that may be harmful to participants.[5]

In regard to consenting sexual behaviors, our culture may need to rethink what it calls acceptable behavior between two persons. Sexual abuse does not always occur in the absence of consent. The issues involved in consent are difficult enough for adults to understand, let alone children. Consenting to engage in sex with another is giving permission to that person to have sexual contact with you. Some believe that in the absence of a verbal prohibition it can be assumed there is a green light to engage in sexual contact. This is not true. Giving consent to heterosexual sexual intercourse, on the other hand, involves many things including several consequences;

- the risk of pregnancy with the attendant responsibility of parenthood

- the risk of contracting sexually transmitted diseases such as gonorrhea, syphilis, and AIDS

- an understanding of intimate relationships and the emotional impact on oneself and one's sexual partner - with or without a long-term commitment

- questions about one's own morals and values

- understanding the good and bad consequences to each individual engaging in the behavior

- responsibility and accountability to one's sexual partner

Consent is an involved decision, not a simple yes or no response. Consent, and especially consent to sexual relations with others, is complex and has potential life-long repercussions, whether it involves a long-term relationship or a one-time experience. Consent is very different from compliance.

Compliance is the act or process of going along with or giving in to another's desire, demand or proposal and may occur under psychological pressure or duress. Compliance may indicate lack of knowledge of consequences, rather than clear and informed agreement.

---

[5] In Chapter Four we give examples of present day sexual practices and behaviors that pose serious health hazards and in some cases loss of life to participants.

Legal Sexual Abuse

When most people think about sexual abuse, they think of it from a legal or criminal perspective. However, every year people fall victim to their own sexual practices. An example would be the accidental deaths of individuals engaging in certain autoerotic acts.[6] Some autoerotic acts are abusive because they put the person, and/or their sexual partner(s) at risk for injury, illness, or death. Recently on cable television, a special program called Sexbytes showed couples talking about and demonstrating the intimate sexual practice of cutting patterns in the skin of their lovers with a scalpel and licking the blood.[7] This practice poses a variety of health risks to the participants including scarring, infection, and transmission of diseases.

While we believe in the protection of individual rights, that same Constitutional protection can inadvertently protect sexual abusers. For example, it is illegal in all fifty states to sexually abuse children; however, it is not illegal to write books and pamphlets about having sex with children. It is legal to organize and/or belong to organizations such as The North American Man-Boy Love Association (N.A.M.B.L.A.), The Pedophile Information Exchange, and The Children's Sensuality Circle that promote sexual relations between children and adults.[8] These groups believe that some types of sexual contact with children are healthy and good. They contend that every child should have his/her right protected to have a sexual relationship with an adult.[9] These beliefs, that it is okay to be sexually involved with children regardless of laws, are attitudes which foster abuse. When an individual has a predisposition or sexual makeup to be sexually attracted to children, as is the case with some N.A.M.B.L.A. members, this inclination should not be an excuse to act on such desires. It should be the catalyst to counseling help for this interest rather than engaging in criminal behavior.

Types of Sexual Abuse

In defining the various forms of sexual abuse, we propose a continuum from non-abusive, consenting sexual behaviors (some legal and others illegal) to the most destructive of illegal sexual behaviors that are traumatic to the victim(s) and may have long-term negative impact.

---

[6] Autoerotic sexual acts are solitary sexual activities that are practiced to produce intense sexual excitement. The individual attempts to heighten his orgasm experience by partially strangling himself and loses control of the situation resulting in an accidental hanging. Some may include asphyxia. The most common form of auto-erotic deaths is accidental strangulation.

[7] "Sexbytes;" Home Box Office (HBO) special. 21, May 1996.

[8] O'Carroll, T. Paedophilia: The radical case. Boston: Alyson Publications, 1980.

[9] Ibid.

We propose that on one end of this continuum of sexual behaviors are sexual relations involving touch between persons[10] or non-touch sexual activities and entertainment (e.g., nude dancing,[11] phone sex) between consenting persons who meet the legal age requirements. The sexual practices between these persons are entered into with the mutual consent and knowledge of all parties. There is no reason to believe that anyone will experience negative consequence from engaging in the sexual activity.

As one moves along the continuum, the next level of sexual behavior involves sexual relations or practices with mutual consent, but with the potential for one or all persons to have an unanticipated negative experience or consequence from engaging in these behaviors. For example, a man and woman have sexual relations after dating for a period of time. The woman says something to the man which reminds him of being sexually abused by his aunt when he was a child. He has a negative emotional experience as a result of hearing the comment, and again experiences the trauma of his own sexual abuse.

Another example of how one might be harmed without another person's knowledge is the scenario in which a man stares at a woman in a restaurant and sexualizes her (a behavior among men that is both common and culturally inappropriate). He does not know that this woman was sexually harassed by a man who is similar to him in appearance. By staring at the woman, he makes her feel uncomfortable, and she flashes back to being harassed. In this scenario, one would not automatically assume that a behavior that appears to be relatively harmless can result in discomfort for another.

The next level of sexual behavior involves practices involving mutual consent, but one or both parties know there is the potential for either person to have a negative consequence from engaging in sexual relations. A married person having an extramarital affair is a common example. An extreme example is a person diagnosed with AIDS having unprotected sex with another individual.[12]

Next on the continuum are the sexual behaviors and select paraphilias[13] (sexual behaviors considered by mental health professionals to be deviations from "normal" sexual behavior) that may or may not be harmful or destructive

---

[10] We acknowledge that consenting sexual relations often occurs between two or more persons of the same or opposite sex. For ease of illustration we will refer to consenting sexual relations as an act between only two persons engaging in heterosexual behavior.

[11] The nude dancer is partially nude or totally nude and in some establishments may sit on the lap of the patron while moving and dancing. The intent is usually the sexual stimulation of the patron.

[12] Depending on the state, either or both of these behaviors may be illegal. Social tolerance rarely results in criminal prosecution for adultery, though its legal status as grounds for civil divorce with some attribution of fault via monetary settlements remains. Case law is now being established as to whether a person with AIDS who has knowingly has unprotected sex without informing his or her partner can be charged with attempted murder or attempted manslaughter.

[13] The paraphilias are sexual deviations from normative sexual behavior as identified and defined in the American Psychiatric Association's Diagnostic and Statistical Manual of Mental Disorders, Fourth Edition (DSM IV), 1994.

to the person engaging in the behavior, and are legal. Fetishism (i.e., sexual arousal to articles of clothing, shoes, or other objects) is one example.

Further along the continuum are acts, behaviors, or events that are not criminal behaviors or illegal acts, but are considered by many to be socially unacceptable. Sexual harassment in the workplace is an example of sexual behavior that may not be a violation of criminal law, does not involve consent, and may be damaging to one or both persons. While there are few laws directly against harassing behavior, it is subject to moral disgrace and negative legal sanctions through civil suits alleging violation of civil rights.

Still moving in the direction of illegal behaviors are sexual behaviors that may or may not involve mutual consent, but are illegal. Prostitution is one example of a sexual behavior that involves mutual consent, is illegal in most states, and may be abusive to one or both persons. Some research suggests that many prostitutes are victims of child sexual abuse. By engaging in prostitution, the woman may be acting out of her low self-esteem and belief that her only purpose in life is to provide men with sexual pleasure.[14]

As we continue to approach the opposite end of the continuum, there are illegal paraphilias, or sexual crimes which include "nuisance" offenses such as exhibitionism, voyeurism, and obscene phone calls. Next are the serious hands-on offenses that are most traumatic to the victims such as child sexual abuse and rape. The impact of the sexually abusive behavior varies from one victim to the next and is discussed in Chapter Nine.

At the extreme far end of the continuum are the sex crimes that cause the victim severe physical harm or death. These include crimes such as sadistic rapes during which the victims are battered and physically injured, child sexual abuse that results in severe physical harm to the victim, and lust murders.

FIGURE 1

A CONTINUUM OF SEXUAL BEHAVIORS

Consenting -	Paraphilic -	Sexual harassment -	Prostitution -	Paraphilic -	Sex crimes/ -	Rape
sexual activities	behavior that doesn't harm others			behavior that harms others	sexual assault	murder

---

[14] Briere, J. Therapy for Adults Molested as Children.: Beyond Survival. New York: Springer Publishing Company, 1989.

Sexual Abusers

Not all sexual abusers are alike. Not all sexual abusers are men. Much of this book, however, is geared toward understanding those who commit the vast majority of sex crimes and sexually abusive behaviors, namely men.

Females also engage in the sex abuse of children, although not nearly as frequently as males, and adult women most often victimize their own children. For resources on female sexual abusers contact the Safer Society Press.[15]

In an attempt to understand the abuse experience, it may be of value to learn some things about sexual abusers' personalities and patterns. If you know someone who has been abused, material in this chapter may help you understand their ordeal so that you can better support them. If you are married to someone or have a friend who has just been charged with a sexual offense, you can now learn more about his hidden side.

Experts in any field are inclined to use a language all their own, and sexual abuse treatment professionals are no exception. In this chapter, some of their terms will be explained to provide you with an understanding of what is being said.

Sex Abuser Terminology

In referencing child molesters, many specialists make a distinction between preferential and situational abusers.

Preferential Child Molesters
Adult preferential child molesters have a sexual makeup that results in a preference to have sexual relationships with children rather than with someone of their own age group. Usually they are intimidated by the thought of a relationship with other adults, fearing they can't negotiate the demands of intimacy with an age-appropriate peer. They find children to be safer partners who can provide adoration, have lower expectations, and are less inclined to reject the adult. These abusers fear rejection intensely.

Some child molesters are seductive.[16] They develop social relationships with children to eventually become involved with them sexually. Others are introverted and prefer sex with children but do not have the necessary social skills to seduce them. Consequently, they may molest strangers and very young

---

[15] The Safer Society Press has published several titles that address female sexual abusers including: The Last Secret: Daughters Sexually Abused by Mothers, by B. Rosencrans (1997); Mother-Son Incest: The Unthinkable Broken Taboo (1995), by H. Miletski; Female Adolescent Sexual Abusers: An Exploratory Study of Mother-Daughter Dynamics With Implications for Treatment (1994), by Turner & Turner; and Female Sexual Offenders: An Exploratory Study (1989), by Mathews, Matthews, & Speltz.

[16] Lanning, K. V. Child Molesters: A Behavioral Analysis. Washington, D.C.: National Center for Missing and Exploited Children. (1986).

children, without a relationship that could buffer some of the child's emotional pain. Still others are sadistic. Fortunately, this type of child molester is rare, but regrettably, he commands intense media scrutiny detracting attention from more common types of child sexual abuse.

A pedophile would fall into the category of a preferential child molester. They are primarily interested in sex with children, preferring intimacy with minors, and usually become sexually attracted to children during their adolescent years.

Situational Child Molesters

Also referred to as regressed abusers, these individuals have exhibited a conventional social and sexual development over the years. Their sexual orientation has usually been focused on age-appropriate peers. As their relationships in adulthood become riddled with tension and conflicts, situational molesters begin to turn their attention to children. In situations of extreme stress and self-doubt, this type of abuser may look to children as adult substitutes and begin relating to the minor as a peer. When the child responds to the abuser's emotional needs, he wants to take the relationship further and initiates a sexual relationship.

Most treatment professionals believe that situational child sexual abusers will respond to treatment and stop interacting with children sexually.

Pedophiles

Often the term, "pedophile," is improperly used to describe all persons who molest children. Actually, there are many types of child molesters, and only some meet the true definition of a pedophile.

It is helpful to view the pedophile as someone who has a strong sexual interest focused exclusively on children. Pedophiles have a persistent habit of searching for opportunities to be with children for social, emotional, and sexual reasons. Consequently, the word predatory is often applied to these abusers.

Because of their sexual preference for children, pedophiles often center their lives around the search for victims - always positioning themselves to be near vulnerable children (children from single parent homes, children who have been previously abused, children who are not well supervised, children who are lonely, etc.).

A pedophile becomes much like a child when in the company of minors. He relates to them at their level and often is regarded as an exceptional communicator with children. At the same time, he often finds himself alienated from persons of his own age. Rarely does a pedophile marry, and if so, the marriage is one of convenience (perhaps to gain access to a child), done for the sake of appearances, and is short-lived.

Once detected, a pedophile may blame his sexual assaultiveness on a variety of problems including alcohol abuse. He may say the decision to be sexual with children was precipitated by heavy intoxication and that most, if not all, of his memories are blocked out. In reality, pedophiles look for child victims whether drunk or sober. The excuse of being drunk is usually just a smoke screen to avoid responsibility for his sexually abusive behavior. He will, in fact, recall almost every assault in great detail.

Intrafamilial Sexual Abusers

Intrafamilial sexual abuse (incest) is narrowly defined as sexual relations between family members prohibited by law from marrying. It includes parents and their children and grandchildren, adults and their nieces & nephews, first cousins (in many states), and brothers and sisters. In practice, step-parents and step-children, and step- or half-siblings involved in sexual interactions are also considered to have committed incest. While adult incest abusers generally prefer adult sexual partners and are usually married, they may, under a variety of circumstances turn to their children to satisfy their emotional and sexual needs. The majority of incest abusers - whether they are men or women - are not true pedophiles. Nevertheless, they can be addicted to sex, and a significant number also sexually assault children outside their families.[17,18]

Even when these individuals are sex addicts, their psychological needs are usually nonsexual in nature; sex simply becomes a narrowly focused way to meet other misidentified emotional needs for attention, approval, or nurturance.

One group of researchers has described male incest abusers as falling into two distinct types: passive-dependent and aggressive-dominant.[19]

Passive-dependent Fathers (or Grandfathers)

These men are emotionally weak, timid, or docile. They lack what counselors call ego strength, self-confidence, and assertion skills. They feel very insecure and inadequate, and see themselves as failures as men, as spouses, and as father figures. Many are depressed, unemployed, and they may abuse alcohol. They often withdraw from their friends and become dependent on their immediate family members to meet all their social, emotional, and sexual needs. Many manipulate their families with sympathy and guilt, and they usually get what they want short of using violence. Often family roles are reversed, with the children parenting their fathers.

[17] Abel, G. G., Becker, J. V., Cunningham, J., Mittleman, M., & Rouleau, J. Multiple paraphilic diagnoses among sex offenders. Bulletin of the American Academy of Psychiatry and the Law. 16 (2). (1988) 153-168.

[18] Carnes, P., The Incest Perpetrator. Newbury Park, CA: Sage Publications, 1990. Horton, A., Johnson, B., Roundy, L., and Williams, D. (Eds).

[19] Burgess, A. W., Groth, A. N., Holmstrom, L. L., and Sgroi, S. M. (1978). Sexual assault of children and adolescents. Lexington: Lexington Books, 1978.

Aggressive-dominant Fathers (or Grandfathers)

These child sexual abusers appear very strong-willed and confident, unlike the image conveyed by the passive-dependent molesters. Yet, this surface behavior is just a cover for the cowering child-like feelings underneath. One such man described himself as a "cast-iron marshmallow." His hardened and gruff public exterior hid his soft and vulnerable inner emotional condition.

An aggressive-dominant abuser uses intimidation, threats, or even violence to command family obedience. He may physically abuse his children and batter or rape his wife. His family helps keep his abusive behavior secret. Family members fear the consequences of exposing him. They frequently fear the ramifications of outside intervention more than a continuation of the abuse itself.

Unlike his passive and dependent counterpart, an aggressive-dominant abuser may be quite charming, outgoing, extroverted, and well-received by his peers. His reign of terror at home stands in sharp contrast to his engaging public facade. At home he "rules the roost," feeling entitled to the sexual services of his property, his wife and/or children. He can control himself, but chooses not to do so at home.

Much like the passive-dependent incest abuser, an aggressive-dominant abuser lives with a deep and pervasive sense of worthlessness, powerlessness, and helplessness. He too is depressed and feels inadequate in the male role. He may also abuse alcohol and other drugs, all in response to his inability to find happiness in life.

Stranger and Acquaintance Molesters

As many as 17% of American men will admit to sexually abusing children.[20] Because men who molest children are so strikingly normal in most social settings, it is often difficult to spot them and describe them in distinct diagnostic terms. To understand them better, it can be helpful to describe their style of abusing and the precipitating motives for the assaults.

Kenneth Lanning[21] of the Federal Bureau of Investigation has compiled a list of traits associated with child molesters who may not be incest abusers nor fit the description of a pedophile. Most are male situational abusers who fall into four categories: regressed, morally indiscriminate, sexually indiscriminate, and sexually inadequate.

---

[20] Finkelhor, D., and Lewis., I.A. (1988). An epidemiologic approach to the study of child molestation. Human sexual aggression: Current perspectives. New York: Annals of the New York Academy of Sciences: 64-78. R. Prentky and V. Quinsey (Eds.).

[21] Lanning, K. Child Molesters: A Behavioral Analysis. Washington, D.C: National Center for Missing and Exploited Children: 1986.

Regressed

These socially awkward, disconnected, and immature individuals turn to children when their adult lives and adult relationships are filled with conflict. During healthier moments they are content to focus their sexual interest on age appropriate peers.

Morally Indiscriminate

Morally indiscriminate abusers opportunistically exploit people in a variety of ways without guilt or remorse. Rather than continuously look for child victims, these men will happen upon vulnerable people - some of whom may coincidentally be children - and take advantage of the opportunity to abuse or otherwise exploit them. They use and abuse nearly everything and everyone with whom they come in contact.

Sexually Indiscriminate

Sexually indiscriminate abusers have a history of experimenting with all types of sexual expression. Often addicted to sex and lacking sexual values and restraints, these abusers are continuously in search of a sexual high, a new experience, or anything novel or bizarre. Children are but one of their many sexual receptacles.

Sexually Inadequate

Sexually inadequate abusers are very isolated and withdrawn from other humans, these men may see children as someone they can play and experiment with as objects.

Sexploitation Abusers

These abusers exploit for two primary reasons: to satisfy sexual needs and to receive some form of monetary gain. They carefully plan ways to get rich from exploiting minors through prostitution, sexual slavery, pornography, and other forms of abuse. Often the children are groomed (set up) and conditioned to accept the abuse while being isolated from normal social interactions.

Exhibitionists

Exhibitionists - exposers, or "flashers" - have historically been seen as nuisances, posing little physical or sexual danger to the public. Society frequently laughs at them. As clinicians have learned more about them they have discovered that without intervention and treatment, the exhibitionist may continue to expose himself and begin to engage in child sexual abuse or rape behavior.

Beginning in the late teens and peaking in the 20's, the tendency toward exhibitionism seems to diminish or terminate by age 40.[22] It is usually an

---

[22] Dwyer, M. Exhibitionism/voyeurism. In Dailey, D. M. (Ed.), The sexually unusual. New York: Harrington Park Press, 1988.

addictive behavior that loses its appeal over time and requires a more powerful replacement. What starts out as a hands-off offense can result in hands-on crimes, including child molestation.

Exhibitionists are commonly classified as one of two primary types: invitational or shocking.

Invitational Abusers

Invitational exhibitionists choose to be sexual from a distance. The impersonal nature of the act is something of an invitation to the victim and oddly feels intimate to the abuser. While hoping for a welcoming response from his victim, most of the men would actually be frightened by such a reaction. Generally, these are the least dangerous exhibitionists.

Shocking Exhibitionists

These individuals are more problematic because of the motivating factors of power and anger. Their goal is to assault the senses. By exposing themselves they can control their victims in a sexual way. Additionally, they can frighten and emotionally scar people. Sexual satisfaction comes from instilling sexual fear in others and in that way, they feel potent and powerful. When the exhibitionist simultaneously degrades his victim, shouts threats, writes, calls, or follows his victim, the potential to engage in rape or child sexual abuse is increased.

Exhibitionists almost always have inadequate personalities, lack maturity and social skills, and are frightened by genuine intimacy. Their biggest fear is that of rejection - of being discovered as inadequate men and sexual partners.

Obscene Callers

The obscene caller makes his social and sexual overtures with the safety provided by anonymity and distance. Having difficulty in developing relationships and feeling inadequate and alienated, the caller immerses himself in a fantasy world in which anything goes. While talking to his victim, he may masturbate and/or cross-dress. Like the exhibitionist, he may find satisfaction in shocking, horrifying, or disgusting women. He feels sexual, powerful, and even intimate during these moments, even if the victim hangs up.

For many years, efforts have been made to categorize obscene callers by their motives and methods.[23] From our clinical experience, three distinct types have emerged: boastful, threatening, and voyeuristic.

The Boastful Caller

The boastful caller brags about his sexual abilities, his sexual prowess, or his physical endowments. Often he describes his masturbatory fantasies or sexual activities in great detail. His boasts are usually motivated by a need to cover up his woefully insecure and inadequate feelings.

---

[23] Mead, B.T. "Coping with obscene phone calls," Aspects of Human Sexuality, 9, June 1975: 127-128.

The Threatening Caller

The threatening caller is a more aggressive type of abuser aroused by making sexual comments that instill fear in his victims. The experience provides a power rush - a sense of sexual control over women. It is a way of shoring up a fragile, sexual self-image.

The Voyeuristic Caller

The voyeuristic caller tries to get his victim to reveal sexual intimacies, sometimes while posing as someone else - perhaps as a phone pollster or researcher. The con leaves him feeling powerful over women and, as a result, sexually aroused and virile.

Many obscene callers are addicted to sex. If their sexual compulsions go untreated, a substantial minority of sex addicts can advance from so-called "nuisance crimes" to far more serious types of sexual crimes. They must be treated seriously from the time of their first arrest.

Voyeurs

Voyeurs receive their sexual pleasure from clandestinely peeking in on private, forbidden, or intimate scenes. Their capacity to be aroused by visual stimuli or imagined sex is often fueled by an addictive use of pornography. With pornography, the man uses sexual images as masturbatory props. This long-standing pattern eventually leads to unsatisfying real relationships, objectification of women, and an isolating routine of masturbation.

Like exhibitionists and obscene phone callers, voyeurs are also sexually immature. They have low self-esteem and limited heterosexual experience, and they must have sex that is safe by virtue of its distance and anonymity. Real intimacy is terribly frightening and elicits fears of rejection and a loss of control. Their most satisfying relationships are in a fantasy world where they successfully conquer and satisfy all partners or vicariously identify with someone they've observed.

Voyeurs prefer strangers, the forbidden, or novel. Interestingly, this is why most "peeping Toms" are not attracted to nude beaches, camps, or resorts. After all, people who frequent such places are likely to be more comfortable with their sexuality than he is, leaving him feeling even more inadequate in their company. Around nudists, he doesn't have the exciting high that comes from sneaking peeks nor the powerful feelings of deceiving and violating someone.

Problems with voyeuristic activities usually begin in early adulthood. About one-fourth of all men arrested for peeping are married. Fifty percent of the men who are arrested for this crime are rearrested for similar acts at later dates.[24] It is common, however, for another type of addictive sex to replace voyeurism once it loses its appeal.

---

[24] Sarason, I.G., & Sarason, B. R. Abnormal psychology. Englewood Cliffs, N.J.: Prentice-Hall, 1984.

Frotteurs

A frotteur also engages in anonymous and impersonal sex. He finds satisfaction by rubbing up against the body of another person, preferably a stranger (known as "frottage") and "stealing" what, to him, feels like intimate sexual touch. Usually the frotteur finds his victims in crowded places like subways, elevators, or shopping malls. There he "sneaks a feel" in what is to appear like an innocent accidental contact. While doing so he may fantasize about his anonymous victim, creating an image of her/him desiring to have a caring and affectionate relationship with the frotteur. He may then leave the scene and masturbate to this image.

Frotteurs are typically ill at ease in social and sexual situations. They have low self-esteem and have experienced few, if any, satisfactory sexual encounters. We most commonly observe the onset of this behavior in the teen years or early twenties. Most frotteurs engage in other forms of compulsive sex as well.

Rapists

Some men who rape other adults begin their assault histories with "hands off" offenses like voyeurism or exhibitionism. Nearly 90% of men arrested for rape are caught by the time they reach their mid-thirties.[25] At least half were high on drugs or alcohol at the time of their crimes. Most are high school drop outs, the majority are unmarried, and nearly all have prior criminal records. Many of these men have previously molested or raped children,[26] while most are quick to claim the opposite and say very disparaging things about child molesters in an attempt to distance themselves from that part of their past.

Rapists have a number of other similarities between them. They rely on aggressive sex as a way to overcome many forms of personal distress. Rape temporarily removes feelings of inadequacy and serves as an outlet for anger and hostility toward women and children who are perceived as dangerous, manipulative, depriving, seductive, and powerful. It also leaves some men feeling dominant or powerful over women.

Most rapists have poorly developed sexual identities. Their lives are purposeless and unsatisfying. They feel unhappy and depressed, carrying a chip on their shoulder that makes them see most everyone as an adversary. Many rapists are also sex addicts.[27]

---

[25] Meyer, L.C., & Romero, J. A ten-year follow-up of sex offender recidivism. Philadelphia: Joseph J. Peters Institute, 1980.

[26] Abel, G. G., Becker, J. V., Cunningham, J. Mittleman, M, and Rouleau, J. "Multiple paraphilic diagnoses among sex offenders. Bulletin of the American Academy of Psychiatry and the Law. 16 (2). 1988: 153-168.

[27] Blanchard, G. (May 1990). Differential diagnosis of sex offenders: Distinguishing characteristics of the sex addict. American Journal of Preventive Psychiatry & Neurology 2:3. May 1990: 45-47.

Nicholas Groth has developed a typology of rapists that helps us understand these men. He describes three primary types motivated by power, anger, and sadistic motives:[28]

Power Rapists

This group of men constitutes the largest category - 55% of all rapists. Power rapists premeditate their crimes which are born out of fantasies. Their offenses are often repeated and tend to show an increase in aggression over time. A power rapist will use whatever force is necessary to gain control of his victim. Usually it is not his intent to leave physical injuries but inadvertently they often do occur. Weapons are frequently employed to assure control of the rape situation, although they are only infrequently used to inflict pain or injury. Power rapists select their victims for their vulnerability with a trend toward choosing persons of their own age or younger.

Language used during the rape often tips investigators off to the type of rapist involved. For instance, the power rapist often uses language that gives orders, is instructional, inquisitive, or seeks reassurance. He may want to have the assault go a certain way and will demand compliance. Another type of power rapist may need to hear that he is attractive, desirable, or quite a sexual gymnast.

The rapes always compensate for some unmet need - usually non-sexual in nature. Desiring to feel powerful and in control, the power rapist finds a victim he then rapes. To banish feelings of insecurity or inadequacy, he rapes. To prop up a flagging sense of manhood, or to quell disquieting homosexual guilt, he rapes. The rape is intended to make him feel strong and manly. Because sexuality is at the core of his identity as a man, a power rapist believes sexual assaults are the solution to most of his image problems. He sees women as threats to his identity; they must be conquered or coerced into cooperating with his obsessional fantasies, lest his fragile image be shattered. Compared to an anger rapist, a power rapist is more inclined to fuel his assaultive fantasies with the use of pornography.

Two sub-types become evident as we learn more about power rapists: power-assertive and power-reassurance rapists.

Power-assertive Rapists

Power-assertive rapists inwardly feel quite powerless and rape is primarily an expression of virility, mastery, and dominance. Usually there are accompanying feelings of entitlement. As one power assertive rapist told us while reflecting on his assault, "I felt that for once in my life things were going to go my f _ _ _ _ _ g way." Another rapist summarized his feelings in one word while he raped and sodomized an unknown pregnant woman. He simply said "Gotcha!"

---

[28] Groth, A.N., with Birnbaum, J. Men who rape: The psychology of the offender. New York: Plenum, 1979.

Power-reassurance Rapists

Power-reassurance rapists assault primarily to resolve disturbing doubts about their masculinity and sexual adequacy. He wants his female victim to be in a helpless and controlled situation in which she cannot reject him. With this conquest he momentarily feels adequate. During the rape he may be heard asking for, or ordering the victim to reassure him of his sexual prowess or manhood. Queries like "How does it feel?," "I'm the best you've ever had, ain't I?," or "I'm better than your boyfriend, right?" are commonly reported by their victims.

Anger Rapists

Anger rapists make up the second largest diagnostic category - 40 percent. Anger rapists are more impulsive, more spontaneous, and more dangerous than most power rapists. Their offenses are episodic and are usually not premeditated. What may start out as only a physical assault can rather suddenly and unexpectedly turn into a rape. He uses more physical force than is required to subdue his victims. Often the victims may be battered and suffer injuries. The assaults occur in a flurry and are relatively short in duration.

Language used during these rapes is abusive, vulgar, and degrading. The rapist declares his superiority while labeling his victim in the way he sees all women - as inferior beings. Victim selection is usually by availability - namely she happened to be in the wrong place at the wrong time. The victims tend to be about the same age or older than the rapist.

Background checks on anger rapists reveal crimes of aggression ranging from breach of the peace and reckless driving to assault and battery against both men and women. This man may have always been volatile and dangerous, but when his relationships with women become stormy and conflictual, the risk of rape intensifies.

There are two sub-types of anger rapists: anger-retaliation and anger excitation rapists.

Anger-retaliation Rapists.

Anger-retaliation rapists usually rape as an expression of hostility toward women. He is motivated to lash out at any woman who represents what he perceives a few women have done to hurt him. The intent is to degrade, hurt, and humiliate the victim as he lashes out in retaliatory rage.

Anger-excitation Rapist.

Anger-excitation rapists link anger to sexual arousal. Excitement, thrills, and pleasure are felt while watching his victim suffer through an assault. For the anger excitation rapist, aggression has become eroticized. Violence is a sexual turn-on. His aim is to punish women. Any small attempt at resistance or noncompliance prompts more anger and more sexual arousal.

Sadistic Rapists

The rarest of all rapists, the sadistic rapist, makes up only 5% of men who rape yet, he commands a great deal of media attention. His assaults are always carefully planned and acted out in a compulsive and ritualistic fashion. Victims are selected in accordance with very specific characteristics that have symbolic importance to him. The victim, however, is almost always a complete stranger until just before the attack.

This serial rapist will use commanding and degrading language. He may alternate between threatening and reassuring comments with the intent of keeping his victim off balance. The result is terrorizing - much to his delight and sexual satisfaction.

Gang Rapists

Gang rape is a crime involving young men - usually of high school or college age. They may be members of athletic teams or fraternities, as well as the image many Americans think of, members of a street gang. For them rape can serve as a way to bolster an image, create some excitement, or generate a sense of belonging or comraderie. Their joint actions suggest to each other that the rape isn't terribly wrong. As one gang rapist said, "After all, if we are all doing it, it can't be that bad." The group psychology is such that no one individual feels capable of confronting the actions of the entire group. As a group, men are more aggressive than when they are acting alone, and they may excuse their collective behavior by saying "things just got out of hand." The New Bedford, Massachusetts rape of a young woman, as portrayed by Jodi Foster in the movie The Accused, is an example of a gang rape.

Marital Rape

Stereo-typically, our society has traditionally thought of marital rape as a case when a woman has "not been in the mood" and her spouse "persuades" her to submit to his sexual or aggressive desires. It is more serious than that.

Until recently, most states had what was called a "marital exemption" in their rape laws. Often the law would define rape as "the forcible penetration of the body of a woman who is not the wife of the perpetrator."[29] Today, laws have changed. It is now illegal to force sex on one's spouse, or for that matter, to harm or humiliate her/him during sex.

Many husbands who rape their wives, use coercive sex as a standard procedure.[30] Domestic abusers frequently rape their wives out of sexual insecurity or as punishment for perceived sexual failings. Often the attacks

---

[29] Russell, D. E. H. "Wife Rape." In A. Parrot & L. Bechhofer (eds.), Acquaintance Rape: The hidden crime (p.129). New York: John Wiley, 1991.

[30] Allison, J. and Wrightsman, L. Rape. Newbury Park, CA: Sage Publications, 1993.

seem like capricious expressions of resentment and anger.[31] Some women are raped at a time when they were leaving, or threatening to leave the marriage. Still other women are raped as a part of their spouses' sexual addiction in which he is preoccupied with sex — always looking for her participation in novel, if not, bizarre sexual scenarios. As many as 10% to 14% of women are estimated to be victims of spousal rape.[32]

A man who rapes his wife can fit the rapist typologies described earlier. In a marriage there can be the violence and even the sadism found in other rape situations. Usually, however, the victim has become habituated to sexual exploitation and humiliation. Without a sudden and isolated incident that stands apart from other sexual activities, the spousal victim may not be able to identify her chronic abuse as rape. Similarly, the husband who rapes may not see his behavior as wrong, often thinking of his wife as his property — someone you can treat as you desire without outside interference.

Psychological Defense Mechanisms

In defense of their distorted lifestyles (also described as abnormal, aberrant, or deviant), sexual abusers demonstrate some predictable defenses once caught:

DENIAL: *"It didn't happen; I didn't do anything."*

He may act shocked or even indignant over the allegations. Claiming to have no explanation for what he terms "false allegations," the pedophile (sexual abuser of children) or incest offender (sexual abuser of children within his own family) will very convincingly use his otherwise good community reputation to attempt to prove his innocence. Often his absolute denial of wrongdoing will be bolstered by community leaders who quickly come to his defense - having seen only the public persona that the pedophile has carefully crafted over the years in fearful anticipation of his eventual exposure.

MISUNDERSTANDING: *"The child misunderstood my innocent affection."*

Sensing there is strong evidence against him, the pedophile will often make a somewhat compromising defense. He may concede to having some contact with the child but qualifies his admission by arguing that no sexual gratification was involved. He may clamor, "Is it a crime to give children innocent hugs?" Some will claim the allegations arise from unhealthy or overly suspicious individuals in the community who have their own sexual problems and are inclined to misinterpret innocent acts of caring.

---

[31] Finkelhor, D. & Yllo, K. (1985). License to rape: Sexual abuse of wives. New York: Holt, Rinehart & Winston.

[32] Allison, J. and Wrightsman, L. Rape. Newbury Park, CA: Sage Publications, 1993.

MINIMIZATION: *"It was an accident; it only happened once."*

Not wanting to be discovered as a chronic abuser, the pedophile may argue that only one or two minor incidents occurred. The perpetrator may claim that there is no cause for alarm because there was no penetration and only accidental contact during play activities.

JUSTIFICATION: *"I'm helping the child"*

Pedophiles - especially those who have had contact with pro-pedophilia organizations - may assert that their relationships with children reflect more sincere care and concern than the natural parents have demonstrated. They may, in fact, be offering bona fide educational, recreational, or artistic opportunities not available from the child's family. In their minds, they are helping a neglected or abused child, but of course that "help" carries the very high price tag of sexual abuse. Often they will counter accusations of improper sexual contact with a demand that the victims' families be investigated by the police or social services, saying that is where the real problem exists.

ATTACK: *"They're lying; I'll get you."*

Feeling his best defense is a good offense, the sex abuser may counter-accuse, harass, or threaten the involved parties. He may bribe victims and/or witnesses. Some can be heard attacking the integrity of investigators, social workers, prosecutors, parents, and even the victims. The problem always lies outside himself.

FABRICATION: *"They're out to discredit me because of my political connections."*

Some sex abusers develop ingenious stories to explain their innocence. Conspiracy theories are common. Another might argue that the children forced themselves on him leaving him the victim of circumstances.

SEEKING SYMPATHY: *"I've given so much to this community and now you choose to do this to me."*

Having positioned himself in the community as a leader, volunteer, or devoted organization member, the sex abuser may look to citizen sympathy for support. The "nice guy defense" is used most often when community members feel indebted to the abuser for charitable acts he performed in the past. Usually, the sex abuser doesn't need to orchestrate this defense, as community members step forward on their own.

NOLO CONTENDERE: *"I didn't do anything, but if it will help the kids, I'll admit."*

Sex abusers may strike a deal with prosecutors to avoid a public trial and conviction. A plea of nolo contendere is tantamount to a "guilty-but-not-guilty" position. Taking this stance, the sex abuser can claim that he is actually protecting the children by saving them from the trauma of a court trial. In actuality, he may be skirting full responsibility for his crimes and not giving the victims any meaningful sense of justice and closure. Further, if a parent or a grown child should later sue the perpetrator to cover the costs of counseling, for example, a nolo plea is inadmissible as evidence of wrongdoing in the civil courts of many states.

When Abusers Deny

Once discovered, the sexual abuser may exhibit several forms of denial. One counselor listed seven types of denial commonly observed in abusers:[33]

1. Denial of facts refers to the position that some things simply never occurred, that the victim is lying or remembering events incorrectly.

2. Denial of awareness is a claim of memory lapse, amnesia, drug- and alcohol-induced blackouts, or dissociation, all of which are possible but unlikely.

3. Denial of impact refers to the minimization of physical or emotional harm that was inflicted on the victim ("I only touched his penis through his bathing suit; it's not like I raped him. Stuff like that happens all the time, it's not hurting him."). In some instances, underdeveloped empathy skills can contribute to this type of denial.

4. Denial of responsibility involves the misplacement of responsibility on circumstances, objects, mental conditions, outside forces, or other people - including the victim. The abuser may blame a medical condition, Satan, the seductive behavior of the children, or drugs as precipitating factors that he feels reduces or eliminates personal responsibility.

5. Denial of grooming or conditioning a child to accept sexualized touch is often used as a way to make the assault appear somewhat less serious. If the abuser can claim that he/she did not plan or set up the abuse, then the crime can be seen as less malicious and perhaps result in less shame or a reduced sentence.

6. Denial of sexual intent is common. "She bumped into me," "I accidentally walked into the bathroom while she was showering" or "she wiggled on my lap" are all ways to give away responsibility for the abuse and make it appear non-sexual.

---

[33] Winn, M. E. The strategic and systematic management of denial in the cognitive/behavioral treatment of sexual offenders. Sexual Abuse: A Journal of Research and Treat ment 8(1), 1996: 25-36.

7. Denial of denial is a refusal to see any level of one's natural and expected minimization or repudiation of what has occurred.

Denial should not be seen as an automatic indicator that an abuser is unsuited for treatment. In fact, denial may be indicative of a person's level of guilt or shame for having been a part of a sexual assault. Denial is a natural, predictable stage in the recovery process that when approached thoughtfully, can be reduced. It is far too simplistic to assume that an abuser is beyond rehabilitation and therefore should be denied treatment because of inability to face his or her crime honestly today. In fact, the Association for the Treatment of Sexual Abusers states, "The existence of some degree of denial should not preclude a client from entering treatment."[34]

---

[34] Ethical Standards and Principles for the Management of Sexual Abusers. The Association for the Treatment of Sexual Abusers. Beaverton, Oregon, 1997.

CHAPTER THREE

What Causes Criminal Sexual Abuse?

The Etiology of Sexual Abuse - The Theories of Cause

A significant amount of research during the past thirty years has looked at the causes of sexual aggression, sexual abuse, and sexual offending. Despite this research, therapists and researchers are still not certain about the causes of sexual abuse. Several theories, each with its case histories and examples, are widely accepted. And as our colleague and noted researcher Janice Marques noted after surveying several leading professionals in the field of sexual abuser treatment about the status of the field, "we may need to toss out our current theories and start with new ideas."[1]

Unfortunately, much of the government-funded research on sexual abusers is winding down. Research about sexual abusers generally occurs within treatment programs for sexual abusers. Government funding sources for sexual abuser research are not likely to develop during a time when treatment of sexual abusers is so controversial. The limited amount of research into sexual aggression, and specifically the etiology of sexual aggression, will further delay prevention efforts, especially primary prevention which holds the most promise of turning around the sexual abuse epidemic.

---

[1] Marques, J. (1996, November 14). The Way Things Were Is Not the Way Things Will Be [Keynote address] Association for the Treatment of Sexual Abusers 15th Annual Research and Treatment Conference, Chicago.

Even research on nonabusive sexual behavior faces obstacles. In regard to previous attempts to do sexual research, Michael and his colleagues (1994) write:

> One reason why sex was not studied was that the government and private foundations were uninterested in paying for sex research ... Further there was a palpable fear of what sex researchers might discover and how it might affect moral and religious standards.[2]

It is no wonder that research into abusive sexual practices and behavior doesn't warrant much attention and continues to receive limited funding.

As the research points out, untreated abuse of a child can (but doesn't always) create another abuser.[3,4] The abuse-reactive model, detailed later in this chapter, offers one explanation for this all-too-common phenomenon. Many additional circumstances and life events have given rise to the public health epidemic of sexual abuse, including governmental policies that ignore children's rights, a profit based media and movie industry that emphasizes sexuality, an explosion of sexual and pornographic materials, multi-billion dollar sex-for-sale industries, our increasingly casual sexual attitudes in America, undiagnosed and untreated sexual behavior problems, and a legal system almost exclusively focused on punishment instead of prevention and treatment.

Learning Theory

The most widely held theory among leading clinicians and researchers in the field of treating sexual abusers is social learning theory.[5,6] This theory suggests that sexually abusive and sexually aggressive behaviors are learned through the course of an individual's development. This learning can occur in several ways, and the learning results in a pairing of sexual behavior with abusive and/or aggressive tendencies.

One form of learning is the result of exposure. A child living in a home where he or she witnesses sexually abusive acts may develop sexually abusive behavior or tendencies. Seeing a sister or brother sexually abused by a relative or friend can initiate the thought of engaging in similar behavior. Exposure to pornography or sexually explicit materials in print, on television, or in the

---

[2] Michael, R. T., Gagnon, J. H., Laumann, E.O., and Kolata, G. (1994) Sex In America: A Definitive Study. New York: Little, Brown and Company.

[3] GAO/GDD-96-178 The cycle of sexual abuse: research inconclusive about whether child victims become adult abusers. (1996). Washington DC: United States General Accounting Office.

[4] Freeman-Longo, R. E. (1986). The impact of sexual victimization on males. Child Abuse and Neglect, Vol. 10, pp. 411-414.

[5] Bandura, A. (1977). Social Learning Theory. Englewood Cliffs, NJ: Prentice Hall.

[6] Greer, J. G., & Stuart, I. R. (1983) The Sexual Aggressor: Current Perspectives on Treatment, pp. 24-25. New York: Van Nostrand Reinhold.

movies may begin to normalize and suggest similar behavior to a child. Witnessing or being exposed to sexual violence is a powerful form of learning. Like domestic violence, just being in a household where sexual abuse occurs can serve as the foundation for a sexual abuse problem later in the individual's life.

Another aspect of the learning theory is related to experiencing one's own traumatic event. A child who is sexually abused by an older child or adult may learn sexually aggressive behavior as a means to release anger and other emotions and regain a sense of power. In other words, a child may learn to be abusive from being sexually abused. The cycle of abuse has been established in the literature for years.[7]

As with other aggressive and violent behavior, some research suggests that sexually abusive behavior has its roots in child physical abuse and neglect. When children are physically abused and/or neglected, the natural processes of attachment and bonding are interrupted. The abused or neglected child does not form a loving or intimate attraction to others, and there is an evident and apparent absence of empathy. In addition, the abused child learns abuse through modeling the behavior done to them as a method of coping with anger, frustration, or helplessness. The result is children who may be at risk of aggressive or violent behavior. These children are often referred to as abuse-reactive, that is, their abusive behavior reflects exposure to abuse.

Biological Causes

The bio-medical school of thought asserts that some people are born with a predisposition to be sexually attracted to children; that sexual preferences are linked physical conditions and not a matter of choice; that some individuals experience biological drives to be sexual with children. Certain medical conditions are found to occur in greater frequency among those who develop sexually assaultive behavior. Risk factors include chromosomal abnormalities, congenital disturbances, hormonal abnormalities, and neuropsychological deficits.[8] The term pedophilia, a formal psychiatric diagnosis, suggests that some persons may be born with a sexual preference for children.[9] These individuals have similar sexual urges as others do, but the target of their sexual desire is children, not peers and adults. While some individuals are

---

[7] Freeman-Longo, R. E. (1986). The impact of sexual victimization on males. Child Abuse and Neglect, Vol. 10, pp. 411-414.

[8] Valcour, F. (1990). The treatment of child sex abusers in the church. In Rossetti, S. (Ed). Slayer of the Soul pp. 45-66. Mystic, CT: Twenty-Third Publications.

[9] Berlin, F. (1996, November 24-26). What practice and research tell us about what works with sex offenders and about our ability to assess risks to public safety. [Panel discussion]. The National Summit: Promoting Public Safety Through the Effective Management of Sex Offenders in the Community; The US Department of Justice, Office of Justice Programs. Washington, DC.

heterosexual, bisexual, or homosexual, others early in life find they have an orientation toward children.

Generations of Abuse

For other individuals, their participation in sexually abusive behavior is the result of generations of abuse, to the degree that the abuse becomes normalized and a way of life. The abuse is not strongly contested despite its damaging affects. For the sexual abusers and the victims of sexual abuse, there has never been a clear understanding that the sexual abuse of children is an abnormal behavior. For example, there are remote native populations in the United States and in Canada where families have lived for hundreds of years. In some of these populations it is believed that the vast majority of the people in these communities have been sexually abused.[10,11] Although there may be an unspoken taboo against this behavior, the taboo does not stop the behavior.

Sexualized Children

The sexual traumatization of a child doesn't always involve physical contact with another person. A child may be sexually abused by exposure to confusing events. They can be harmed by what they see or hear. A sexually charged home environment can create sexual associations to everyday objects and processes that generates a continual and damaging sexual arousal. This type of influence is an example of why sexual abuse has become a public health problem.

When children are harmed in sexual ways, their behavior can take on sexual characteristics that are unusual. The terms being used today to describe these children are sexually-reactive and sexualized children.

Sexually-reactive children may be responding to physical traumas that involved sex and aggression. Their reaction may involve replaying confusing experiences or things they have observed. Included in the reenactment will be sexually explicit and sometimes sexually exploitive behavior. This behavior may be subconsciously motivated by a need to manage or master their original trauma.[12]

The sexualized child may appear to be excessively focused or strongly drawn toward sexual interests and activities when most of their peers are not. In essence, they are trained and conditioned by their environment to behave in

---

[10] LaBelle, J. W., Rural Coordinator, Commissioner's Office, State of Alaska. Personal Communication May 10, 1996.

[11] Kennedy, D. Hollow Water Community Holistic Circle Healing Program, Wanipigow, Manitoba, Canada. Personal Communication February, 1997.

[12] Schwartz, M. (1992). Sexual compulsivity as post-traumatic stress disorder: Treatment perspectives. Psychiatric Annals, 22:5, 333-338.

sexual ways. Although the two terms - sexually- reactive children and sexualized children - are used interchangeably, they are not the same.

The terms being used today have been around as concepts since the days of Sigmund Freud. It was Freud who coined the term *repetition compulsion* to describe this phenomenon whereby children replay painful events in an attempt to understand and control them.

Origins of Sexualized Behavior

When a youngster displays sexual behaviors far beyond his/her age or developmental level, therapists can often describe environmental factors and individual characteristics which seem to be associated with the behaviors. Typically, one or more of the following apply:

- The child comes from a single parent home, usually with a female head of the household; there is an uninvolved, absent, or unknown father, with frequent visits by many different men looking for sex and/or drugs.

- A chaotic home where activities are unplanned/unstructured and events revolve around the needs and interests of the adults, while the children are frequently overlooked or are expected to meet the needs of the adults.

- A family in which boundaries are loose and unclear, and where adults may sleep or bathe with the children, or even engage in sexual activities in front of them; at the very least, inappropriate discussions of sex regularly occur in the presence of children.

- The mothers are depressed, emotionally immature, and extremely dependent with low self-esteem, unresolved childhood trauma (usually sexual abuse), who tend to be isolated and alienated from their communities and use sex as a substitute for the love they never truly felt.

- The children are often thrust into adult roles as comforter, confidant, or sexual partner, or are used by the men in the home for their sexual pleasure, much like the mother is used and abused.

- Authoritarian discipline, is used but only sporadically, leaving the children confused and feeling off balance.

Social Isolation

A few individuals grow up in environments filled with rejection from adults as well as from peers. Their pain was so severe that a sweeping fear of criticism and rejection consumes them. Being hypersensitive to rejection, they grow increasingly cautious about entering any relationship unless unusually strong guarantees of uncritical acceptance are felt.

A number of child molesters report that these experiences and fears were the catalysts that led them to form criminal sexual relationships with children. Children were perceived as desirable sexually, often as less threatening, and more accepting than most adults.

Attachment Disorders

When a parent has been physically and/or emotionally unavailable to a child, normal attachment and bonding may not occur. When denied a secure attachment and cheated of a warm two-way relationship with another human being, some children develop into adults who are unable to give and receive care or to empathize with others. They become extremely selfish and self-centered.[13] Their attachment may also be weak because of abuse inflicted by the parents. This experience leaves the child distrustful, or even hateful, toward other people.

Whatever the reason behind the failure to attach, the damage to a child can be very harmful. As adults these abused, neglected, isolated people may show disregard for others, break laws, fail to learn from their experiences, exhibit no guilt, and lie incessantly. Having never been loved, they are incapable of true love. Typically their sex lives are impersonal and trivialized and their sexual partners are quickly discarded after being used and abused.

Psychologists have labeled these individuals as psychopaths, sociopaths, and antisocial personalities. These persons, usually men, engage in chronic criminal lifestyles that may include assault and battery, burglaries, robberies, drinking offenses, as well as sex crimes. Psychologists believe theses individuals rarely get better, even with the best of therapy. Still others have found therapy may make them worse.[14]

---

[13] Magid, K., and McKelvey, C. (1989). High Risk Children Without a Conscience. New York: Bantam.

[14] Hare, R. (1995). Without conscience: the disturbing world of psychopaths among us. New York: Pocket Books.

Narcissistic Wounds

A narcissistic wound is any childhood trauma, subtle or blatant, that leaves the child ill-prepared for later independent living. The wounds common to sex addicts are very obvious. For others, however, such wounds may be harder to see.

When most of us were born, we were at the center of adult attention. When tired, we were rocked to sleep. When we were hungry, food appeared. When wet and in discomfort, our parents tended to our needs. As time went on, we were weaned from this total dependence to a more autonomous way of living. This gradual move to independence was perhaps difficult at times, but usually not traumatic.

For some children, as John Crewdson writes in *By Silence Betrayed,*[15] the distancing process goes awry. When parents withdraw their attentiveness and emotional support too abruptly, external supplies of admiration are missed. The child may not feel capable of developing internal substitutes. Worse still, the death of a parent can leave some children floundering in a void of self-worth. Crewdson likens this type of narcissistic wound to a child who is learning to ride a bike and his/her training wheels are quickly and prematurely removed.[16]

As a result, some children conclude that the world is an unreliable place, a cruel and painful environment. They may conclude that other people can't be relied on to give them what they need and deserve. In fact, some children conclude that they are entitled to more, and they aggressively take what they need from what they perceive as a "dog-eat-dog" world.

Other children are so pampered and protected by their parents - so emotionally smothered - that they too conclude that the world owes them whatever they desire. For both types, a selfish (narcissistic) response is generated.

As these children enter adulthood, they carry with them a sense of entitlement, deep insecurities, a lack of empathy, and an exaggerated, fragile, and false sense of their own importance. They impulsively meet their self-centered needs with little regard for the hardship it causes other persons. A few turn to the combination of pleasure and excitement to assuage their misunderstood emotional pain. Sex, especially forbidden and clandestine sex, becomes an overpowering "drug."

Contrast the child molester with the adult rapist who generally is less addictive (in one study, 39% of rapists were diagnosed as sex addicts),[17] and less driven to find sources of uncritical love. The rapist is more inclined to use

---

[15] Crewdson, J. (1989). By silence betrayed. New York: Perennial Library of Harper & Row.

[16] Ibid.

[17] Blanchard, G. (1990). Differential diagnosis of sex offenders: Distinguishing characteristics of the sex addict. American Journal of Preventive Psychiatry and Neurology 2:3, 45-47.

sexual abuse as a way to pursue the power and control that he has was lacking for much of his life. Some child molesters, on the other hand, need to believe that children enjoy sex much like he does.

Brain Trauma

In our clinical experience with sex abusers, we have noted how apparently normal men without a childhood history of child maltreatment could, following a brain injury, suddenly commit a violent sex crime. Canadian researchers have suggested that damage to the temporal lobes in the brain may be linked to sexual behavior.[18]

Others have noted how brain damage is significantly correlated to violent criminal activity.[19] Again and again the literature points to the role head trauma can play in the unfolding of sexually abusive behavior. In fact, significant neuropsychological abnormalities have been detected in as many as 96% or more of abuser samples studied.[20,21] This implies prompt and proper post-injury medical care may help prevent many incidents of sex abuse.

Shame

A risk factor for sexual violence is the fear of shame and ridicule. Violent abusers have an overwhelming need to prevent others from laughing at them, to the point where they may harm others to prevent it.[22] Much of the fear of humiliation comes from childhood trauma that was left untreated. When even the slightest hint of an interpersonal slight is sensed, the shame-based individual prepares to lash out in an effort to regain pride through violence. Our prisons are filled with these insecure men, some of whom would rather be killed than submit to a put-down. The same "emotional logic" underlies many acts of sexual abuse.

Still other men are so shame-based that they feel the only persons who would find them acceptable or worthwhile are children whom they can impress with superior knowledge and abilities, and who don't know any better.

---

[18] Pukins, J., & Langevin, R. (1985). Brain correlates of penile erection. In R. Langevin (Ed.) Erotic preference: Gender identity and aggression in men. Hillsdale, NJ: Lawrence Erlbaum.

[19] Pallone, N . (1990). Rehabilitating criminal sexual psychopaths. New Brunswick, NJ: Transaction Publishers.

[20] Yeudall, L., & Fromm-Auch, D. (1979). Neuropsychological impairments in various psychopathological populations. In Gruzelier, J. & Flor-Henry, P. (eds.), Hemisphere asymmetries of function in psychopathology. Amsterdam: Elsevier/North Holland Biomedical Press.

[21] Corley, A., Corley, D., Walker, J., & Walker, S. (1994). The possibility of organic left posterior hemisphere dysfunction as a contributing factor in sex-offending behavior. Sexual Addiction & Compulsivity, 1 (4), pp. 337-346.

[22] Gilligan, J. (1996). Violence: Our deadly epidemic and its causes. New York: Grosset/Putnam Books.

When shame is at the root of a sexual crime and society imposes its punishment on the abuser, he or she feels additional shame while healthy guilt and genuine love are diminished; the abuser becomes more violent.

Imagine for a moment the implications of these shame dynamics on our child-raising techniques, the importance of intervening early and effectively with sexual abuse victims (especially boys who may feel the most shame regarding being victimized and become our most dangerous offenders), and the way our criminal justice may escalate criminal violence through shaming sentencing techniques and other forms of punishment.

Sexual Addiction

Sexual addiction can be defined as a dependence on the mood altering experience that sex can provide. Sex is used "medicinally" as a way to alter moods and escape everyday stressors. Amidst the pleasure and excitement that sex provides (especially if it is clandestine or forbidden), the addict's emotional pain is momentarily pacified. When the sexual act has been completed, guilt and shame usually flood the addict, leading to a search for still more sex to numb the discomfort. The addiction escalates with the addict taking more and more risks to get a fix. Values are compromised in search of the next sexual encounter. Some addicts eventually violate laws and abuse people as their compulsive sexual behavior spirals out of control. Consequently, it is important to find ways to reach these individuals early in their addictive cycle before others get hurt.

On a psychological level, much has been written about the emotional condition of the men, women, and children who become sex abusers. Some personality features and adjustment patterns are clear. Sexual addiction is an often neglected malady that gives impetus to sexual abuse. This is not to say that all sex addicts become sex abusers, but an alarming number of sex abusers are untreated sex addicts.

A Wyoming survey of incarcerated sex offenders found over half of the men (55%) were diagnosed sex addicts.[23] Nearly three of every four (71%) child molesters shared the same diagnosis. Yet, most prisons fail to test for sexual addiction or treat that component of an offender's life. Outside of prison, only a handful of facilities specialize in the treatment of sexual addiction. Most charge fees far in excess of what most people can afford - as much as $45,000 for one month of care. Treatment is out of reach for most Americans, which leaves a volatile sub-population of addicts at risk for assaulting our loved ones or ourselves.

---

[23] Blanchard, G. (1990). Differential diagnosis of sex offenders: Distinguishing characteristics of the sex addict. American Journal of Preventive Psychiatry and Neurology 2:3, 45-47.

Research at the Institute for Behavioral Medicine in Golden Valley, Minnesota revealed that 81% of sex addicts self-reported that they had been sexually abused as children, 72% said they had been physically abused, and 97% disclosed that they had been victims of emotional abuse.[24] Most sex addicts grow up believing they are unworthy, "damaged goods," or undeserving of love. Sex becomes their pacifier and best friend, a medication for emotional pain.

The triple impact of the stigma of being a victim, guilt for their participation, and shame for being who they are, has led many innocent victims down the path of sexual dependency. Unfortunately, addictive behaviors are often progressive and what may have started as sexualized childhood behavior or compulsive masturbation eventually evolves into victimizing behavior for some of these children.[25] But the actions of an addictive minority can affect an incredible number of innocent people. Although sexual abusers may only have one victim or few victims, surveys have shown that some sexually compulsive sex abusers assault hundreds of times before they are apprehended.[26, 27]

Our national obsession with sex has been described by some as an addiction, on both an individual and a societal-cultural basis. One organization, the National Council on Sexual Addiction and Compulsivity, has been founded to serve those individuals who are "hooked" on sex. One council spokesperson, Dr. Patrick Carnes, has written widely on this subject. It is his belief, and that of many others, that it is emotional pain - not an abnormally strong sex drive - that fuels most addictive, out-of-control sexual behavior.[28] Personal shame, or a sense of being totally unworthy, drives many a person in search of a mood-altering experience, just as the chemically dependent person goes in search of a mood-altering drug. Pleasure and excitement, which generate powerful chemical and hormonal changes in the body, serve to obliterate emotional pain when used in heavy doses. Much of that pain comes from a childhood that was submerged in abuse and neglect. The sex addict learned early on that sex was one of the few ways to receive anything resembling love or affection. As a result of abuse, a sense of unworthiness, and their familiarity with sex, many addicts come to believe that sex is their most important need.

[24] Carnes, P. (1991). Don't call it love. New York: Bantam Books.

[25] Carnes, P. (1983). Out of the shadows. Minneapolis: CompCare.

[26] Rosenfeld, A. (1995). Discovering and dealing with deviant sex, Psychology Today, pp. 8-10.

[27] Freeman-Longo, R., & Wall, R. (1986). Changing a lifetime of sexual crime, Psychology Today, March (20)3 , pp. 58-64.

[28] Carnes, P. (l989). Contrary to Love. Minneapolis: CompCare.

We can't talk seriously about preventing sexual abuse, including criminal sexual abuse, without examining the variety of causal factors, including sexual addiction. Recognizing this affliction is the task of every person working in the sexual abuse field. A few warning signs include:

- The inability to stop certain sexual behaviors despite repeated promises to do so
- Significant consequences to oneself and others
- Compromising one's values in search of a sexual experience
- Using sex in a medicinal way to escape unpleasant feelings
- Obsessing about sex
- Taking more and more risks to find a sexual outlet
- Being unable to walk away from a sexual encounter once the opportunity presents itself
- Sexual relationships are without sincere care and commitment for partners
- Regularly feeling shame after sexual experiences
- Going to great lengths to keep sexual activities hidden and secretive
- Feeling degraded and depressed by one's sexual activities
- Obtaining less and less pleasure from sex over time

Overcoming abuse and developing a healthy sexuality are essential in the recovery from an addiction to sex.[29] Researcher and sexual addiction clinician Ginger Manley has described healthy sexuality as the experience of feeling whole and worthy as a sexual person, being willing and able to consent to sex, responding sexually in a way that is consistent with one's value system and connected to a spiritual core, and being able to enjoy sex and even laugh about it.[30] But if all the media teaches in America is a highly eroticized version of sexuality along with the abuses of sex, few will have the chance to experience or even recognize healthy sexuality once they reach adulthood. Education then is a key, and it must expose the youth of America to information about sexuality that is loving, consensual, enjoyable, spiritual, and healthy.

---

[29] Irons, R. (1994). Healthy sexuality in recovery. Sexual Addiction & Compulsivity. 1 (4), pp. 322-336.

[30] Manley, G. (1995). Healthy sexuality: Stage III recovery , Sexual Addiction & Compulsivity, 2(3), pp. 157-183.

Dr. Charlotte Kasl Davis has written, "To heal from addiction in an addictive society is a little like an alcoholic trying to recover in a bar."[31] A sex addict can best recover when his/her host culture has entered the healing process. A major challenge of this book is to point the way toward creating a sexually healthy America.

Pornography

Pornography is a controversial topic because there are many case examples that demonstrate both its value and its potential harm. In regards to pornography some research reveals:

- pornography can heighten unacceptable sexual urges in some persons,

- some sexual abusers never use pornography, and

- it can decrease sexual tensions in some men (and some behaviorists use it in therapy for this reason).

By itself, pornography does not turn people into sex abusers. Persons who are predisposed to sexually aggressive behavior may use soft- and hard-core pornography to increase their arousal or justify their behavior.[32] Because of some of the risk factors previously discussed, some are addicted to sex. Others have a high tolerance for violence and aggression while some have been raised to regard others as sexual objects to be used at their whim.

What some learn from pornography is called objectification - an attitude that others are nothing more than objects - not human beings. Women and children may be seen as eager, yet passive, sexual toys whose function in life is to satisfy a man. Males may be viewed as sexual machines, always ready, or as pawns who are vulnerable when aroused. In our clinical experience we have seen a growing number of sexually abusive boys identify the use of pornography as the source of their ideas regarding objectification of and sexual aggression toward women.

Some males may see women's worth as linked to the perfect body, a link established and continually reinforced by the images pornographers and many consumer product advertisers present. Personality factors are always secondary to body parts. Others might be aroused by scenes involving bondage and violence being inflicted on women. A steady diet of violent pornography can desensitize viewers to this type of mistreatment. No longer inhibited by any

---

[31] Kasl Davis, C. (1992). Women, sex and addiction. New York: Ticknor & Fields.

[32] Rosenberg, J. (1989). Fuel on the fire: An inquiry into "pornography" and sexual aggression in a free society. Orwell, VT: Safer Society Press.

sense of revulsion toward violent images or empathy toward the victims, it isn't much of a leap for some men to live out the fantasies portrayed in the pictures by engaging in a sexual crime.

Nonpornographic Sexploitation

Obviously, there is a demand for nonpornographic material that "sexploits" others because they are a part of our economy and generate billions of dollars in sales. As time goes on, the language and messages have become more explicit. Our society has become more permissive of what is tolerable and, over time, we have consistently tested our limits and stretched our boundaries. There are examples of explicit sexual images everywhere. They create an environment conducive to sexual abuse.

In addition, we promote our children in sexual ways. The classic example of children portrayed as sexual objects is the Calvin Klein advertising campaign that was so controversial in New York City and made national news in 1995.[33] Even conversations about children have sexual messages; for example, comments about children often include "Isn't she a sexy little girl," "He's gonna be a real lady's man," and "She's gonna break all the boys' hearts." These sexual comments clearly convey to young children that their value relies on sex appeal.

At the same time, we try to protect our children from being exposed to age inappropriate materials by rating movies and removing books from the public libraries. Despite pervasive sexual messages in our culture, coupled with the threat of AIDS and other sexually transmitted diseases, many parents are still opposed to teaching sex education in the schools. For example, Joycelyn Elders, our former Surgeon General, was fired because she supported teaching older school children about masturbation.

Explanations or Excuses?

An understanding of what contributes to the development of sexually abusive behavior is helpful in treating abusers and thereby reducing their chances to continue to abuse others. Some people may use knowledge to excuse their conduct. But unless an abuser understands the repeating pattern or cycle of sexual abuse, accepts full responsibility for his abusive choices, and actively learns and practices new, nonabusive habits and behaviors, he is at risk for continuing to abuse. Insights are helpful but without a sincere commitment to institute changes based on those understandings, danger remains.

---

[33] Ingrassia, M. with Nayyar, S., Kalb, C., Miller, S., and Mabry, M. (1995, September 11) Calvin's World. Newsweek, pp. 60-66.

Sexual abuse has been around for such a long time that pinpointing its origin is difficult. The rape of women has been documented for thousands of years, as has the sexual abuse of children. However, most societies have decided that these behaviors are wrong and cannot be ignored. We know there are damaging effects from sexual abuse and that the sexual abuse cycle will continue to be a problem in America unless we do something different to stop it and prevent it.

Unfortunately, a complete understanding of the origins of sexual abuse does not exist. Such an understanding would make developing treatments and prevention easier. As with other public health problems such as cancer, AIDS, and substance abuse, when time and funding resources are made available to explore the causes of sexual abuse and violence in our society, it will become easier to find solutions and cures for the problem.

The Sustainers

The term "sustainers" is used to identify aspects of our culture that reinforce unhealthy, deviant sexual attitudes and behaviors. Examples include pornography and other sex-for-sale industries, sexualized ads and media messages, adult entertainment establishments, and more. Sustainers place many barriers and temptations in front of even highly motivated sex offenders who are trying to change their sexually abusive patterns through their involvement in responsible, intensive, long-term treatment programs.

Abusers tell us that once an individual has engaged in sexually abusive behavior, turning the problem around is difficult. If will power alone worked, many abusers would gladly stop their abusive behavior before they risked legal penalties and the resulting disruption to their lives. Unfortunately, sexual abuse is a complex problem that requires more than will power and simple punitive solutions. As we will discuss in Chapter Seven, time and experience have taught us that our current laws are not effectively addressing this problem. Tough laws, with stiff penalties, will only continue to drive the sexual abuse problem underground, generate more victims, and tax limited government resources.

Sexual abuse is not going to go away because the public is tired of hearing about it. Sexual abuse and the abuse of sexuality are deeply ingrained in the American culture. As long as there are so many cultural components that sustain sexual abuse, the problem will continue, despite the public's intolerance of sexual abuse. As a society, we must be willing to examine our values as well as our tolerance for public portrayal of deviant and abusive sexual behaviors. If we are to discover the roots of violence and abuse we must critically examine our own beliefs and behaviors as well as those of abusers.[34]

---

[34] Strean, H. & Freeman, L. (1993). Our wish to kill: The murder in all our hearts. New York: Avon Books.

We must question our tolerance and support of messages and products which sustain behavior we abhor.

There is a reason people who suffer from sexually abusive urges and thoughts do not seek help. Few individuals who experience sexually abusive urges are willing to risk the public's wrath. Our culture does not make it easy for someone with a sexual abuse problem to step forward and get help, nor does it provide any options for them. In fact, our country doesn't have national public service announcements inviting the sexual abuser to seek help for his problem. For an individual who is acting out sexually, any agency he or she visits is mandated by law to immediately report the abuse to the authorities. Depending on the severity of the sexually abusive behavior, and the laws in each state, an abuser who turns himself or herself in may face penalties as harsh as life in prison, hardly a motivator to seek help. The public's demonization of sexual abusers also discourages self disclosure.

For example, a sexual abuser who wanted to stop his sexually abusive behavior turned himself in to the authorities. He was arrested and sentenced to 37 years in prison. One can be assured that other individuals, who have had similar ideas of getting help, but heard about this case, are not likely to report their problem to anyone.

• CHAPTER FOUR •

Promotion of Sexual Abuse

Pro-Pedophilia Organizations

Although it may be hard to believe, there are organizations in America that advocate adult sexual relations with children. Because we have First Amendment rights of freedom of press and speech, these organizations are legal and able to foster behavior, render opinions, and advocate abusive actions that are contrary to state and federal laws. In the late 1980's several of these groups were organizing and planning to lobby state governments to lower the age of sexual consent for children to as young as 12 or 13 years old.[1] In the 1980's, the Dutch government proposed lowering the age of sexual consent from 16 to 12.[2] Even publications available on newsstands contain articles that invite Americans to reconsider the positive side of pedophilia (child sexual abuse). Mary Eberstadt, an adjunct fellow at the Hudson Institute, writes " ...even as the the public rhetoric about prosecuting America's children has reached deafening levels, a number of enlightened voices have been raised in defense of giving pedophilia itself a second look.[3]

---

[1] Detective Laren Glover, Oregon State Police. Personal communication September 10, 1988.

[2] Sideman, A. (Writer/Producer/Director). (1994). Chicken hawks: Men who love boys. UGF-TV, New York University, New York.

[3] 3 Eberstadt, M. Pedophilia chic. The Weekly Standard. News America Publishing Incorporated, New York. (17 June, 1996) 1(39), p. 19-28.

Several organizations and networks promote sexual relations between adults and children and some are incest-specific, advocating sexual relations between children and family members or relatives. Three organizations stand out as more public in their advocacy and mission, the North American Man-Boy Love Association, the Childhood Sensuality Circle, and The Rene Guyon Society.

In his book *Paedophilia: The Radical Case*, Tom O'Carroll discusses some of the organizations that promote sexual relations between children and adults that are described below.[4] Below are brief descriptions of a few such organizations.

The North American Man-Boy Love Association

The North American Man-Boy Love Association (N.A.M.B.L.A.), is a national organization that promotes, as its name implies, men having sex with young boys. In the past N.A.M.B.L.A. has attempted to ride on the coattails of gay rights organizations, despite the fact that the majority of men who sexually abuse male children do not refer to themselves as gay or identify with the gay rights movement. Thus, many people falsely believe that part of the child sexual abuse problem is a result of homosexuality. The truth of the matter is that the vast majority of child molesters lead heterosexual lifestyles and the gay rights movement has refused to embrace their cause.

In addition, N.A.M.B.L.A. has protested, to varying degrees, conferences and educational training events on child sexual abuse. These efforts to promote their cause have gone to extremes.[5]

N.A.M.B.L.A. has produced publications such as the NAMBLA Journal. Information about N.A.M.B.L.A. is freely available on the Internet, including articles and "non-pornographic" pictures of boys in seductive poses.

Childhood Sensuality Circle

The Childhood Sensuality Circle, founded in 1974, also promotes children as sexual beings and fosters sexual relations between children and adults. An article by the Associated Press reads:

Pedophile Writings Alleged.

AUSTIN TX (AP) - A clerk with then-Austin Independent School District will be fired immediately if it's proven he is the author of pamphlets urging adults to have sexual relations with children, a school official said Friday.

---

[4] O'Carroll, T. (1980). Paedophilia: The radical case. Boston: Alyson Publications.

[5] Sideman, A. (Writer/Producer/Director). (1994). Chicken hawks: Men who love boys. UGF-TV, New York University, New York.

A story published by the Houston Chronicle maintained that clerk D.S., age 43, had published several such pamphlets.

According to the newspaper, Mr. S. also is listed as associate editor of a newsletter published by Childhood Sensuality Circle, a California group that advocates sexual relations between adults and children and repeal of age-of-consent laws.

The Rene Guyon Society

The Rene Guyon Society, formerly located in Beverly Hills, California, promoted sexual relations between children and adults. This membership organization was known for its slogan "Sex by year 8, or else it's too late!" and published newsletters and brochures to promote its mission. At one time the Rene Guyon Society, listed in the Gale Encyclopedia of Associations, had as many as 5,000 members.[6]

Although the Rene Guyon Society may not be in operation today, organizations with similar purposes and messages, such as PAN (Pedophile Alert Network) and PIE (Pedophile Information Exchange), continue to be formed throughout the United States and overseas. The adult pornography market is filled with videos and books whose titles clearly suggest sexual liaisons with children, teens, and young female relatives.[7]

To attempt to track down and cite every organization that promotes children having sexual relations with adults would be a difficult task. By examining just a few organizations we point out the fact that organizations can legally promote this behavior despite national laws prohibiting it.

Other Organizations

V.O.C.A.L.

While not a pro-pedophilia organization, Victims of Child Abuse Laws (V.O.C.A.L.) has fought against many laws that protect children from abuse and enable state officials to investigate sexual abuse allegations. V.O.C.A.L. was started in the 1980's by individuals who allege they were falsely accused of child sexual abuse.

It is tragic whenever an individual is falsely accused and successfully prosecuted for a crime he or she did not commit. But even when the occurance of sexual abuse has been substantiated through investigation, those accused of child molesting are much more likely not to be prosecuted (for a variety of

---

[6] Child Lures - "The Safety Solution" @ www.childlures.com. 03/07/97.

[7] Examples of titles from actual child pornography publications are given in Chapter Six.

reasons including the victim being too young to testify) than to be prosecuted on the basis of false or malicious allegations. Research has consistently found that young children rarely fabricate accusations without coaching from an adult, and adolescents who falsify reports are easily discovered.[8] Inconsistency in false reports are usually discovered rather quickly by trained investigators. Because of our increasing knowledge and ongoing data collection on the accuracy of children's disclosures of sexual abuse, there are reduced opportunities for false reports to be followed through to arrest and conviction.

Some people may belong to V.O.C.A.L. and similar groups based on their passionate belief that the state has no right to interfere with families. But unfortunately, many real child sexual abusers may also join such groups as camouflage against detection and/or for support if prosecution is imminent. While these groups may help the individual avoid prosecution or assist in fighting charges, their efforts do little to prevent sexual abuse. To the contrary, when child sexual abusers are successful at avoiding prosecution or conviction, the avenue for further abuse remains open. We also note it is probably not coincidental that the philosophies of such groups fit very neatly with several characteristic defense mechanisms used by sex abusers, such as justification, denial, and reliance on conspiracy theories.

To rid themselves of the taint of potential complicity in the perpetuation of child sexual abuse, organizations such as V.O.C.A.L. must be willing to put as much effort into prevention of sexual abuse and the identification and treatment of abusers as they put into helping the minority who are truly the victims of false accusations in the criminal justice system. Narrow, one-sided efforts will not contribute to the greater cause of sexual abuse prevention.

Sexual Behavior Trends

Over the past fifteen years we have observed many human sexual behavior trends that reflect both the seriousness of the sexual abuse problem and the pervasiveness of deviations from what Americans might consider to be appropriate, healthy human sexual behavior. We briefly review a few of these trends below.

Teen Pregnancies

Teen pregnancy is a multi-faceted issue that directly affects the American standard of what constitutes family. National economics, health care, cultural values, and standards for child rearing are all effected by changes in family

---

8 Ryan, G. The Kempe National Center for Child Abuse & Neglect. Personal Communication. July 8, 1997.

structure. Many teenage girls who become pregnant have been victims of sexual abuse or incest. As researcher Dr. Debra Boyer of Seattle's University of Washington reminds us,

> In the midst of these issues are adolescent girls who have been sexually abused and are most vulnerable to pregnancy in a society that offers little protection. If public policy and prevention efforts are to be meaningful, child sexual abuse and exploitation must be understood in relation to the other "causes" of teen pregnancy.[9]

In a study conducted by Dr. Boyer on 535 parenting and pregnant adolescents from 35 sites in nine counties in Washington state, "62% had experienced contact molestation, attempted rape, or rape prior to their first pregnancy."[10] Participants were 9.7 years old on average at the time of their first molestation, with 24% reporting their first sexual abuse experience at age five or younger.

There is an alarming number of teen pregnancies in the United States. As researchers D.S. Herrmann and J. J. McWhirter note, "The rate of teenage sexual involvement is at an all-time high. Of every 10 girls in the United States between the ages of 15 and 19 years, 1 becomes pregnant each year, with 5 of 6 of these pregnancies being unintentional. By the time they turn 19, 74% of girls and 83% of boys have engaged in sexual intercourse and are thus at risk for HIV infection."[11]

In the newsletter *Youth Today,* B. Howard notes, "Unfortunately, Congress has committed taxpayers to spending $50 million dollars each year to teach girls and boys to say no to sex - until they marry."[12] It is unfortunate to commit public funds to programs already deemed ineffective. An independent 12-member scientific panel convened by the National Institute of Health concluded that abstinence-only education cannot be justified in the face of other, more effective programs. According to Brian Wilcox of the University of Nebraska, "... credible evidence is lacking to show the effectiveness of abstinence-only programs ... there is mounting evidence suggesting that these programs are generally ineffective."[13] Besides, if teen pregnancies are often the result of past (or current) sexual abuse, it seems the $50 million for abstinence might be better spent on sexual abuse prevention.

---

[9] Boyer, D. (November/December 1995). Adolescent pregnancy: The role of sexual abuse. NRCCSA News, 4(6) Pg. 1. NRCCSA News is the newsletter of the National Resource Center on Child Sexual Abuse of the National Center on Child Abuse & Neglect.

[10] Ibid, p. 3.

[11] Herrmann, D.S., & McWhirter, J. J. (1997). Refusal and resistance skills for children and adolescents: A selected review. Journal of Counseling & Development, 75(3), 177-187.

[12] Howard, B. (March/April 1997). 'Best Friends' Snag $50 Million for 'No-Sex' Ed. Youth Today 6(2). P. 1. Youth Today is a bimonthly publication of the American Youth Work Center, 1200 17th St. NW - 4th Floor; Washington, D.C. 20036-3006.

[13] Ibid.

According to Jill Hutton, an education outreach coordinator in Vermont, "Three out of four births to high school aged girls are fathered by men older than high school age usually in their twenties. Men over 20 years old are responsible for 5 times as many births among junior high girls as are junior high boys, and 2.5 times as many births among high school girls than high school aged boys."[14] Gail Ryan of the Kempe National Center on Child Abuse and Neglect notes:

> "It is ironic that an adolescent boy who convinces a child more than 5 years younger will be charged with a sexual offense, and yet many men in their mid 20's impregnate similarly young girls and are rarely arrested. One California judge actually allows these young men to chose between marrying the girl or being charged."[15]

Teen pregnancies are both a serious social problem and a public health issue. Senators Olympia Snowe (R-Maine) and Joseph Lieberman (D-Conn.) described unwed teen mothers as "a plague on the nation."[16] That so many of these teen mothers have been sexually abused, and that in some cases the children may be the product of forcible rape or other sexually abusive behavior is testimony to the need to look at sexual abuse and the abuse of human sexuality from a new and different perspective. Because many of these teenage girls have been sexually abused, they are at risk of having problems that can persist throughout their lives, as we will discuss in Chapter Nine. The problems from being sexually abused, if left untreated, can pose many difficulties and concerns for teenagers attempting to raise children.

Date Rape Drugs

Another recent trend has been the introduction of drugs, some sold over the counter, that have come to be known as "date rape drugs." Rohypnol and GHB (Gamma-hydroxybutyrate) are two examples.

GHB is a central nervous system depressant that has been investigated as an anesthetic. Rohypnol is a medication prescribed by physicians for people with severe sleep disorders. It produces a sedating effect in the user, and with large doses can generate impaired ability to remember details of events.[17]

---

[14] Hutton, J. (1997, April). The true shame. GOSSIP: News and notes from the Burlington women's council, 4(4), pp. 1-2.

[15] Ryan, G. The Kempe National Center on Child Abuse and Neglect. Personal Communication. July 8, 1997.

[16] Unwed teen moms called 'plague on the nation'. Youth Today July/August 1997, 6(2). P. 1. Youth Today is a bimonthly publication of the American Youth Work Center, 1200 17th St. NW - 4th Floor; Washington, D.C. 20036-3006.

[17] When Drugs Are Used For Rape. Brochure funded through a public service grant from Hoffman-LaRoche. DC Rape Crisis Center, Washington D.C.

These drugs are usually given to women before they are taken advantage of sexually or sexually abused. Typically, the man slips the drug into the woman's drink. The drugs normally cause amnesia in the user, making it difficult for victims to report sexual assaults that have occurred. Even worse, some women have become comatose and others have died from overdoses.

Made for Television Shows about Human Sexual Behavior

The media is highly charged with sexual material that challenges even the most liberal-minded person's attitudes regarding human sexuality. Television is the most powerful and accessible of the media and provides the elements of sound and vision over time to produce highly stimulating programming and has tremendous potential to influence viewers. Several cable channels offer programming that is centered around human sexual behavior, such as the HBO show described in Chapter Two featuring couples carving designs on each other's bodies with razor blades and licking the blood from the wound. Although these couples claim this to be consenting intimate sexual relations, the image delivered to the viewer is mutilation and sadistic sex.

Another example is a program titled "Sex in the 90's."[18] This series addresses human sexuality and sexual relations of consenting couples. One episode described the fantasies of individuals and simulations of the fantasy were acted out. A woman talks about being taken by her man and made to engage in certain behaviors. This image portrays women as desiring rape and forcible sex. In some segments the viewer is left not knowing what or how to distinguish fantasy from reality. The use of aggressive images in fantasy portrayed on television sends a message that may normalize rape as an acceptable sexual behavior.

The portrayal of these behaviors (or any behavior for that matter) on television begins to normalize the behavior. The more we are exposed to ideas or see actual behaviors in practice, the less sensitized we become and the more likely it is that individuals will take the opportunity to try the behavior, even if it is just "one time."

Sexualized Literature and Films

Adult pornography consists of books, magazines, videos, and other images that usually emphasize body parts and/or specific sexual behaviors. The emphasis on body parts and behavior has the potential to depersonalize and dehumanize sexual relations and refocus sexual behavior solely for the purpose of self-gratification. In some cases, the materials focus on the "size" of human body parts or sexual behavior in a way that can negatively affect the way people

---

[18] Sex in the 90's was a series aired on Music Television (MTV) during the 1996 television season.

engage in sexual relations with each other. To make it "legitimate," the producers of the materials promote them in a variety of ways. In some instances, the materials are advertised as providing helpful sexual behavior information and promoting a healthy sexual lifestyle.

One catalog makes the following statement to its customers:

> Because we are committed to a healthy exploration of sexuality, a team of psychologists review our video cassettes to ensure that they do not appeal to a prurient or unhealthy type of interest in sex. There is never any violence, nor are there words or actions that are demeaning to men or women. Our films have scientific value because they offer information on human sexual activity and may help individuals to become more comfortable with certain acts, thus leading to greater sexual fulfillment.[19]

The same catalog offers the following video titles: Women Who Crave Facial Orgasms, Massive Black Erections, Women Behind Bars, Anal Lust, Titty Bar Part 2, Sex Extremes - Beyond the Norm, Girls with Huge Vaginas, and Group Sex to name a few. In addition, this catalog provides advertisements for phone sex (see Chapter Six).

Although some of the video titles may seem harmless, the messages they portray in their titles imply the sexualization of others, accentuate the abnormal or unusual, and often exaggerate the frequency of sexual behavior between persons. In the book *Sex In America,* Michael and colleagues note the case of a woman who experienced anxiety in her sexual life and was quoted as saying, "Sex is all around you. In the ads, in the movies. You start thinking that if you're not having great sex all the time, then there's something wrong with you."[20] Given what the research says, compared to what the sex-for-sale industry promotes, one might ask, what is the purpose for promoting sexual behavior and sexual relations in this fashion, other than for purely financial gain, and why do so many people want to watch this material?

Cybersex on the Internet

Increasingly, more and more people are becoming socially withdrawn as a result of their addiction to computer use. The computer, especially now that it offers a banquet of sexual activities, has caused many a person to become dependent on it for the pleasure and excitement it offers. This addiction can

---

[19] Sensations: A Catalog of Adult Products Designed to Educate Stimulate and Enhance Your Sex Life. Gary, IN: Leisure Time Products.

[20] Michael, R. T., Gagnon, J. H., Laumann, E. O., and Kolata, G. (1994). Sex in America: A definitive study. New York: Little Brown.

often serve as a replacement for healthy human relations and, as the addiction progresses, encourage some users to find partners for the deviant sex they have been exploring on the Internet. An otherwise empty and unsatisfying life is given a boost by the mood-altering experience the computer provides.

Sowton (1987), was one of the first to explore the problem of computer addiction.[21] Milkman and Sunderwirth (1987), gave us a model for understanding the way computers can transport us to a fantasy world of relationships and experiences that enables the user to avoid the unpleasant side of life.[22] They described the "fantasy addict" who, with immediacy and very little effort, can "punch out", immerse themselves in a world of sex, and leave their stress behind.

The Internet has brought our world closer together and has opened up vast opportunities to access information on almost anything at any time. One of those opportunities is access to adult sexual material, pornography, and cybersex. Loosely defined, cybersex is the interactive experience of engaging in sexually explicit talk with another person or persons on the Internet. It is similar to phone sex (described in Chapter Six). The real-time interaction (or "chat," often initiated by invitations to "private rooms") may be accompanied by self-stimulation of the genitals.

It is not difficult to find live interactive "chat rooms" where the focus of conversation is sex. Users must indicate that they are at least eighteen years of age and agree to the rules and guidelines of the sponsoring organization. Some sites have several rooms to select from once the individual signs into the chat function. The chat rooms may limit the number of participants in the room at any given time and the titles given to the room imply the level or depth of conversation. For example, one chat location offers separate rooms that cater to straights, couples & swingers, gay men, lesbians, etc.

Once on the Internet (and free of charge) the user can enter a sexual oriented "chat room" and engage in literally any level of sexual discussion he or she chooses, as long as the user can find a willing participant. Finding a user willing to engage in sexual talk at any level is not difficult since this is why many of the users have gone to the site.

Since nobody knows who you are, it is easy to play any role and be any type of person you want to be, including an underage participant. If you are underage and log on, you can engage in explicit sexual language and describe participating in any sexual act you wish. The interactions can be between adult participants who are heterosexual, homosexual, lesbian, and bisexual. But serious problems arise when at least one of the participants is a child and the other is an adult.

---

[21] Sowton, M. (1987). Computer Addiction. Bristol, PA: Taylor and Francis.

[22] Milkman, H. & Sunderwirth, S. (1987). Craving for ecstasy: The consciousness & chemistry of escape. Lexington, MA: Lexington Books.

Cybersex has become popularized in many ways. One of the most interesting ads we found was discovered by accident when looking through a publication profiling potential talk-show guests for radio and television producers. Gennifer Flowers, the woman who claimed a 12-year affair with President Bill Clinton, now has her own cybersex website, "Gennifer's Girls." In a promotional ad for her website, it is noted that Gennifer Flowers "knew what it took to turn on Bill Clinton and now she's turning on others" with her new online cybersex website.[23] The ad goes on to read:

> "Attention Producers - Gennifer Flowers is also willing to discuss her views on the Paula Jones case which is currently before the Supreme Court. Jones claims President Clinton has some 'distinguishing characteristics' on his body, however, Gennifer says 'absolutely not.'

Such ads take advantage of others, and can be destructive to those they exploit, for personal gain.

Unfortunately, misuse of the Internet has led to documented potentially dangerous situations. In one instance, a man was accused of soliciting someone over the Internet to kidnap, rape, and torture his wife.[24] In another instance, a 15-year-old boy from Washington state met a man on the Internet who sent him a bus ticket to California. The man listed his hobby as "engaging in fellatio" and his motto: "The one who dies with the most boys – toys wins."[25] In Kentucky, a 13-year-old girl was "lured away after an e-mail correspondence with someone identified only as George in California. 'We can run around our room naked all day and all night,' George had suggested in the computer message printouts left behind by the girl."[26]

In another tragic case, 35-year-old Sharon Lopatka traveled from Maryland to North Carolina to meet the man who agreed to fulfill her sexual fantasies of being tortured and killed. Sharon Lopatka was murdered by Robert Class, the man she met on the Internet, who described how he was going to sexually torture her and ultimately kill her.[27]

[23] Gennifer Flowers offers presidential quality cybersex through the Internet. (1997, May). Radio-TV Interview Report, p. 79. Lansdowne, PA: Bradley Communications Corp.

[24] Anderson, Liz. Internet Sting: Accused Man Seeks A Delay. Rutland Daily Herald. Friday, February 7, 1997 Page 13.

[25] Murphy, K. (June 11, 1995) Youngsters falling prey to seducers in computer web. Los Angeles Times. p A1.

[26] Ibid.

[27] Young, G. Woman set up her murder on net. Available 4/23/97: http://www.web.co.za/mg/pc/96 nov/08nov-netmurder.htm.

Autoeroticism

Autoeroticism is sexually pleasuring oneself using a variety of nontraditional acts. It often involves extremely dangerous behaviors designed to heighten the pleasure of the sexual experience and orgasm. These sexual practices are different from self-stimulation through simple masturbation and can be life threatening. Each year people die while engaging in autoerotic behaviors.

One of the more common autoerotic practices or acts used as a means of achieving a sexual high and maximum sexual gratification, involves engaging in some form of self-strangulation. By engaging in limited self-strangulation at the point of orgasm, participants report a substantial increase in the sensation and pleasure of orgasm unmatched by that reached through traditional sexual practices.[28] Although the practice of attempting to partially hang oneself (in a foolproof way that will not result in death) is not widespread, it is the cause of death in a number of cases each year.

Other unhealthy sexual behavior trends that are damaging to individuals and to us as a society continue to exist and others are probably being developed as you read this book. Our point of mentioning them is simply to make you aware that such practices exist.

Rising Concern

Now you are aware of a few of the trends in human sexual interest and behavior occurring in America. They concern us for a variety of reasons. First, we are concerned about eroding boundaries regarding healthy sexual attitudes, interests, and behavior. Is society moving in an "anything goes" direction without regard for the impact on our culture and upcoming generations? As society becomes more accepting of abusive, addictive, nontraditional, and sometimes dangerous human sexual behavior, and as it becomes more relaxed with what it accepts in the media for children to see and learn, society may reach a point at which it will become very difficult to redirect its sexual values, attitudes, and behaviors.

Second, there is concern how these new directions in human sexuality will influence and possibly reinforce sexual abuse in our country. There is no research regarding how this material is impacting our culture. By the time responsible research is done and negative findings suggested, it may be beyond our ability to turn the problem around.

Some studies show that children are becoming sexually aware - and in some cases sexually active - at younger ages. One such study, whose purpose was to look at the pervasiveness of sex in the American culture and its impact on

---

[28] Money, J., Wainwright, G., & Hingsburger, D. (1991) The breathless orgasm. Buffalo, NY: Prometheus Books.

children, was conducted at Syracuse University with 35 elementary school children ages 5-12.[29] On ABC television's news magazine *Prime Time Live,* experts blame a popular culture that bombards children with sexual images from all sides, from comic books to the Internet.[30]

There is good reason to be concerned about pro-pedophilic organizations and deviant sexual trends in American culture. While adults are not as easily influenced as children by what they see and hear, some research now suggests that some adults are wrongly concerned that they are not within the "sexual norm" because of the sexual messages they are exposed to.[31]

While one or two studies do not necessarily constitute grounds to stop everything we are doing in the realm of human sexuality, they are a wake-up call. If we are going to prevent sexual abuse and discourage the abuse of human sexuality, we must act now, before it's too late. We must challenge traditional thinking and responses to sexual abuse.

[29] Theodore, J. (May 10, 1995). Local kids' sex views topic of tv show. The Post- Standard. Syracuse, NY. p. 1.

[30] Gavin, R. Reports on Kids and sex features Syracuse H S. May 10, 1995.

[31] Michael, R. T., Gagnon, J. H., Laumann, E.O., and Kolata, G. (1994). Sex In America: A Definitive Study. New York: Little Brown and Co.

CHAPTER FIVE

Sexual Abuse is Widespread in America

It has been decades since we considered rape and child molestation as crimes of the lower class, crimes affiliated with poverty, or crimes committed by uneducated people. Because sexual abuse is perpetrated by persons from all socio-economic strata and by persons with a variety of backgrounds, all Americans must take time to understand this social problem and address sexual abuse from a public health perspective.

When one class of people holds the majority of wealth and power over other classes, it is easy for members of the privileged class to incorrectly attribute blame for crime to another class of citizen, i.e., the wealthy blame crime on the poor. When a social problem cuts across all classes, it becomes easier to attribute blame to a specific group or class of individuals. In other words, non-abusive people separate themselves from those who are abusive, instead of accepting that abusive behavior can be perpetrated by anyone regardless of class or affiliation. Sexual abuse is not about intelligence, race, class, or social status. The follow sample of headlines from newspapers demonstrates that sexual abuse knows no boundaries.

- U.S. Soldiers Face Sex Case Charges [Frankfurt, Germany (AP)]

- Federal Judge Charged With Child Sex Offense [Ocean City, MD (AP)]

- Boy Scout Leader Jailed For Molesting Campers [St. Petersburg, FL (AP)]

- Priest Resigns after Sex Arrest [Portland, OR (AP)]
- Teacher Convicted in Sex Abuse Case [Corvallis, OR (AP)]
- 2 Congressmen Admit Sex Affairs with Young Pages [Washington, DC (AP)]
- Minister Indicted On Sex Charges [Waukegan, IL (AP)]
- Abuse by Judge Alleged [Caldwell, ID (AP)]
- Ex-Sheriff's Sergeant Guilty of Sexual Abuse [Marion County, OR]
- Home Operator Gets Rape Charges [Gainesville, FL]
- Anti-Smut Crusader Arrested For Sexually Molesting Minors [Tampa, FL (AP)]
- Nursery Worker Faces Child Abuse Charge [Gainesville, FL]
- Prosecutor Admits to Crime [Nashville, TN (AP)]
- Foster Father Denies Charge of Sexual Abuse [Dallas, TX]
- Female Therapist Must Stand Trial in Alleged Sexual Assault on Teen [Golden, CO]
- Rabbi Released on $100,000 Bail [Petaluma, CA (12/96)]
- Officer Indicted in Sex Case [Coquille, OR (AP)]

Clergy, doctors, politicians, and a host of professional people are being charged with sexual abuse, sexual misconduct, sexual harassment, prostitution, and are engaging in sexual behaviors disapproved of by our society. Criminal sexual abuse is not our only sexual abuse problem. America is in a human sexuality abuse crisis.

Sexual abuse can happen anywhere or at any time. For example, on an international flight between Sydney, Australia and Los Angeles, California an airline flight attendant relayed the following incident.

> In the first-class section, a female flight attendant was invited by one of the male passengers to sit and talk once the meal was served and things calmed down. After the meal the attendant joined the passenger while the movie was being shown. During the conversation, the passenger reached over to the attendant, grabbed her hand, and forced it down on his exposed, erect penis.[1]

The flight attendant who was describing this event said the victim of this abusive act did not intend to report it to the airline company or the authorities even though the captain of the aircraft encouraged her to do so. Her response

---

[1] Anonymous flight attendant. Personal communication January 1991.

to the natural question, "Why not?" was, "The airline company would not support her because of the negative publicity it would create."

As it turns out, this story is not unique in the airline industry. Other flight attendants relate similar stories about male passengers, men who refuse to fasten their seat belts and tell the attendant to do so, passengers in first class who take the hot moist towels offered them and drop them on their laps expecting the attendants to pick them up, and men who grab at the attendant's genital areas and breasts. These incidents occur frequently and sexual abuse treatment professionals identify all of them as abusive.

What is alarming about such instances is that they usually go unreported. Fears of reporting and concern about subsequent reactions by management and consequences if such reports go public, are a few reasons the problem continues. These problems don't simply go away on their own.

Sexual Abuse by Prominent People and Professionals

Probably the most glaring example of alleged sexual abuse by a prominent individual is the accusation of sexual harassment and exhibitionism made against President Clinton by Paula Jones.[2] However, as the sample of previously cited newspaper headlines indicate, people in prominent positions are no exception to sexually abusive behavior. For example, presidential advisor and campaign consultant Dick Morris admitted to having sexual relations with a prostitute. The media's disclosure of this event ended his career and was a major embarrassment to President Clinton.[3]

The Survivor Activist, a newsletter published by Survivor Connections, Inc., notes in one of its issues the filing of a lawsuit in January 1997 against Jeff Smith, age 58, TV's "Frugal Gourmet," for molesting a 15-year-old boy.[4] Also in that issue are accounts of allegations and/or investigations of sexual abuse by teachers, policemen, the former president of Zimbabwe, former congressman Mel Reynolds, and a hypnotherapist among others.

Frequently, a national headline features the story of a sexually abusive act perpetrated by an individual with an honorable profession held in high esteem by the community. Below, we review some of the demonstrative news stories about prominent persons and professions to illustrate the point that sexual abuse is widespread, pervasive, and a problem that requires more than just a criminal justice response.

---

[2] Greenhouse, L. (The New York Times) Clinton bid to delay lawsuit is rejected. (1997, May 28) The Rutland [VT] Daily Herald, p.1.

[3] Hunt, T. Whitehouse Correspondent. Chicago (AP) 1996, August 29. Clinton loses chief political strategist in sex scandal..

[4] Celebrity Accused. The Survivor Activist. (14) Vol.5, no.1. Spring 1997. Published by Survivor Connections, Inc. 52 Lyndon Rd. Cranston, R.I.

Sexual Harassment

As we noted in Chapter Two, consent means that all participants involved understand the consequences, both good and bad, for engaging in a particular behavior. Consent entails responsibility and accountability at many levels. Unfortunately, individuals who sexually harass often don't see anything wrong with their behavior and don't think about it as an issue of consent. The most important cases of sexual harassment in recent times involved the allegations by Anita Hill against then-nominee Supreme Court Justice Clarence Thomas. Also, the resignation of Senator Robert Packwood of Oregon was hastened when more than 20 women reported incidents of sexual harassment.

Sexual harassment has become such a concern that most workplaces are mandated by law to develop and post policy regarding sexual harassment in the workplace. Despite current laws and increasing public awareness, the media continue to expose television viewers to situations depicting sexual harassment that often makes light of the issue. In one study, according to researchers Grauerholz and King:

> Forty-eight hours of prime television viewing, representing a total of 81 shows, were recorded and content analyzed for this study. The unit of analysis is a particular act of sexual harassment. Within the 81 programs sampled, only 13 had no sexually offensive incident. Of those that had sexually offensive incidents, 231 incidents were recorded; the average number of acts, per program, was 3.4. In this study, a laugh track was heard in 70.6% of the cases (all occurred in situation-comedies; none was used in any of the dramas).[5]

The professional literature is growing with articles and research that examines how the media contributes to a cultural climate that is supportive of attitudes facilitating violence against women. Some research suggests that this type of media may diminish concern for female victims and produces negative changes in women's views of themselves.[6] If sexual abuse is to be prevented, such contributions to public attitudes regarding sexuality must be addressed. This is another example of how our media can take a behavior that is problematic and through repeated exposure, normalize it in the minds of its viewers, listeners, and/or readers.

---

[5] Grauerholz, E., and King, A. (1997). Prime Time Sexual Harassment. Violence Against Women, Vol. 3 No. 2, April 1997. 129-148. Sage Press.

[6] Krafka, C., Linz, D., Donnerstein, E., & Penrod, S. (1997). Women's reactions to sexually aggressive mass media depictions. Violence Against Women, 3(2),.149-181. Sage Publications.

Sexual Abuse and the Military

During the past few years there have been numerous news stories regarding the sexual abuse of female recruits and military personnel by male military officers and trainers. The scandal involving the sexual harassment and abuse of female naval officers at the Tailhook Conference in California is one of the stories that received the public's attention. It triggered Congress and the military upper echelons to focus on sexual abuse and harassment within its ranks.[7] The rape of a teenage Japanese girl by three Marines illustrated male military abuse of civilians and made international news.[8] The incidents of sexual abuse and harassment of female recruits by male Army personnel at the Aberdeen Proving Ground developed into a scandal involving multiple charges of sexual abuse and harassment against many officers and military personnel.[9] Also, the rape charges against two U.S. Army sergeants made the rapes of women soldiers at Darmstadt military training center "the most serious sex-abuse scandal at a U.S. military installation in Germany in years."[10]

These are just a few of many media-reported incidents involving military personnel and sexual abuse. Other than their sexually abusive behavior, many of these men are outstanding individuals with distinguished military careers. They have done much good for our country and have otherwise led law-abiding lives. Alleged and convicted sexual abusers are not always dirty old men from the lower class, or mentally impaired. Rather, they are subject to societal influences and have developed sexual behavior problems that must be addressed. If we look at sexual abuse as a public health issue for which help could be offered without severe, long-term punishment we may be able to encourage these individuals and others who may have similar problems to seek help before they act out, or in the early stages of an assault pattern. Such instances in the military are preventable when proper education and services are available to help those in need of treatment.

Sexual Abuse and the Church

As is the case with most helping professions, the churches of America have few, if any, set psychological standards for the selection of ministers or priests. Not surprisingly, many unhealthy individuals find their way into the ministry and

---

[7] Lancaster, J. Jury is still out on Tailhook scandal's effect on navy attitudes. (1994, February 17). The Washington Post, p. A10.

[8] Associated Press. (1995, November 7). U.S. Serviceman pleads guilty to rape in Japan, two others admit plotting. NAHA, Japan (Nov 7, 1995 - 01:24 EST) .

[9] Capt. pleads in sex case. (1997, March 21). The Rutland [VT] Daily Herald, p. 3.

[10] U.S. Soldiers Face Sex Case Charges. (1997, March 1) The Rutland [VT] Daily Herald. p. 2.

are confronted with the many burdens that being a cleric entails. With their own personal pains and the stress of their position in the church, giving much and receiving little, it is not surprising that many are tempted to extend their spiritual intimacy with some parishioners to physical intimacy. The frequency of pastoral sexual exploitation is in question. Some believe the incidence is near 9% of clergy.[11]

While the Catholic Church has been the focus of media attention as a result of the abuses of children by priests and nuns, no church is exempt from this problem.[12,13] The dynamics that give rise to clerical abuse are similar to those of father-daughter incest, with comparable amounts of suffering for the victims. Whenever you find a tremendous power imbalance matched with a deep and abiding trust, there is a risk of some form of abuse. As in the case of incest where entire families are torn apart by the aftermath, congregations are split and feel victimized by the pastor's betrayal. Some clergy describe addictive relationships with pornography and acknowledge the use of pornography helped open the door to the sexual abuse of members of the church congregation.

Today there are a number of treatment centers throughout the nation which are specifically designed to treat ministers and priests who have sexually exploited their parishioners. Churches, like families, want to treat their own outside the glare of the public spotlight. Consequently in some churches a dynamic develops in which the secret of abusive clergy is kept from outside scrutiny, and accountability, is only infrequently brought to bear.

Sexual Abuse and Health Care Professionals

Physicians and psychologists have traditionally received only a modicum of education and training regarding the avoidance of sexual exploitation of patients. Despite the power physical and mental health care professionals wield in their patients' lives, a code of ethics and the professional's sworn allegiance to it may be all there is to prevent the abuse of patients. As a result, many doctors and psychotherapists have sexually assaulted the very people they were expected to heal.

---

[11] Seat J., Trent, J. & Jwa, K. (1993, Winter). The prevalence and contributing factors of sexual misconduct among Southern Baptist pastors in six Southern states. Journal of Pastoral Care, 47, 363-370.

[12] Associated Press. (1996, November 15). Mormon church spokesman arrested in sodomy investigation. Http://www.newstimes.com:80/archive/nov1596/nal.htm. Available 03/08/97.

[13] Jennings, C. (1994, May 4). Church elder arrested for sexual assaulting a child. The Tromball [TX] Potpourri Newspaper, 7(3), p. 1.

The history of client abuse has its origins in the practices of some of the most famous names in the counseling field. Otto Rank turned a patient into a mistress. Sandor Ferenczi rationalized his fondling of female patients as a way to give them needed comfort. Carl Jung had affairs with several of his patients.[14] It is now estimated that 10% to 20% of health care professionals will sexually exploit a patient.[15,16] This type of abuse isn't surprising when one source reported that some therapists suffer from serious mental disturbances.[17] Finell,[18] Miller,[19] and Sussman[20] believe that some individuals who chose to enter the field of psychotherapy are inclined to have narcissistic disturbances. Obviously the self-monitoring done by physicians and therapists hasn't served a preventive function. The registering, certifying, accrediting, and licensing of health care providers is little more than window dressing when it comes to eradicating sexual abuse in the helping professions. (Appendix B lists positive qualities of a good mental health therapist and warning signs of problematic therapeutic relationships.)

Once trust has been betrayed as a result of sexual abuse, there must be a safe place to turn for healing. Therapy requires vulnerability, and vulnerability can easily be exploited by any helping professional. The vast majority of therapists operate ethically. A minority - 10 to 20%[21] will overstep sexual boundaries or even rape patients. Each profession (social work, psychotherapists, psychologists, and psychiatrists) currently is attempting to internally eliminate patient abuse - usually by treating these assaults as a non-criminal breech of ethics requiring censure, training, and/or decertification. Many state legislatures are saying this isn't enough - that any violation that so closely resembles incest must be treated as a crime. No matter the response, most everyone now agrees that therapist abuse is a serious problem.

Each year in the United States, thousands of people are victims of professional sexual misconduct The offending professional is typically male and the victim is typically female. A list of the professions where sexual misconduct occurs includes, but is not limited to, clergy, lawyers, physicians,

---

[14] Strean, H. (1993). Therapists who have sex with their patients. New York: Brunner/Mazel.

[15] Gabbard, G. (1989). Sexual exploitation in professional relationships. Washington, DC: American Psychiatric Association.

[16] Pope, K. (1986). Research and laws regarding therapist-patient sexual involvement: Implications for therapists. American Journal of Psychotherapy, 40, 564-571.

[17] Bermak, G. (1977). Do psychiatrists have special emotional problems? American Psychoanalytic Association, 21, 61-76.

[18] Finell, J. (1985). Narcissistic problems in analysts. International Journal of Psychoanalysis, 66, 433-445.

[19] Miller, A. (1981). Prisoners of childhood. New York: Basic Books.

[20] Sussman, M. (1992). A curious calling: Unconscious motivations for practicing psychotherapy. New York: Jason Aronson.

[21] Sanderson, B. (1985). Task force on sexual exploitation by counselors and therapists. St. Paul: Minnesota Department of Corrections.

and mental health professionals. The National Network for the Treatment of Professional Sexual Misconduct, developed by Dr. Gene Abel, was designed to address this growing problem. The network specializes in protecting parishioners, patients, and clients while returning professionals safely to practice.[22] The network, a new concept in sexual abuser treatment, offers a system to protect the public by providing long-term monitoring of the professional's interactions and continued therapy by specialized sexual abuse therapists. As with abuse in the church, closer outside supervision, better university training, ongoing education, and an informed public are all needed to reverse the trend of this part of the sexual abuse epidemic.

Summary

Sexual abuse is not a behavior limited to persons from a lower socio-economic class, nor is it always perpetrated by persons who have a psychopathic personality and desire to harm others. As we have described, sexual abuse is often a behavioral problem that can afflict persons who otherwise are law abiding citizens and are leaders in their chosen professions.

As a society we can hold these people accountable for their behavior without devastating their lives and the lives of their families and friends. We do not always have to remove them from the professions. America can turn to the use of the restorative justice model (as we describe in Chapter Eleven) in which the abuser is held accountable and gets help, and the abuser, the victim(s), and community all take an active part in the healing process.

---

[22] The National Network for the Treatment of Professional Sexual Misconduct. 3280 Howell Mill Road. Suite T-30; Atlanta, Georgia 30327.

• CHAPTER SIX •

Sex for Sale

Sex as an Industry

Many people do not think of sex as an "industry." Instead, we think of sex as a behavior people engage in for expressing affection and for experiencing pleasurable physical sensations. However, the collection of "sex-for-sale" businesses, establishments, organizations, and agencies promoting sexually oriented products and services generate billions of dollars of revenue every year.

Sex as an industry has both positive and negative impacts on our culture. Unfortunately, as we assess it, there is much more harm than good in the sex-for-sale industry. On the positive side, some elements of this industry may educate people about the value of human sexuality, its beauty, and its rewards. Some elements of the industry have been developed to protect us, such as books and materials developed for sex education, AIDS education and prevention, and prevention of other sexually transmitted diseases. Other aspects of the sex-for-sale industry, however, often have a deleterious effect on the consumer and the people who work within the industry.

It does not take a lot of imagination to see how American lifestyles are enmeshed with sex-for-sale commodities. Although the various aspects of sex as an industry do not necessarily cause sexual abuse, they often play a role in sustaining sexually abusive behaviors in individuals who are predisposed to or presently engaging in sexually abusive acts, as well as contribute to the ongoing problems of the sexual addict.

Most people who are familiar with the sex-for-sale industry do not think of these services and products as abusive. However, sex-for-sale commodities such as prostitution, pornography, phone sex, adult entertainment establishments, and other sexually oriented money making enterprises can be abusive to the consumer, the service provider, and persons participating in the enterprise.

Through many of the industry's products and services consumers can be victimized through the alteration of their perceptions about human sexuality, by acquiring distorted views of human sexuality, and/or by spending excessive amounts of money in purchasing products or services. For example, sexual addicts who become dependent on pornography report spending tens of thousands of dollars on their addiction.

In addition, the consumer is usually bombarded with sexual messages that are destructive and distorted. As a theme, love is absent in most of the sex-for-sale products and services, while sexual performance is lauded. It comes as no surprise that our country has problems with human sexuality, especially when pornography becomes a means of learning about and/or practicing behaviors and attitudes.

The Kinsey studies of the late 1940's and early 1950's found that 94 percent of American men and 40 percent of women had masturbated. Current research confirms the high percentage of men and finds that the percentage of women has doubled (Reinisch, 1990), reflecting how much women's roles, and views on sexuality have changed dramatically in the years since Kinsey first studied human female sexuality. Today, women are far more active and experienced sexually than they were in the fifties.

The higher level of tolerance for masturbatory behaviors in today's world is manifest in many ways. Newspapers and magazines run advertisements for phone sex, the Internet affords people access to sexually explicit materials through their home computers; pornographic videos can be brought, rented, and viewed in privacy. Sexual materials that offer the vicarious experience of unconventional as well as traditional sexual activities, and cater to the varying sexual lifestyles, are available not just to specialty buyers but to even the most conventional consumers, a great percentage of whom use them for self-stimulation.[1]

On the positive side, no longer are boys routinely told that they will go blind if they masturbate. Boys and girls feel less shame about exploring their sexual feelings within their own bodies. Exposure to conventional gay sexual activities may help some people recognize their own gay sexual feelings or

---

[1] Miccio-Fonseca, L.C. (1997) Personal Sentence Completion Inventory. Brandon, VT: The Safer Society Press.

become more accepting of gay people. But we must also ask, "Are we exposing our future generations to values and attitudes that promote the abuse of human sexuality and sexual abuse? Are we perpetuating the damage done to victims of sexual abuse by subjecting them to the sex-for-sale industry?" Some research suggests that we may be exacerbating the trauma of sexually abused children and adults by repeatedly subjecting them to images that distort human sexuality, "sexploit" children and adults, or depict sexually abusive acts.

In a news article titled "Cigarette Advertising Linked to Smoking Behavior" it was noted, "Students who saw cigarette advertisements in magazines were 21 percent more likely to experiment with smoking than those who said they hardly ever or never saw ads."[2] In addition, it is interesting to note that companies such as Absolute Vodka and Anheuser-Busch, Inc. are being accused of using their Web sites to attract youth (as future consumers of their products) through games, bottles changing disguises, entertainment, and chat forums with messages touting drinking and smoking.[3] Kathryn C. Montgomery, President of the Center for Media Education, a Washington-based non-profit group that released a report detailing the online efforts of tobacco and alcohol companies, states:

> The marketers of alcohol and tobacco see the Internet and the World Wide Web as a powerful way to market their products and reach youth…A lot of what we see has been happening under the radar of most parents. They have created Web sites that are really more like playgrounds. They are really very, very appealing to youth.

Are there similar attempts to influence youth within the sex-for-sale industries and other sexual oriented entertainment? Does American culture run the risk of encouraging children and teens to engage in sexual behavior because of the sexual advertising and images portrayed in the various forms of media? We believe the answer to both questions is yes.

Because most of the sex-for-sale industry is legal, only child pornography and prostitution (in most states) is illegal, people don't think of these enterprises as abusive. Those who purchase sex-for-sale services (prostitution, nude dancing, phone sex, etc.), believe the services represent a simple business arrangement (albeit an illegal one in some instances). The person providing the service is viewed as an individual voluntarily engaging in the behavior and selling a service to an individual who knowingly, willingly, and voluntarily purchases the services or goods. Thus, it looks like a supply-meets-demand, win-win situation.

---

[2] Child and Adolescent Behavior Letter, 12(2), p. 4. Vol.12 No. 12, December 1996. Page 4.

[3] Schiesel, S. (1997, March 7). Liquor, Cigarette Sites Beckon Kids Online. The Rutland Daily Herald, p. 1.

Even though the sex-for-sale industry generates billions of dollars in revenue each year, there is no way to determine the exact amount of money that exchanges hands between patron and business proprietor. It is impossible to track sales of illegal activities or purchases with any degree of accuracy, but there is little doubt that it is a huge segment of the economy and that it is growing. The flourishing illegal segment of sex-for-sale trade suggests that regulation through legislation will not be effective at controlling these activities. Since legislation is not effective in curtailing illegal sex-for-sale activities, the best prevention is to educate future generations about the potential damage it has on the consumer.

As we will discuss in Chapter Ten, one of the best efforts at preventing sexual abuse and changing sexual abuse trends in our society is to educate the public about human relations, human sexuality, sexual abuse, self-respect and respect for others, as well as the often hidden abuses and traumas related to the sex-for-sale enterprises. Educating the public about the harm done to our society as a result of this industry, may help us better understand how each citizen can do their part to effect change.

Prostitution and Escort Services

When people think of "sex for sale," prostitution often comes to mind. The typical images are of women dressed in provocative clothing posed on street corners, or the legalized houses of prostitution in Nevada, Denmark, Thailand, and elsewhere.

Prostitution is everywhere. It is estimated that prostitution is a $14 billion a year operation in the United States, and that nationwide prostitutes service an estimated 1.5 million customers a week.[4] The most common avenues for soliciting prostitution services are the districts where women (and some girls in their early teens) stand on the streets or work in massage parlors or for escort services (which may be listed as such in telephone directories or disguised as massage or dating services). Although labeled as the world's oldest profession, during the past ten years prostitution has become so popularized that several motion pictures and made-for-television movies have used it as a central theme or have developed primary characters as prostitutes.

Movies often glorify prostitution. For example, the made-for-television movie *Mayflower Madam* depicted the true story of a woman who ran a high class call-girl service. A major motion picture, *Pretty Woman,* is the story of a prostitute hired by a wealthy businessman as a companion - a business relationship that evolves into a romantic one. Also popular was the movie *Milk Money*, a story about a young boy who goes to a prostitute with the milk

---

[4] Magdalana Grace Burke. Project WISH, Inc. Merrimac, MA. Personal communication June 26, 1997.

money he saves from his school lunches to help buy his father a new wife. Even books have been written in recent times about prostitution and its history.[5]

Prostitution is not just a profession of women. Escort services offer both male and female escorts, catering to men and women. Unfortunately, there are large numbers of male and female children in their early teens who also sell their services to men in the child sex trade.

Prostitution has often been referred to as the victimless crime, however, this is far from the truth. While many prostitutes are free agents, some are not. On the streets, many women work for pimps (men who 'own' and take half or more of the fee). The pimps may beat, rape, or encourage prostitutes to become drug dependent, all in an effort to control them.

Regardless of how they sell their services, prostitutes are subject to verbal, physical, and sexual abuse by the men who hire them. In addition, some estimates suggest that 80% of women involved in prostitution are victims of incest, physical abuse, or child sexual abuse.[6] Many prostitutes are also victims of domestic violence and rape. Other research indicates that untreated child victims of sexual abuse may engage in criminal behavior later in life. In an article published by the National Institute of Justice, it was noted that, "compared to victims of childhood physical abuse and neglect, victims of childhood sexual abuse are at greater risk of being arrested for one type of sex crime: prostitution."[7] Therefore, we must rethink criminal sanctions for prostitutes and consider educating women and children who engage in prostitution as well as the consumers of this service.

The Child Sex Trade

Each year, a growing number of children are being abducted, tricked, lured, or sold into commercial sexual exploitation, or child prostitution.[8] With this growing trend is the fear of 1) AIDS, and 2) increased trafficking of as many as one million children worldwide each year.

Although many people do not believe this is a serious problem in America, an estimated 100,000 to 300,000 children are in prostitution in the U.S. and Canada and the numbers are growing, with the largest number of children

---

[5] Seagraves, Anne (1994). Soiled doves: Prostitution in the early west. Hayden Idaho: Wesanne Publications.

[6] Barry, K. (1981) Female Sexual Slavery. New York: Discus Books.

[7] Widon, C. S. (March, 1995). Victims of childhood sexual abuse: Later criminal consequences. National Institute of Justice Research in Brief, p. 1. Washington, DC: U.S. Department of Justice, Office of Justice Programs, National Institute of Justice.

[8] The child sex trade: Battling a source. A series reprint from The Christian Science Monitor. August and September 1996. PO Box 37123; Boone, IA 50037-0123.

from the United States coming from Kansas and Florida. To avoid detection, pimps move from city to city and the children are kept penniless.[9]

More than 80 percent of children entering the sex trade admit to being physically or sexually abused at home. In downtown Minneapolis, the child sex trade flourishes. Children as young as 12 enter the multimillion dollar business, despite claims by the myriad sex-for-sale businesses that they do not employ underage persons.[10]

There is a growing appetite among American and Canadian men for sex with young girls and boys. The typical customer looking for child and adolescent prostitutes are "middle-aged, white, affluent, male[s] living in suburbia... [with a] a good job, wife, and children."[11]

Society often sees child prostitution as a choice. However, Kimberly Daum, author of a recent report on juvenile prostitution in Vancouver, B.C. states,

> "These are sexually abused kids, they're not prostitutes... In any other sector of society what happened to these children would be called sexual abuse. If a teacher does this to them in school it is abuse. But the minute a kid is persuaded by a pimp to stand on the street, society denies them their rights as a child."[12]

Pornography

Pornography is a 7- to 10-billion dollar a year business in America. In towns and cities across the country it is not difficult to find adult book stores with racks of pornography. Soft-core pornography or "erotica" also has a major share of the market.[13] An increasing number of adult "oriented" magazines are making their ways onto the shelves of bookstores, magazine stands, and news stands across America.[14]

Other magazines, although not erotica or pornography by design, promote the sexualization of women and/or men. The most popular example is the

---

[9] Clayton, M. Prostitution 'circuit' takes girls across North America. A series reprint from The Christian Science Monitor. August and September 1996. PO Box 37123; Boone, IA 50037- 0123.

[10] Clayton, M. Minneapolis 'shouldn't have to sell its daughters.' A series reprint from The Christian Science Monitor. August and September 1996. PO Box 37123; Boone, IA 50037- 0123.

[11] Clayton, M. In United States, Canada, new laws fail to curb demand for child sex. A series reprint from The Christian Science Monitor. August and September 1996. PO Box 37123; Boone, IA 50037-0123.

[12] Clayton, M. Girls entering sex trade may say it's a 'choice' ... but are they victims of master manipulators? A series reprint from The Christian Science Monitor. August and September 1996. PO Box 37123; Boone, IA 50037-0123.

[13] There is disagreement as to what constitutes pornography versus erotica. Generally, erotica tends to display nudity, but unlike pornography does not show explicit pictures of persons engaging in sexual behavior or acts with each other.

[14] Playboy, Hustler, Penthouse, Forum, and Club, are but of a few of the titles of magazines that deal with sexually explicit materials on magazine racks in quick-stops and mainstream bookstores open to the general public.

Swimsuit Edition of *Sports Illustrated* magazine. Magazine racks are loaded with covers of men and women bodybuilders. Even some of the specialized magazines dealing with cars and trucks have women in bathing suits on the covers.

Pornography is a volatile topic of discussion. The issue is emotionally charged one it often generates anger and disgust among discussants, especially women's groups. If nothing else, the lines of support are divided between the sexes with men often being the primary consumers while women are often the primary opponents.

Many people hold the misguided belief that pornography creates or is the cause of rape and sexual abuse in America. The 1986 Meese Commission Report didn't clarify matters when it concluded that there was a causal relationship between pornography and sex crimes.[15] However, other well researched publications on pornography reveal that there is no direct causal relationship between pornography and sex crimes.[16] What is supported in the literature and rings true to the thousands of professionals who treat sexual abusers is that pornography reinforces the deviance associated with sexually abusive behavior. It lowers inhibitions and "fuels the fire" of many individuals who are inclined to sexually abuse.

Pornography is a challenging issue to address because 1) it is hard to define, 2) most pornography is protected by our constitution, and 3) few people have recognized the harm it causes to the mental and emotional health of its primary consumers; men. Most people who broach the issue of pornography have a difficult time remaining objective because it elicits/excites our own feelings, emotions, thoughts, morals, values, religious views, feminist view points, personal experiences, politics, economics, and so forth.

Like prostitution, pornography is not a victimless industry. Many of the people involved in the making of pornography are 1) abused in the process (some of the actors in this material are forced into sexual behavior they don't wish to engage in) and 2) are at risk of contracting sexually transmitted diseases, including AIDS.[17] Although releases to be photographed and the photographs to be published are allegedly signed, it is likely that several of the models who pose in pornographic magazines and books and act in pornographic movies are under legal age.[18]

---

[15] In March 1985 the U.S. Justice Department announced plans for a commission to study pornography. This commission became the Meese Commission, which would address, in part, the question of whether there was a connection between pornography and violent sexual crimes such as rape. The 1970 report of the national Commission on Obscenity and Pornography refused to conclude that exposure to erotic materials is a risk factor in the etiology of sex crimes or sex delinquency.

[16] Rosenberg, J. (1989). Fuel on the fire: An inquiry into "pornography" & sexual aggression in a free society (1989). Orwell, VT: The Safer Society Press.

[17] John Holmes, a famous pornography star, died of AIDS in 1988.

[18] This is especially the case in pornography with titles that depict sex with children and teenagers.

Hard-core pornography is generally sold through mail order catalogs or in adult book stores. In the adult bookstores, racks of pornography are sorted by topic and most shops have an assortment of "XXX-rated" books, videos, and sex accessories, i.e., condoms, dildos, and assorted "sex toys." Some adult bookstores advertise private viewing booths where, for a fee, the customer can view portions of adult pornography movies.

In many instances, the consumer of pornographic material is bombarded with sexual images that sexualize body parts, are absent of loving relationships, and in which sexual performance is lauded. The titles of these materials are often centered on particular themes to promote sales of the materials.[19] Although there seems to be an endless number of sexual practices that two people can engage in, the focus of these materials on bondage, domination, sadism, masochism, rape scenarios (including the misattribution that women desire and enjoy rape), adult-child sex, and children having sex with each other, coupled with the lack of emotional intimacy is cause for grave concern. When these materials become the basis of sexual education and learning for people, there is the potential for the consumer to develop seriously distorted sexual beliefs and values.[20]

Child Pornography

Children are increasingly becoming the focus of sexual attention for a growing number of sexual abusers. It wasn't until 1982 that the United States Supreme Court outlawed child pornography.[21] Although illegal, there is a tremendously persistent and widespread underground of child pornographers and an international market for their products.[22]

Child pornography has been in existence for a while. However, "It was in the 1970's that the problem of child pornography came to public attention."[23] By the mid-1980's "there were approximately 260 different monthly magazines published in the United States depicting child pornography."[24]

---

[19] In one catalog, titles such as Facial Cum Shots, Anal Delights, are common.

[20] This statement is based on the assumption that sexual behavior between consenting adults is a private and intimate act inclusive of care, respect, mutual concern, and mutual pleasure.

[21] Child pornography on the Internet. (Fall, 1996). Virginia Child Protection Newsletter, 49, p. 8.

[22] 20/20 News Magazine. 1996, May 10. ABC News, New York. Produced by Vic Walter.

[23] Child pornography on the Internet. (Fall, 1996). Virginia Child Protection Newsletter, 49, p. 8.

[24] Ibid.

The child pornography literature is filled with titles depicting children as sexual objects and as sexual beings. Some of these titles include:

School Girls & Boys: New Action

Her Uncle Tucked Her In

Nymph Lover

Angelic Annette

Nudist Moppets

Lolita Chick

Schoolgirls

Teen Girls and Animals

Daddy Made Them Do It

Little Girls are Best

Person to Person Directory[25]

In 1981, there was a concern about rating a film entitled *Endless Love* starring Brooke Shields. The film was about the love affair between a 15-year old girl and 17-year old boy. The initial rating was "X" before it was edited down to a "PG" rating.[26] Making films of this nature normalizes sexual relations between teenagers and is not necessary for public entertainment. The movie *Pretty Baby,* a movie about a young girl being raised in a house of prostitution, is another example of the film industries willingness to openly "sexploit" children for financial benefit in the name of entertainment. Neither of these movies provides healthy sexual messages, both exploit children as sexual beings, and one's central theme is based upon illegal sexual activity.

Nevertheless, child pornography flourishes today. On May 10, 1996, the ABC television news magazine 20/20 featured a story on "Operation Special Delivery," a US Postal Service sting operation to identify and arrest distributors and consumers of child pornography. Many of the persons arrested were respected members of their community. Many of the photographs and video materials confiscated revealed children crying, being tortured, and being subjected to physical and sexual abuse.

In France police detained over 250 people and confiscated more than 5,000 videocassettes of child pornography.[27] The police stated that those arrested were from all walks of life: "No social class has been spared. They are mainly

---

[25] Person to Person Directory: An Adult Perspective of the Developing Nymphet. Issue #1

[26] Beck, Marilyn. (1981, June 18). Brooke Shields' Film, 'Endless Love,' Faces Fight Over 'X' Rating. Hollywood, CA. Associated Press.

[27] Simons, M. (1997, March 14). French Police Arrest 250 Men Linked to Child Pornography Ring. The New York Times, p. A4.

married professionals. Some apparently made the videotapes, others distributed them, and some just brought them."[28]

All children who are the subjects of child pornography are victimized in one fashion or another; however, many children in pornography are being photographed either before, during, and/or after they have been sexually abused.

Adult Entertainment Establishments

Adult entertainment has grown in popularity during the past two decades, and this entertainment field has capitalized on the sex-for-sale industry. Catering to a variety of people and situations, the various forms of adult entertainment are a growing enterprise. Some of the more popular forms of adult entertainment include:

Strip-o-grams

For a fee, one can hire a stripper for bachelor parties or private events. The stripper will dress up in costume, i.e., as a maid, secretary, nurse, etc., and sing and/or dance and do a striptease act. Depending on the individual stripper and company policy regarding members of the audience touching the dancer or touching of people in the audience by the stripper, some sexual touching may occur.

Live Peep Shows

Peep shows are establishments that charge a fee for the customer to enter a private booth. In the booth is a glass partition and a small room behind the glass. The glass partition has an opening through which the patron can talk to the performer and pay the performer tips. He may have a choice of women performers to select from. The performer usually engages in erotic dance while taking off her clothing. In some establishments, patrons may masturbate while watching the women dance and perform.

Modeling Establishments

Modeling establishments advertise women who model lingerie. Upon entering, there are a few racks of women's lingerie for the customer to select from. The customer can then pay a fee to go into a private room with a choice of available models and she will model the lingerie of choice.

---

[28] Ibid.

During the session, patrons are usually not permitted to touch the model who may completely disrobe. She may dance, move seductively, and/or manipulate her breasts and genitalia. In many of these establishments, the patron is allowed to engage in masturbation during the "performance."

Some "modeling agencies" provide "out call" services where the woman comes to the client's home or hotel room. The sessions are often sexual in nature and are a cover for prostitution.

Nude Dancing

Nude dancing establishments are another part of this growing industry. In recent years, nude dancing has been popularized on weekly television shows, and is the focus of made-for-television movies and major motion pictures. The most recent example is the movie *Striptease* starring Demi Moore.

In nude dancing establishments, the majority being bars that serve alcoholic beverages, patrons often pay a cover charge and are entertained by women or men who dance and disrobe on stage.[29] In addition, patrons can pay from ten dollars to well over one hundred dollars to have a table or nude dance with a chosen performer.

Depending upon state and/or local laws, and the rules of the establishment, customers can engage in various kinds of physical contact with the dancers. Some establishments have rigid no touching policies while others let women engage in lap dances. Some nude dancing establishments have VIP rooms in which the patron pays a fee to have private performances with a dancer or the patron can slow dance with her.

In some of the major cities throughout America, there are free publications in news racks that advertise various nude dancing and modeling establishments, massage parlors, and escort services. It is not difficult for the consumers of these services to locate the businesses they prefer.

Clubs

There are several organized clubs that promote various types of sexual encounters. One example is "Swingers Clubs" for which a fee is often paid to join. The member writes, calls, or receives calls or letters from other interested parties. A sexual liaison is set. Sexual preference doesn't matter. Sometimes there may be multiple partners or partner swapping. If one is patient and persistent, he or she can find exactly what he or she wants.

---

[29] In recent years male strip shows and all male reviews such as "Chippendales" have grown in popularity.

Phone Sex

In the back of adult magazines and other catalogs and publications that focus on sex, one can find a wide variety of ads. Phone sex is so popular that a movie titled *Girl 6* was recently aired on Home Box Office.[30] *Girl 6* is about an unemployed actress who goes to work at a phone sex agency as an operator and engages callers. The phone sex industry is a business that legitimizes, normalizes, and encourages obscene phone calling behavior.

Phone sex is at the tip of one's fingers. Phone sex is simple, private, and the services are usually discreet. Anyone can get the numbers out of the back pages of many adult magazines. They call the number and the service asks for a major credit card number. When calling a "900" number the per-minute charges are billed directly to the caller's phone number and appear on the monthly billing statement. The consumer then tells the person on the other end what they like sexually and a dialogue ensues. You request it and the person on the other end of the line pretends that he or she is there with you as a detailed description of various sexual acts is spoken. Costs typically range from $1.95 per minute and up.

Some of the phone sex ads in one publication encourage people with specific sexual interests to call. They read:

> Your hard c__k in her tight a__! Anal sex is what you need!
>
> I love it when you suck and screw my massive t__s!
>
> I want my p___y & a__ filled ... at the same time!
>
> Shoot your wad onto my face while I play with my p___y![31]

The messages in these ads are not consistent with what researchers know about human sexual behavior. According to Michael, Gagnon, Laumann, and Kolata, "... the public image of sex in America bears virtually no relationship to the truth. The public image consists of myths, and they are not harmless, for they elicit at best unrealistic and at worst dangerous misconceptions of what people do sexually. The resulting false expectations can badly affect self-esteem, marriages, relationships, even physical health."[32]

---

[30] Girl 6 was aired on Home Box Office on May 13, 1997.

[31] Sensations: A catalog of adult products designed to educate, stimulate and enhance your sex life. Gary, IN: Leisure Time Products.

[32] Michael, R. T., Gagnon, J. H., Laumann, E. O., & Kolata, G. (1994). Sex in America: A definitive survey. New York: Little, Brown.

More than Meets the Eye

Other activities are available to tempt the sexuality of a human being. Sex, in a variety of ways, is there for the asking. Again, much of it gives the impression of being harmless, yet it effects the lives of its takers in more ways than are imaginable. For some, the victimization is swift and obvious, such as being sexually harassed or abused. Sometimes the abuse is blatant, occasionally it is subtle. But for many people who engage in the sex-for-sale industry, use sex-related products, or involve themselves with the sexual products and services described above, they may be taken advantage of or abused without recognizing the personal impact they may experience later. Most of the time it goes undetected by the person being victimized until further down the road, often when it is too late to prevent the person from developing a problem.

Thousands upon thousands of people fall prey to sexual addiction in one form or another.[33] Some are addicted to pornography. Some go to topless bars every night. Some hire prostitutes off the streets or use adult escort services. Some are constantly trying to find persons to have sex with, one after another. Some engage in masturbatory practice with or without a partner 5-10 times per day. Addictions are considered to be a progressive disorder that can gain control over the individual. Our country has numerous clubs, activities, and outlets designed to feed the cravings of sexual addicts.

The Harm Done

Many people simply do not see any harm in the majority of sex-for-sale industries, however, according to Dr. Magdalana Grace Burke of Project WISH, Inc., many women enter prostitution, nude dancing, making pornography, and other sex-for-sale trades with an abusive background and their trauma or problems are only worsened by their continued participation in these professions. "Virtually all of these women have been victims of child abuse, and have found themselves caught in a downward spiral of violence and addiction. Women in prostitution are labeled as criminals when in fact most were victims of abuse. Statistics indicate that virtually all of them were, as little girls, victims of either sexual, physical, or emotional abuse, typically leaving home between the ages of 14-17 to escape an abusive situation. Only the prostitutes, not their customers, are treated as criminals under the law."[34]

---

[33] For more information on sexual addiction read Out of the Shadows by Patrick Carnes; (CompCare, 1983).

[34] Magdalana Grace Burke. Project WISH, Inc. Merrimac, MA. Personal communication June 26, 1997.

Summary

While arguably there may be reasons to continue the many businesses of the sex-for-sale industry without restrictions or regulations, there are equally good or better reasons to look at the need to regulate or otherwise eliminate them. If in fact they contribute to damaging human sexuality, should we not put warnings on these products and businesses much like we do with cigarettes and alcohol products? Prohibition didn't work to stop alcohol consumption, but public education has helped decrease the incidence of drunk driving and alcohol-related illness or medical problems. At a minimum we should require the businesses of the sex-for sale industry to warn customers and consumers that they may contract sexually transmitted diseases, experience psychological problems, or develop sexual behavior problems?

The field of medicine considers sexual functioning, sexual behavior, and overall sexual health as part of comprehensive health care and an important component of human health and well-being. Because sexual health is important, all aspects of human sexual behavior - including the use of sex-for-sale services and products, their impact on human sexual functioning - must be viewed in the context of human health and human sexual health. Therefore, not just criminal sexual behavior, but all aspects of human sexual behaviors and practices, should be addressed as a public health issue.

CHAPTER SEVEN

The Politics of Sexual Abuse Prevention

Legislation to Reduce Sexual Abuse

In the late 1960's and early 1970's there was very little known about child abuse and neglect. There was almost no public awareness and little if any political interest.[1] Stemming from the feminist movement's revelations of adult rape and past childhood sexual abuse and neglect, as well as the growth of social work as an investigative field, national efforts to address child abuse and neglect began in the late 1970's. By the mid- to late 1980's child abuse was a national issue and it was paramount in the minds of the public, with 9 out of 10 Americans viewing child abuse as a problem.[2] Subsequently, people turned to the government to fix the problem and prevention efforts began.

From the mid-1980's until now the United States has witnessed a tremendous growth in the number of laws written and passed to address the sexual abuse problem in America. While in theory and intent states have developed laws intended to reduce the incidence of sexual abuser or prevent it from occurring, abuse has continued to increase each year. Some laws have been targeted at all

---

[1] Donnelly, A.C. (1997, May 14). Public education about child abuse and neglect from 1972- 1997: Educating ourselves and the future. [Keynote address]. The 25th Annual Child Abuse and Neglect Symposium, Keystone, CO. Sponsored by the Kempe Center, Denver CO.

[2] Ibid.

repeat or violent offenders including sexual abusers, while others have been aimed at sexual abusers exclusively and especially child sexual abusers.

Three Strikes and You're Out

Laws such as the *Three Strikes You're Out* bill, first publicized and passed in California in March 1994, have grown in popularity and directly impact repeat sexual abusers. Some of these laws require the third-time felon to spend the rest of his or her life in prison with no chance of probation or parole.

In an analysis of the *Three Strikes* approach, Winett and Wallack (1994) note, "The Three Strikes concept, though seemingly straightforward, has the potential for far-reaching adverse social and economic consequences for California."[3]

There is some evidence that the *Three Strikes* law may not working as anticipated by California legislators and the public. As Gregg Schoenfeld, a member of the Judicial Process Commission Inc. in Rochester New York reports, "There is little evidence that third strike laws deter criminal behavior, the rationale for their implementation. Most crimes are committed without rational forethought. Those who know of the law may become more violent so as to eliminate possible witnesses."[4] The Campaign for Effective Crime Policy has also studied the impact of these laws. In California, the study found marked racial disparity in sentencing under these laws, severe jail overcrowding, bogged down courts, and early release of sentenced non-violent offenders.[5]

On March 27, 1997 National Public Radio reported states with *Three Strikes* laws had higher crime rates than those that did not have such laws.[6] A state-by-state analysis of the FBI's Uniform Crime Report data for 1994 and 1995 revealed "larger decreases in crime rates in states without three-strikes laws. That finding held both for violent crime rates and total crime rates."[7] Assuming that the law would perhaps lower crime rates simply by incapacitating criminals through locking them up, rather than deterring future crime, it is projected that the *Three-Strikes* law will triple California's prison

---

[3] Winett, L. & Wallack, L. (1984, August). An Analysis of three strikes in California newspapers: September 1993 - March 1994. Berkeley, CA: Berkeley Media Studies Group.

[4] Schoenfeld, Gregg (1996, November). Are the "three strikes and you're out" laws working? Justicia. Newsletter of Judicial Process Commission, Inc. Rochester, NY. pp. 5-6.

[5] bid.

[6] National Public Radio news broadcast on March 7, 1997. All Things Considered Morning Edition.

[7] Drop in crime said to be less in states with three-strikes laws. (1997, March 18). Criminal Justice Newsletter, 28(6), p. 1.

[8] Parent, D., Dunworth, T., McDonald, D., & Rhodes, W. (1997, April). The effects of mandatory sentencing laws: Excerpts from Mandatory Sentencing, part of the U.S. Department of Justice's Key Legislative Issues in Criminal Justice series. Corrections Compendium, 22(4), p.9.

population over the next 25 years. This increase would mean that California's prison population in the year 2020 would about equal the entire U.S. prison population in 1980.[8] Some researchers suggest that the drop in crime rates is not based on tougher laws such as the "Three Strikes" laws, but rather upon an aging baby boomer population, and a waning of crack cocaine usage.[9,10]

Marc Mauer, assistant director of the Sentencing Project, a Washington, DC group that looks at alternative sentencing, said, "There is no evidence that locking more people up translates to safer streets."[11] Some researchers also believe that "get tough" laws will not reduce the incidence of juvenile crime.[12]

Sex Offender Registration

Sex-offender registration laws became popular in the late 1980's. The laws are designed to help law enforcement agencies and corrections departments track the whereabouts of known sexual abusers, became so popular that the Federal Crime Bill of September 1994 (H.R. 3355), the Jacob Wetterling Act mandated that all states adopt a registry by October, 1997 to avoid losing federal funds. The law includes the Megan's Law Amendments and mandates the registration of juveniles convicted as adults of certain sex offenses.

Generally, sex-offender registration laws make good sense for the limited purpose of finding a repeat offender after a crime has been committed. They require law enforcement agencies, corrections departments, and probation and parole agencies to track the locations of convicted sexual abusers. Often, a description of the abuser's criminal patterns and modus operandi are also kept on file. When a sexual abuse crime is reported and there is no obvious suspect, sexual offender registration can help investigative agencies obtain leads to track down the abuser.

Among the drawbacks to sex-offender registration laws is the lack of compliance by convicted sexual abusers, as well as its application to children and teenagers. In California, for example, approximately 72% of convicted sexual offenders comply with the registration law.[13] This means that corrections and law enforcement agencies cannot account for the whereabouts of over one-quarter of convicted sexual offenders. The state of Washington

---

[9] Ibid.

[10] Drop in crime said to be less in states with three strikes-laws. (1997, March 18). Criminal Justice Newsletter 28(6), p.1.

[11] Brinkman, P. (1995, March 2). Stiffer criminal penalties assailed. Wisconsin State Journal, p.1.

[12] 'Getting tough' won't deter most juvenile criminals. (1995, November). The Brown University Child and Adolescent Behavior Letter, 11(11), p. 5.

[13] Nidorf, B. (1996, November 26). Megan's Law and Beyond — Forging Effective Policy from the Legislative Perspective. Panel discussion. National Summit: Promoting Public Safety through the Effective Management of Sex Offenders in the Community. Department of Justice. Washington, D.C.

reports approximately an 80 percent compliance rate. Currently, Illinois has only a 50 percent registration rate by sexual offenders.[14] One might argue that sexual offenders who do not register are the most dangerous, have not participated in treatment programs, and pose the greatest risks of reoffending.

In one case, an adolescent who sexually abused another child when he was seven years old is now registered for life as a sexual abuser due to retroactive application of registration laws.[15] Even more common is the registration of children 10 and 12 who, developmentally, are not yet clear about their sexual identity. These children may believe the registry label more than the treatment provider's optimistic message of change.[16] Imagine the impact of this label on the child's psychological and social development. Is this labeling a form of child abuse in itself?

Another drawback to sex offender registration laws is that they do not provide primary prevention. They may provide some limited deterrence for compliant parolees, but they do not prevent hard core, untreated, noncompliant abusers from re-offending or address the large number of sex abusers who have not yet been identified.

If our country is going to legislate the registering of sexual abusers, it makes sense that the law be uniform nationally, rather than developed and applied with individual state discretion. When one state's law is more harsh, applied to young people, or is more damaging to the individual abuser, the law may encourage a family to migrate or abusers to avoid registration as is presently occurring. Punitive laws do not encourage compliance by abusers. It does not make sense to drive a problem from one state to another.

Public Notification of Sex Offender Release

First developed in the state of Washington as a provision of the Community Protection Act of 1990, the most popular notification legislation of recent times is Megan's Law, a law developed and enacted nationally after the brutal rape and murder of seven-year-old Megan Kanka on July 29, 1994. Megan's Law, which provides for the public notification of sex offender release into the community, was enacted in New Jersey on October 31, 1994[17] as a result of Megan's parents' campaign to make parents and others aware of known sexual

---

[14] Burden of Proof. 1997, April 10. Produced by Lauren Oltarsh. Cable News Network (CNN) Washington, D.C.

[15] Steve Bengis, Ed.D. Co-Director, New England Adolescent Research Institute, Holyoke, MA. Personal communication July 25, 1997.

[16] Gail Ryan. Facilitator, National Adolescent Perpetrator Network. Kempe Center, Denver , CO. Personal Communication July 15, 1997.

[17] Fischer, C., & Parrish, M. R. (eds). (1995, Summer/Fall). Introduction. Criminal Justice Ethics, 14(2), pp.3-4.

abusers living in the community. This law became so publicized and popularized that Congress passed without debate and President Clinton signed the federal version of Megan's Law in May 1996.

Megan's Law, or Public Notification of Sexual Offender Release, is designed to let agencies, organizations and, in some cases the public know the addresses of convicted sexual offenders released into their communities. There are variations of how this law operates from state to state, though they are similar in many instances. Most states have developed a risk criteria checklist or process designed to identify an abuser's risk level (dangerousness to the community). Based upon the individual's risk to the community, the notification of law enforcement officials, schools, service organizations, and even the public may occur.

While there are many inherent problems with public notification laws, several stand out.[18] First, more than 90 percent of cases involving the sexual abuse of children are perpetrated by someone the child knows, not strangers.[19] In these cases, public notification will have little impact in preventing sexual abuse, especially when denial (which is very common in intra-familial sexual abuse) is present. Further, when the victim is related to the abuser, she or he unfairly suffers the same publicity under notification as the offender, resulting in punishment of the victim.

Second, there is no scientific research or data to support the effectiveness of this unfunded and expensive federal mandate. A Washington study of public notification of sexual offender release showed there was no reduction in the incidence of sexual abuse reports.[20]

Third, sexual offenders are mobile, there is nothing to stop the sexual abuser who wants to molest children or rape women from going into neighboring communities, where he or she is not known and select a victim there. Even if the abuser chose to reoffend within his neighborhood or community, one must wonder how many names, addresses, and faces a parent or child can remember.

Fourth, the outcome data from sexual abuse prevention and education for children has mixed results, suggesting that this type of education may occasionally traumatize certain children rather than assist them in feeling safe. Public notification may wind up having similar results. Children may become afraid to venture out into their neighborhoods and surrounding areas for fear that 'a sex abuser may get me.' Therefore, although sexual abuse prevention education for children has many benefits, the methods of delivery and type of

---

[18] Freeman-Longo, R.E. (1996). Feel good legislation: Prevention or calamity. Child Abuse & Neglect, 20(2), pp. 95-101.

[19] Association for the Treatment of Sexual Abusers (ATSA). (1996, November 6). Reducing sexual abuse through treatment and intervention with abusers.

[20] ATSA statement. (1996, November 6). Public notification of sexual offender release.

information disseminated may create problems for some, and unfortunately, it places responsibility on them for their safety.

In addition, "Doing community notification without doing community education is like smoking a cigarette while you're standing in a pool of gasoline," says Seattle police detective Bob Shilling, who keeps the public informed about his city's 1,031 offenders. "You are setting yourself up for a disaster."[21] Neighbors and residents must be advised that threatening or harassing convicted sexual offenders who are subject to public notification laws may result in more crimes because sexual abusers are more likely to commit new crimes if they feel their lives are out of control.[22] Likewise, additional nonsexual crimes may occur when fearful neighbors engage in vigilante behavior through vandalism and/or assaults on the property or person of the identified sexual abuser.[23] Are we creating more crime in the name of prevention?

Finally, the impact of this unfunded mandate has added to the workload of an already overloaded justice system. "Probation officers, police, and other criminal justice officials with new responsibility for notifying the public of the presence of convicted sex offenders in their neighborhoods are finding the task 'very time-consuming and burdensome,' according to a study of the programs in eight states."[24] This particular law takes time away from more meaningful police work.

We continue to hear the problems associated with this law. Increasing numbers of adolescent and adult sexual abusers are plea bargaining down to non-sexual offenses to avoid public notification. There are also reports that child protective workers and other child advocacy agencies are now less likely to report sexual abuse perpetrated by juveniles and young children due to the concerns they have about how the system will abuse the abuser.

Chemical and Surgical Castration

The latest agenda in sex offender laws is the chemical castration laws such as the one passed in 1996 by the California legislature. Most recently, Montana became the second state to pass such a law for repeat child molesters. "Officials [in Montana] estimate that the injections will cost $21 a day, while incarceration costs $44 a day."[25] At least seven other states, Colorado, Florida,

---

[21] Tyson, A.S. (1997, April 8). How communities respond to sex offenders next door. The Christian Science Monitor, p.1.

[22] Ibid.

[23] Matson, S. with Lieb, R. (1996) Community notification in Washington State: 1996 survey of law enforcement. Washington State Institute for Public Policy. Olympia, WA.

[24] Sex offender notification laws add to justice system workloads. (1997, April 15). Criminal Justice Newsletter, 28(8), p. 3.

Louisiana, Massachusetts, Michigan, Texas, and Washington are considering similar legislation.[26] Such laws require convicted sexual offenders to submit to anti-androgen hormone treatment to reduce their sexual drive. The most commonly used drugs are Depo-Provera and Depo-Lupron medications that when administered lower the blood serum testosterone levels in males. Testosterone is the hormone that influences sexual drive and aggression in men. Nevertheless, taking a drug by itself is not a guaranteed solution. In fact, and surprising to many, a person can engage in both noncriminal and criminal sexual behavior while taking these drugs.

Dr. Fred Berlin, in noting that pedophilia cannot be punished or legislated away, and that it is as much a public health problem as it is a matter of criminal justice, states:

> "The bill [California's chemical castration bill] passed without support from the scientific and medical communities. There is no requirement for an individual assessment of the parolee to determine the medical necessity for the treatment, which is administered involuntarily, without informed consent. The California legislation is problematic for two reasons. It imposes a medical intervention in the absence of evidence that forced (as opposed to voluntary) treatment is likely in and of itself to be effective. The legislation makes no provision for an individualized assessment to determine whether a given person belongs to this group."[27]

The use of these drugs alone will not benefit most sexual abusers. Any pharmacological approach must be used in conjunction with specialized cognitive-behavioral treatment to maximize the drug's potential to intervene in sexually abusive behavior. Furthermore, anti-androgen therapy (chemical castration) should only be used when a) other treatment alternatives are not appropriate; b) prescribed by a physician after a sex-offender-specific evaluation; c) it is part of a comprehensive medical assessment and treatment plan, and d) informed consent can be obtained from the individual.

In addition, the use of chemotherapy does not make any guarantees regarding an individual's future behavior. Such interventions do not stop behavior and only work for those persons who want to change their behavior.

Anti-androgen therapy is not appropriate for use with all sexual abusers. Anti-androgen medications carry considerable risk, and should only be administered with ongoing medical supervision. These medications should never be used as a

---

[26] Hoversten, B. (1996, August 29). Bill requires chemical castration. USA Today, p A1.

[27] Berlin, F. S. (1997, April 3). "Chemical castration" for sex offenders. [Letter to the editor]. New England Journal of Medicine 336(14), p.1030.

sole method of treatment.[28] And, certainly it is inappropriate for politicians to be, in effect, prescribing drugs. Only physicians should do that.

In regard to surgical castration, sex offender treatment professional, national trainer, and author Dr. Barry Maletzky writes:

> Castration as part of a court-imposed sentence cannot be distinguished from corporal punishment and, as such, has lacked a serious support base in this country, despite the frenetic and vengeful clamor among cursory observers to cut it off. We lack follow-up studies of castration and it is unlikely now that they will be done. It would be of interest to learn how castratos now go about their lives and how they regard their prior surgical decisions (or more likely their European governments' decisions).[29]

Using involuntary surgical procedures and medical procedures to carry out governmental policies for managing criminal behavior is counter to ethical medical practice. Moreover, given the availability of anti-androgen medications, surgical castration should rarely be necessary for the reduction of sexual drive. As the Hippocratic Oath taken by all physicians states: "First, do no harm." Such laws move away from a humanistic approach to working with human beings, and are comparable to the now-defunct laws that required sterilization of mentally handicapped persons.[30] However, we should mandate the availability of such treatment for those who want it and who could be helped by it.

Sexual Predator Laws

A growing number of states are developing laws that address sexually violent predators. The laws have tremendous potential for abuse. Generally, they are intended for convicted sexual abusers who are determined to be so dangerous to the community, that they are confined to state mental hospitals and institutions. These individuals are held for observation and treatment after the expiration of a criminal sentence until it is determined they are no longer a threat to society. In many instances these few, but dangerous, sexual predators are not amenable to treatment and may have no interest in changing their violent sexual behaviors.

While sexual predator laws have some value in keeping dangerous predatory sexual offenders off the streets, these very expensive laws address less than one percent of sexual abusers in America. For these individuals who have no interest

---

[28] ATSA statement. (1997, February 7). Anti-androgen therapy and surgical castration.

[29] Maletzky, B. (1997). Castration: A personal foul. Sexual Abuse: A Journal of Research and Treatment, 9(1) pp. 1-5.

[30] Lapon, L. Mass murderers in white coats. Available http://alpha.mic.dundee.ac.uk./ft...s/truthseekers/tr8murderers.html, April 26, 1997.

in and are least likely to benefit from any form of treatment, the safest and most cost-effective way to protect society is to conduct a comprehensive evaluation of the person's dangerousness. If the individual is determined to be a high-risk offender, he should be sentenced to lifelong incarceration without parole.

In December 1996, the United States Supreme Court heard arguments regarding challenges to a Kansas law that confines sexual predators to an institution after they are released from prison. The Kansas law requires a judge or jury to decide whether someone convicted of a sexually violent crime has a mental abnormality and is likely to commit new predatory (sexual) acts.[31] Five other states, Arizona, California, Minnesota, Washington, and Wisconsin have similar laws, and New Jersey, New York, and 35 other states filed a friend-of-the-court brief urging the justices to uphold the law.[32]

There is concern about such laws because they "incarcerate people solely because they have the possibility of committing a criminal act," said Thomas J. Weilert, the lawyer for Leroy Hendricks whose case was argued before the Supreme Court.[33] Such laws may violate an individual's due process rights because they allow states to confine the person without proof of mental illness or defect. There is also considerable debate about treating these individuals because they have engaged in multiple and extremely violent, sadistic acts against their victims. Many professionals question the capacity of these individuals to respond successfully to treatment and the ability of current treatment methods to change their behavior.

On Monday, June 23, 1997, the U.S. Supreme Court ruled that states may confine violent/predatory sexual abusers in mental health facilities after they have served a criminal sentence.[34] The 1994 Kansas law was upheld by a 5-4 decision. The Kansas Supreme Court declared the law unconstitutional on the basis that the definition of "mental abnormality" was too vague, and that the law was a violation of 14th amendment right of due process. Despite the division of the court, the court found that the confinement was not punishment.[35]

In addition to the recent Supreme Court decision, new sexual predator legislation has been introduced at the federal level by Rep. Louise Slaughter (D-NY).[36] The proposed legislation a) allows for federal prosecution of rape

---

[31] Laurie Asseo, Supreme Court: Can Sex Predators be Held After Sentence Served? Associated Press, December 10, 1996, National Wire.

[32] Greenhouse, L. (1996, December 11). Justices sound sympathetic but troubled by sex- offender law. The New York Times, p. 24.

[33] Laurie Asseo, Supreme Court: Can Sex Predators be Held After Sentence Served? Associated Press, December 10, 1996, National Wire.

[34] Greenhouse, L. New York Times writer. (24, June 1997) Sexual predators can be confined after jail term. The Rutland Herald. P. 1.

[35] Ibid.

[36] The Protection from Sexual Predators Act of 1997 (HR 305), authored and introduced in the 105th Congress by Rep. Louise Slaughter, January 7, 1997.

and serious sexual assaults committed by repeat abusers; b) requires that repeat abusers convicted under this law be automatically sentenced to life in prison without parole; c) gives local district attorneys the option of pursuing federal prosecution to ensure that the abuser will remain in jail; d) adds a condition that allows courts to sentence repeat sex abusers to life in prison without parole; and e) authorizes a study of persistent sexual predators by the National Institute of Justice. Such a law would generate billions of dollars in prison construction and maintenance costs and in the majority of cases would not serve as a deterrent to undetected sexual abusers committing additional sexual crimes.

The Use of Laws to Prevent Sexual Abuse

The initiation of laws to prevent and eradicate sexual abuse is a noble cause. However, we are concerned about the motives behind most of the laws developed to date. We believe that politicians are passing laws that reflexively capitulate to the public's fear of sex crimes, and passing legislation based on emotions is dangerous. At a meeting held in Washington, DC, one lawmaker stated, "Politicians often pass laws because we are concerned about getting votes. We do not necessarily vote our conscience."[37]

Relying solely on laws that prosecute and punish sexual abusers is not a perfect solution, nor will it prevent sexual abusers from committing future crimes. Many sexual abuse cases are not reported to the authorities. Some families and/or victims are afraid to turn their abusers in or report the abuse to police or the authorities for a variety of reasons. Many abusers who are charged have the charges dismissed or are not prosecuted because the case does not present substantial evidence for prosecution.

Passing legislation should follow a process by which legislators research the issue, have some supportive evidence that the law will work, and are willing to allocate funds at state and federal levels to ensure states will carry out and uphold the law. During the passage of Megan's Law, no public hearings were held, no supportive research existed, and no federal funds were allocated.

The criminal justice system plays a role in addressing the sexual abuse problem. The primary role is to protect the public and enforce laws, and an additional role is to punish the abuser. The criminal justice system is not a prevention-based system. There is no evidence that punishment is an effective method of educating the public, preventing injurious behavior, or promoting public health concerns. If laws alone could stop crime, the passage of sexual abuse laws would have already reduced or eradicated sexual abuse in America.

---

[37] Member of a state House of Representatives and chairperson of that chamber's judiciary committee speaking at the National Summit: Promoting Public Safety through the Effective Management of Sex Offenders in the Community. Department of Justice. November 24-26, 1996. Washington, D.C.

Laws are only as good as a state's ability to uphold and enforce them. The growing number of identified and convicted sexual abusers in America will continue to test the effectiveness of such laws. Will they be helpful in reducing sexual abuse and specifically sexual crimes in America? Our belief is "no," although the test of time will be the final determining factor.

To develop effective laws, a variety of issues must be addressed. First, we need to look at the etiology (the causes) of abuse. It does not eradicate abuse when we punish people afflicted with mental, emotional, or health problems that can be treated. Instead, we need to encourage, not discourage, these individuals to seek professional help. We need to develop and adequately fund treatment programs, not close them.

Second, we need to develop funded legislation that promotes responsible prevention programs using the knowledge we have acquired regarding sexual abuse prevention. Some legislative mandates, such as "Megan's Law" and sex offender registration laws, are not funded, placing additional financial and personnel burdens on states.

Third, we must differentiate between the various types of sexual abusers. As was discussed in Chapters Two and Three, not all sexual abusers come out of the same mold. The more common forms of criminal sexual abuse include child molestation, adult rape including marital rape, teen date rape, and other abusive paraphilias. Each of these types can be divided into sub-types. Some are treatable, while others are not. Some pose extreme risks in the community, and others pose minimal risks. Laws must provide treatment options for those who will respond to treatment as well as protecting society from those who will not respond to or do not want it.

To address the sexual abuse problem in America, Americans need to know that as many as 30 to 50% of all sex crimes are now perpetrated by juveniles, including one third of all rapes and almost 50% of child sexual abuse incidents.[38] Addressing youth crime and adolescent sexual abuse by trying young people in adult courts has become popular during the past two years. Unfortunately, this fails to take into account a basic developmental principle: adults are presumed to know the consequences of their actions, while juveniles often are not.

These new stringent and highly punitive laws also fail to take into account that juveniles are potentially salvageable as productive human beings, they are still in a fast-track learning mode, and many are preparing to enter college. Irresponsible decision making and behavior on the part of some adolescents are just two reasons why we don't allow young people to drive cars, vote in elections, sign contracts or join the military. If they are not afforded adult

---

[38] Hunter, J. (1996, November 24). [Panel presentation]. National Summit: Promoting Public Safety through the Effective Management of Sex Offenders in the Community. Washington, DC: Department of Justice.

rights and privileges in these areas, does it make sense to hold them accountable as adults when they have sexual behavior problems? Severe punishment such as incarceration, does not take advantage of their developmental ability to learn correct behavior and, in fact, may contribute to developing a criminal lifestyle. Therefore, addressing adolescent criminal behavior from an adult perspective is irresponsible.[39] Raising children in jails develops criminals.

There is a growing number of teen and adult females who perpetrate sexual abuse, primarily on children. Therefore, legislation mandating the use of chemical castration or surgical castration is ineffective in addressing female perpetrators and preventing their reoffenses.

Legislation to punish sexual offenders continues to be used as a means of preventing it. Unfortunately, society cannot legislate away problems. There is a place for legislation regarding sexual abuse; however, legislation will be most effective when is uses a balanced approach that holds sexual abusers responsible and accountable coupled with the opportunity to change their behavior. Our country needs to stop passing laws in the name of prevention that are untested, expensive, and ineffective. If the current trend continues, we believe that we will see these laws fail and in some cases backfire, making the problem worse.

Summary

Laws that result in the incarceration of sexual abusers prevent them from engaging in further criminal activity during that period. To that end they are effective. However, tough laws don't always prevent crime, may single out minorities or others groups of individuals, and often have many problems associated with their implementation. That is because they are punishment-based, not prevention oriented.

Creating laws to punish sexual abusers instead of treating them is a narrow approach that has demonstrated its ineffectiveness over decades. These laws do not reduce the incidence of sexual abuse nor do they prevent it. The criminal justice system sets up an adversarial relationship between the individual perpetrator and the system which all to often further harms the victim. Laws punish individuals who violate them and often discourage, rather than encourage, the individual from seeking help and/or treatment for his or her problem. This is why we can not solely rely on them to prevent sexual abuse and why we need to address the sexual abuse problem as both a public health issue and a criminal justice issue.

---

[39] Cummins, K. Scattershot youth violence war still gropes for answers. (1997, May/June). Youth Today: The Newspaper on Youth Work, 6 (3), p. 1.

We must begin to encourage the abuser and potential abuser to seek help for their problem as soon as they detect its presence, just as we encourage people through public service announcements and anonymous testing to be checked for AIDS, cancer, or other illnesses, and receive treatment as soon as they show any symptoms. We must open avenues for sexual abusers, as well as those who believe they may be developing this problem to get help rather than closing doors and driving them into isolation and seclusion through threats of incarceration, public notification, and chemical or surgical castration. Few people will subject themselves to such abuse by the system, especially in the absence of treatment and hope for recovery.

Sexual abuse effects not only the victim of the abuse, but also the perpetrator of the abuse, the families and friends of both perpetrator and victim, and the greater community. The affected people face both physical and psychological problems and may need professional service. We can better help all of the people involved and affected by sexual abuse - victims, offenders, families, friends, and members of the community - when we approach the problem from a public health perspective.

• CHAPTER EIGHT •

The Media's Role

S ex is fascinating! Sex is intriguing. It gets people's attention. Sex makes for good stories and headlines. Sex is in and sex is trendy. Sex sells clothes, cars, hairdos, and much, much more including books. The fact that this book deals with sexual behavior, albeit sexually abusive behavior, may be one reason people have made a decision to read it. Likewise, even when the media is trying to do a good, responsible reporting job, their motives are often tainted by the use of sexual subjects to sell their news products. Consider how many stations broadcast their in-depth reports on strip clubs and adult entertainment during their "sweeps" weeks (the three times per year that viewer preferences are monitored). It is no wonder that the media's focus is often related to extreme stories about criminal sexual behavior and sexual abusers.

Up until the 1960's and early 1970's very little was written about sexual offenders or the victims of sexual abuse. Virtually nothing was written about child sexual abuse prevention or rape prevention, because there were few reported incidents and abuse was not popularized. However, we know from the personal accounts of thousands of adults who were sexually abused as children, and by victims who have stepped forth to talk about being raped, that sexual abuse has occurred for decades. Historically, reports indicate that rape, before it was ever called sexual abuse, existed for centuries. Sexual abuse is not new, but our awareness of its existence and our attempts to control and stop it are primarily documented over the past twenty-five years.

The media has played an historic and important role in the public's understanding of sexual abuse and specifically criminal sexual abuse. In the 1970's victims of rape began to increase public awareness about the nature of rape. Until then, it was common for women who were raped to be blamed for their own victimization. Women who were raped were considered loose or of low morals and they were criticized for the way they dressed or for going to places they "should not have been." Rape awareness programs began to educate the public, and these initial efforts were eventually covered by the media. As a result of the media exposure Americans began hearing that rape was a crime of power, anger, and control, not primarily a crime of lust in which a man had uncontrollable urges to have sex with a woman or was led on by a woman to the point of being beyond control. The sexual addiction issue was not being addressed at all.

In the late 1970's social workers, rape crisis center volunteers, clinicians, researchers, and feminists, were educating the public to the view that women have the right to dress as they chose and to frequent the places they want to visit. These activities by women were no more an invitation to be raped than a well-dressed man carrying large sums of cash in his wallet was an invitation to be mugged or robbed. As more cases of the sexual abuse of young children and assault on elderly women were addressed in the news, people began to take notice of rape as a serious sexual crime.

In most states, public records revealed only a handful of child sexual abuse cases in the 1970's; before that cases were rarely brought to the attention of the authorities and only 1 in 10 people had heard about battered child syndrome.[1] In the early 1980's Americans began to learn about child sexual abuse through the media. As people became aware of child advocacy and treatment programs, child protective services began receiving reports of an increasing number of sexual abuse cases. What happened? The media brought the public awareness of sexual abuse to a new level and as a result an increasing number of sexual abuse resource centers for children and adult victims were established. As a direct result of media coverage and with more resources for child sexual abuse being developed, more people recognized cases and felt comfortable reporting sexual abuse.

By the 1980's crime prevention programs developed by law enforcement agencies and sexual abuse services were being promoted throughout the country. Neighborhood crime prevention programs, corporate safety programs, and school prevention programs were offering classes on sexual crimes and ways to prevent sexual abuse. The once-taboo subjects of rape and child sexual abuse had come out of the proverbial closet.

---

[1] Donnelly, A.C. (1997, May 14). Public Education about Child Abuse and Neglect from 1972-1997: Educating Ourselves and the Future. Keynote Address. The 25th Annual Child Abuse and Neglect Symposium, Keystone, CO. Sponsored by the Kempe Center, Denver CO.

With this new awareness, data on the number of sexual crimes reported each year and projections of how many people were sexually abused during their lifetime began to appear in the media. The numbers were shocking. One in three women may be raped over a lifetime! One in five children may be sexually abused prior to their eighteenth birthday! The figures were enough to put fear in the minds of even the most confident person.

By the early 1990's, nine out of ten people knew about sexual abuse.[2] However, some in the professional community became polarized between two sides of the child sexual abuse issue. The extremes included the witch hunt side of the coin, and the backlash side. The witch hunt is characterized by the tendency to exaggerate the incidence and severity of child sexual abuse, to emphasize believing the children (regardless of the lack of corroborating evidence or the outlandishness of the testimony), and to criticize the criminal justice system for refusals to prosecute, for plea bargaining with abusers, and subjecting children to abusive interrogations. The backlash is characterized by the tendency to minimize child sexual abuse, to characterize victim recantations as false allegations while exaggerating their numbers and prevalence. The backlash criticizes the criminal justice system for maliciously or recklessly victimizing innocent, respectable pillars of the community and branding them with the shameful label of sexual abuser.[3] Kenneth Lanning, a Supervisory Special Agent at the FBI Training Academy, notes:

> Both sides aggressively try to influence the media. They will cooperate with any level of the media if they believe their views will be aired and supported. In their zeal to manipulate the media, they forget that the media often manipulate them. The media often fluctuate between witch hunt or backlash stories depending on which way the wind is blowing. Today, backlash stories tend to have the upper hand. But this too will change. Much of the media also seem to gravitate toward emotional rather than professional responses when covering these issues.[4]

Often, it is aggrieved parents and attorneys that provide a social base for this backlash.[5] Seldom do they have a plan of their own; they simply stand against the sexual abuse prevention movement.

Public education is the best way to help society understand a problem and promote sensible solutions to it. Sexual abuse is no different. We have found that most people have opinions about sexual abuse, its causes, and its remedies,

---

[2] Ibid.

[3] Lanning, K. (Winter, 1996). The "witch hunt," the "backlash," and professionalism. The APSAC Advisor, 9(4), p. 8. Published by the American Professional Society on the Abuse of Children, Chicago, IL.

[4] Ibid.

[5] Finklehor, D. (1994). The 'backlash' and the future of child protection advocacy. In, Myers, J. (Ed.) The Backlash: Child Protection Under Fire. Thousand Oaks, CA: Sage Publications.

but few have an accurate understanding of sexual abuse and what can realistically be done about it. For example, a public survey conducted in Vermont by STOP IT NOW!,[6] a sexual abuse prevention program, compiled the following statistics:[7]

- 93% of people surveyed considered drinking and driving a problem in Vermont

- 90% said they would attempt to confront a drinker if they knew someone was going to drink and drive

- 73% of persons surveyed believe child sexual abuse is a problem in Vermont

- only 8% said they would attempt to confront the abuser

You may have sat in front of televisions, listened to radios, and read accounts of the sexual abuse problem in America and been astonished regarding the levels of people's understanding of this problem. Perhaps you have listened to professionals make statements about sexual abuse with no data or scientific research to back up their claims. Rightfully, you may be concerned about single-track and extreme views the media, the public, and many professionals have regarding this social issue, such as putting all sexual abusers into the same category of sex offender, proclaiming sexual abuser treatment as ineffective and a waste of public funds, or statements that suggest victims of sexual abuse are damaged for life.

As was mentioned in Chapter One, in the past few years there has been growing concern about the media's ability to cover news and topics of interest without bias or distortion. One of the authors was quoted in The New York Times as saying, "This [sexual abuse] is a major public health issue in this country and people need to look at it as such instead of trying to enact all these bizarre laws like public notification and chemical castration."[8]

That single quote resulted in four additional contacts from other media sources. In subsequent radio and TV interviews citing The New York Times quote, the media interviewer countered the attempt to focus on the public health perspective from the quote. The interviewer's immediate interest was the highly charged subject of sexual abuser treatment (the focus of the preceding paragraph in the New York Times article). When attempting to address sexual abuse prevention, the interviewee was repeatedly cut off by the media interviewers and the topic was changed to the interest of the interviewer. Thus the issue of why sexual abuse is a public health problem was never addressed.

---

[6] The STOP IT NOW! VERMONT program is discussed in Chapter Eleven.

[7] STOP IT NOW! Report number three, 1995. STOP IT NOW! Haydenville, MA.

[8] Navarro, Mireya. Years After Outrage Faded, a Woman Dies. The New York Times. National Report February 21, 1997, p. A16.

But the media and its portrayal of sexual abuse and human sexuality extends well beyond popular radio and television news magazines and news shows. Two examples of distorted messages about sexuality are the focus of movies on illegal sexual behavior and the commercials that use human sexuality to sell a particular product.

Popular culture has softened traditional lines of resistance toward prostitution.[9] Mark Clayton, a staff writer for the Christian Science Monitor states, "Music videos, advertising, movies, and television talk shows frequently portray teenagers as sex objects and prostitution as an alternative career "choice." Ross MacInnes, a retired Calgary, Alberta police officer trying to help children leave prostitution, claims, "Movies like "Pretty Woman" and "Milk Money" glorify prostitution and make it socially acceptable."[10]

Pater Dalglish, who heads the Quebec-based Youth Service Canada, which works with youth organizations nationwide, says North America is hypocritical. "Our society rightly condemns sexual exploitation of children," he says, "but at the same time it condones and promotes the use of 12- and 13-year old girls to sell household products - their sexualized images are used to sell everything from jeans to soap."

Recently, a study was conducted that specifically looked at how the media affected denial in juvenile sexual abusers. Juvenile sexual abusers in a major metropolitan area treatment facility were assessed for an eight year period between 1989 and 1996. In 1995, the local and national media provided extensive coverage of the trial for a sadistic adult sex offender and murderer. In his study, Dr. James Worling, a psychologist and researcher with the SAFE-T Program found, "The proportion of adolescent sex offenders denying their offenses in 1995 and 1996 (40%) was significantly higher than in previous years (21%). [The] results suggest that heightened public awareness of a notorious sex offender impacts on the denial of adolescent sex offenders."[11] One could argue the denial was a result of the negative messages attached to the individual on trial and the adolescents fear of similar public attack or scrutiny.

This is not to say that all media reports on sexual issues are inaccurate or negatively focused. Many television shows, movies, radio talk shows, and magazines provide valuable information about human sexuality and sexual abuse. There are many case examples of children who watched a television program about sexual abuse and the next day disclosed being sexually abused. But somehow, it seems, the good materials are washed away by a tidal wave of media hype and sensationalism that lures people to its channels, dials, and pages.

---

[9] Clayton, M. Pop culture paves the way. A series reprint from The Christian Science Monitor. August and September 1996. PO Box 37123; Boone, IA 50037-0123.

[10] Ibid.

[11] Worling, J. R. (1997). Impact of a high profile case on denial of adolescent sex offenders. Unpublished manuscript. Thistledown Regional Centre, Ontario, Canada.

It is unfortunate that the media is overwhelmingly filled with stories and images of abusive and violent sex that range from fictional to true accounts of sexual scandals, sexual abuse, serial rapists, and sex murders. Politicians, people in the public eye, and TV evangelists have all filled the headlines in recent years with sexual scandals. Even daytime soap operas are becoming more lewd and explicit.

Media representatives maintain that what they report represents the views of Americans. However, this is not necessarily the case. The question is raised, "Does the public influence the media or does the media influence the public?" In the case of sexual abuse, we suspect that much of the public's opinion and attitude is influenced by the media, not the reverse. As was noted in Chapter One, many people have concerns regarding the media's influence on the public. Even some of television's most celebrated news anchors share similar concerns as indicated by the following quotes:[12]

"We have to stop underestimating the intelligence of people."
–Carol Marin, Co-anchor, The Evening News, WMAQ, Chicago

"This survey [conducted by the Roper Center in conjunction with Newseum] refutes those cynical voices who say the public does not take our work seriously."[13]
–Dan Rather, anchor, The CBS Evening News

"I feel, as any citizen, that more and more media in fewer hands, in the abstract, is reason to be concerned."
–Peter Jennings, anchor, ABC World News Tonight

"[Coverage of big stories] can give the impression of a feeding frenzy. People feel bombarded."
–Tom Brokaw, anchor, NBC Nightly News

Gavin de Becker, in his book The Gift of Fear: Survival Signals That Protect us from Violence, addresses the contradiction between official statistics that suggest violent crime is down, and our instincts that warn us we are still vulnerable to violent crime.[14] Additionally, Morganthau and Miller write:

As de Becker rightly emphasizes, most Americans exaggerate the risk of random crime. Like other experts, he blames local news media, which frequently overplay crime stories in a desperate

---

[12] Valente, J. Do you believe what the newspeople tell you? (1997, March 2). Parade. The Sunday Rutland [VT] Herald and The Sunday [Montpelier, VT] Times Argus, p. 4-6.

[13] The article by Judith Valente was written in part based upon a public survey of American's views regarding the media and the news. For further information about this survey write to: News Survey, PO Box 5099, Grand Central Station, New York, NY 10163-5099.

[14] Morganthau, T., and Miller, M. with Rogers, A. and Foote, D. (21, July 1997). Don't ignore your fears: instincts, a best seller teaches, can ward off crime. Newsweek, p. 78.

search for audience. "The local news has a financial investment in making us believe in the randomness of violence," he says. "We live in a country in which only 20 percent of the homicides are committed by strangers, and yet look at the news-media coverage. The phrase 'random and senseless' is bulls__t ... we are focused on fears [because] we aren't interested in hearing about the risks posed by the people in our lives."

Since 1995, an increasing number of laws have been proposed and enacted aimed at moving violent teen offenders into adult courts. Similar legislation is also being proposed at a national level. "In 1994, Children Now, a nonpartisan policy and advocacy group, published a study by a professor of communications on how five major newspapers and three television networks create and perpetuate the public's fear of children. During the month of the study, almost half of the stories about children on television (48 percent) and 40 percent of the stories in newspapers equated children with crime and violence."[15] According to *The Children's Beat* newsletter,

> Two reasons suggest why the media presents such a one-sided picture of youth. First, the media is obsessed with crime. 'News coverage of crime, especially on TV, really didn't take off until after the fall of the Soviet bloc,' Soler says.[16] 'There are no more headlines about the bomb scare, and we need something to occupy people's attention. Crime fills that vacuum.
>
> Second, and more significantly, public policy is complex and often turgid. Policy and statistics make for dull television and back-page newspaper stories. The media focuses instead on what is known as 'anecdotal' information, which is often presented from the view point of terrified adults. The problem with anecdotal information is that it can be terribly misleading.[17]

The media can serve an important role in sexual abuse prevention and contribute quality information to the public. However, until the media are willing to take time and effort to thoroughly research and accurately report in an unbiased fashion and without unnecessary sensationalism, the public must be informed about sexual abuse in other ways. The best method may be

[15] Children, crime, and the media. (Winter 1997). The Children's Beat, 4(2), pp.3-8. A newsletter of the Casey Journalism Center for Children and Families. College of Journalism, University of Maryland at College Park.

[16] Mark Soler is the former executive director of the Youth Law Center, a nonprofit public interest law firm that does advocacy work in juvenile justice.

[17] Children, crime, and the media. (Winter 1997). The Children's Beat, 4(2), pp.3-8. A newsletter of the Casey Journalism Center for Children and Families. College of Journalism, University of Maryland at College Park.

through community education, community-based action groups, public education events, distribution of printed public service announcements, and pre-recorded public service announcements not ultimately controlled by media.

Beyond the News

What the media reports on and how they chose to report on the issues are two aspects of the problem. Media's primary role in providing entertainment is generating growing concern about the content of broadly accessible shows and the rating systems used. For example, the themes in the cinema and on television are all centered on prostitution and nude dancing in the following movies, *Mayflower Madame, Milk Money, Pretty Woman, Striptease, and Showgirls*. Most recently, "Pamela Isaacs was nominated for best leading actress in a musical 'The Life,' a nostalgic look at prostitutes in Times Square."[18] In addition, it is not uncommon to find scenes in many movies and television shows that take place in nude dancing establishments or city streets with prostitutes on the sidewalk. These plots and scenes are not necessary in movies and shows. They do not contribute to plot or character development while promoting responsible sexual behaviors, values, and attitudes. They there simply to titillate.

Sexy Kids

The cover of US magazine's May 26, 1981 issue reads, "TV's SEXY KIDS: On the tube, they play gawky teens, but off camera - wow!" In a time when most Americans have serious concerns and fears regarding child sexual abuse, we have to ask why advertisers are portraying children as sexy human beings. Such efforts invite us to sexualize children. For persons prone to sexually abuse children, the messages can normalize and validate aberrant feelings, desires, and beliefs.

The advertisements for Calvin Klein clothing and products are examples of how children are sexualized. In August of 1995, Calvin Klein launched an advertisement campaign for "CK Jeans" that caught the public's attention, drawing comments such as, "His ads were 'absolutely' pornographic.', 'This ads up to porn.', and 'Where are the parents who are allowing their child to do this?"[19]

---

[18] Stearns, D.P. (1997, May 6). Tony list is notable for exclusions: 'The Life' and 'Steel Pier' earn the most nominations. USA Today, p. D1.

[19] Ingrassia, M. with Nayyar, S., Kalb, C., Miller, S. & Mabry, M. (1995, September 11). Calvin's world. Newsweek. pp.60-66.

An article in Newsweek magazine notes:

> To veteran watchers of Calvin Klein, Inc., it has seemed like just another marketing splash. For the last 15 years, Klein has built a fashion empire largely by tapping both the charge and the cultural unease about youthful sexuality. In the early '80s, feminists like Gloria Steinem protested his crotch shots of a 15-year-old Brooke Shields cooing that nothing came between her and her Calvins, and some TV stations refused to air the spots. [20]

For the many thousands of professionals who treat child sexual abuse victims, sexual abusers, and specifically child sexual abusers, the sexualization of children in the media is problematic for many reasons. In particular, the influence they may have on sexual abusers who are in treatment and recovery is problematic. As was noted above, these ads play a similar role in arousing some child sexual abusers as does pornography to others. For the child sexual abuser, something as harmless and common as the children's underwear section of clothing catalogs can be used for creating fantasy and deviant images of sexually abusing children. Imagine then, the power of suggestion to child sexual abusers generated by sexualized portrayals of children.

The tragic murder of JonBenet Ramsey illustrates an important point. It is heartbreaking to hear about this six-year-old child who since her death in December, 1996 has been portrayed in the media continuously and consistently as a young beauty queen. The sexualized pictures of this child are flashed across television screens and the covers of magazines and tabloids over and over again. While many people do not consider turning a young child into a beauty queen as problematic, sexual abusers tell us different.

In the medium-security state prison at Lino Lakes, Minnesota, one or more prisoners painstakingly built a list of 3,000 children containing descriptions of them taken from local newspapers. Pointers about the vulnerability of individual children were given including such specifics as 'latchkey kid' or 'speech difficulties.' One girl was described as 'Little Ms. pageant winner.'[21]

The more explicit the media and its messages, the more child sexual abusers will use the materials to support their distorted thinking that children are appropriate sexual partners and enjoy engaging in sexual behavior with adults and others. Once again, when individuals are continuously exposed to sexualized materials it normalizes the actions or behaviors being depicted. At the least, such images may begin to desensitize even the most critical individual. With repeated exposure, the sexualization of children becomes tolerated, then accepted, and eventually commonplace.

---

[20] Ibid.

[21] Abuse via Internet (1997, Spring). The Survivor Activist, 5(1) Cranston, RI: Survivor Connections.

Children and adolescents are sexual beings. Adolescents are at a critical stage in sexual development. While society must acknowledge children and adolescents as sexual beings with feelings, interests, and desires, it must be cautious about the nature of the materials and messages provided regarding sexual issues.

Sexual Situations

Many television shows and movies, as well as the movies in the cinema, have at least one reference to sex. Some have several such references, from the 30-minute sitcoms, day-time soap operas and talk shows, to full-length motion pictures. This includes those television shows aired between 8 and 9pm weekdays, the time period considered to be the prime "family" hour.[22] As we revealed in Chapter One, the Kaiser Family Foundation's study found that three out of four family-hour shows on the four major networks (ABC, CBS, NBC, FOX) contain some sexual content.

While these references are not necessarily inappropriate or in bad taste, the question remains as to whether they contribute to the overall development of the story. Though many people would consider these sexual references harmless, Robert T. Michael and his associates have found the continuous bombardment of people with sex in the media is having negative effects. As noted in Chapter Six, there may be a destructive aspect to the public image of human sexuality. Michael and his colleagues state, "This exotic world of movies, television, and novels may be more a disincentive than an incentive to sex with a partner."

Television's New Rating System

The movie industry has a rating system that warns potential viewers and parents about the amount of nudity, violence, language, adult situations, and sexual content in a given movie. In the fall of 1996, the television industry released its new rating system for television shows. Like the movie rating system now does, the new television rating system advises for age levels, but does not address the nature of programming regarding language, sex, violence, or other issues of concern for television viewers. Many child advocates, educators, and others are unhappy with this system.

On National Public Radio's *Morning Edition* news broadcast for December 20, 1996, the new TV rating system was characterized as "a bust." Its many critics suggest that the current system is of little value to parents and educators because it does not describe the content of the television show.

---

[22] New study finds increase in sexual content on TV's family hour. [News release]. (1996, December 11). Sex, Kids, and the Family Hour: A Three Part Study. The Kaiser Family Foundation.

According to the American Academy of Pediatrics (AAP), "Content rating for sex, violence and strong language, not age groups, should be the basis for effective television ratings ... Content-based systems, such as those developed by the Recreation Software Advisory Council (RSAC) and the cable system, are effective in helping parents make informed decisions about the program selections."[23] The AAP goes on to say, "... next to the family, the television is the most important influence on child development and behavior in American society."[24]

Media Distortion of Sexual Abuse

We have discussed and provided several examples of the media's ability and willingness to distort stories. For example, the media will use sensational headlines to create a "story" that will get the attention of the viewer, listener, or reader, especially when in competition against other newsworthy events or stories on the same topic by competing media sources. Drs. Fred Berlin and Martin Malin conducted a study to address the public's perception of treatment outcome regarding sexual abusers. Their study concludes "Inaccurate media presentations about psychiatric rehabilitation that ignore treatment successes and focus only on alleged failures do a disservice to patients, mental health workers, and society at large."[25] They further note that, "Until the news media begins to consider the occurance of good events, such as successes in treatment, to be as newsworthy as the occurance of tragedies, the public's perception of psychiatric interventions may continue to remain unfavorably skewed and distorted."[26]

Unfortunately, the more recent focus of child protection agencies, child advocates, and child therapists has shifted onto negatives. Child protection services and other organization with a mission of serving and protecting children are faced with many problems, but they are not corrupt, nor do they deliberately attempt to negatively impact children or families. Fear of lawsuits and failing to do their job properly, are taking precedence over their focus and purpose of helping children and succeeding. As Thomas Morton, Executive Director of the Child Welfare Institute suggests, "We have allowed the press to shift our vision to failure from succeeding."[27] Negative media messages

---

[23] Pediatricians say TV ratings should label content, not viewers' age. (1997, March). The Brown University Child and Adolescent Behavior Letter, 13(3), p.5.

[24] Ibid.

[25] Berlin, F. S., & Malin, H.M. (1991, November). Media distortion of the public's perception of recidivism and psychiatric rehabilitation. American Journal of Psychiatry 148:11, November 1991.

[26] Ibid.

[27] Morton, T. (1997, May 14). The past and future of the child protection services system. [Keynote address]. The 25th Annual Child Abuse and Neglect Symposium at Keystone, CO. Sponsored by the Kempe Center, Denver CO.

emphasizing failure give little hope to the abuser who wants to stop his behavior or to the potential abuser who would like to get treatment for his problem before he takes the first step to sexually abuse someone. Imagine the response of cigarette smokers, alcoholics, or drunk drivers if they were told not to bother getting treatment for their problem because the treatment doesn't work.

Selective Airing and Printing of Materials

Getting public service announcements aired on radio, and letters to the editor printed, has been problematic in the recent experience of STOP IT NOW!, the cutting edge prevention program described in Chapter Eleven.[28] For example, one particular public service announcement (PSA) featured a recovering abuser in therapy speaking to current abusers, challenging them to seek help. A STOP IT NOW! representative was told that the PSA was too slick for the listening audience. STOP IT NOW! recognizes stations depend on maintaining their listening audience. If listeners are uncomfortable with a PSA, they may simply switch to another station and the original station loses a part of its audience. The stations don't want to portray an image that their listeners are sexual abusers.

Thus, unfortunate end results are that some information never gets to the public or the information may be altered based on an economic, rather than an educational rationale. When vital information is censored, this becomes a betrayal of the public trust under which broadcast stations operate. It is easy to see, given this example, that the politics of the media may very well impact what information the public receives.

STOP IT NOW! had a similar experience with the printed media. On two separate occasions, the organization sent an op-ed piece to 14 weekly papers, one written by a leading professional, the other by a recovering abuser in treatment. All 14 papers printed the op-ed piece written by the professional while only two papers carried the piece written by the recovering abuser, even though it was a very compelling and well written piece.

If the goal of sexual abuse prevention is to encourage abusers or would-be abusers to get help, personal appeals by recovering abusers should be published as well. The media determines what is covered based upon financial gain, political bias, or plain ignorance and refuses to educate us on uncomfortable issues. This doesn't foster truth in reporting, when the public is given only one slant of a particular story.

---

[28] Tabachnick, J. (1996, May). Eight Month Program Evaluation: STOP IT NOW! Vermont. STOP IT NOW! , Haydenville, MA.

Summary

The media play an important role in the lives of Americans. Print, broadcast and subscription media entertain us, provide educational materials, inform us about what is happening in the world, and deliver information instantaneously from anywhere in the world. The media have the ability to shape views and opinions and influence the way Americans make decisions and run their lives. In short, the media plays a role in determining the health of Americans.

Unfortunately, in too many cases the media are destructive by misinforming or misguiding. A case in point is the media's treatment of sexual abuse and their complicity in the abuse and misuse of human sexuality. They have provided negative influences on sexual abuse prevention and treatment. Some media contribute to the sexual abuse problem in America.

Third-party censorship is not an answer. Ours is an information-based society. The media has a function in the lives of Americans. Media, after all, are the means by which we will educate and positively influence how America deals with its multitude of problems. Media must take a more responsible position regarding the use of sensationalism to sell stories and generate profits at the emotional, moral, and spiritual expense of Americans.

At a recent training for sexual abuse professionals, a member of the audience related how one state has attempted to encourage reporting on sexual abuse-related issues in an accurate and educational manner. In that state, the professionals review all of the sexual abuse media pieces submitted. They then elect a writer/reporter/media that does the best job at reporting on sexual abuse issues and present an award.[29]

Finally, if research continues to suggest that children and adults may be negatively influenced by what the media offers to them, society must take notice. Society should hold the media responsible for delivering a balanced approach to human sexuality. To do so, the media may need to show a willingness to forego the financial benefits of current practices that contribute to and sustain sexual abuse.

---

[29] Freeman-Longo, R. & Tabachnick, J. Workshop entitled "Utilizing the Media in Our Work." ATSA 15th Annual Research and Treatment Conference. Chicago, IL. November 14, 1996.

CHAPTER NINE

Experiencing and Overcoming Sexual Abuse

The Victims of Sexual Abuse

Sexual abuse is a national health problem in America. Estimates vary, but the most common statistic cited is that one in five children may be sexually abused prior to age 18 and that one in three women may be raped during her lifetime. By themselves, or in comparison to other national health concerns, these figures suggest a pattern of epidemic proportion.

In 1988 Dr. Gene Abel and colleagues published data from a long-term study of over 560 sexual abusers and their victims. His eight years of research revealed sexual abusers typically continue to repeat their sexually abusive behaviors until they are detected.[1] Another study with 53 sexual abusers yielded similar results (see Appendix A, Tables 1, 2, 3, & 4), as did a study in Australia.[2] These studies suggest that many sexual abusers repeated their abusive behaviors and the most likely victims were children.

That sexual abuse can result in trauma for the victim is not in doubt. Because most abusers' crimes go unreported, many victims continuously experience emotional pain and may not get the professional help they need and deserve.

---

[1] Abel, G. G., Becker, J. V., Cunningham-Rathner, J., Mittelman, M. & Rouleau, J. (1988). Multiple paraphilic diagnoses among sex offenders. Bulletin of the American Academy of Psychiatry and the Law, 16(2), p.153-168.

[2] Margo French, Clinical Psychologist. Perth, Australia. Personal communication January 19, 1991.

None-the-less, no one can predict exactly what any single individual victim of sexual abuse will experience, the degree of trauma, or how long the effects of the abuse may last. In the early 1970's and 1980's, victim advocates characterized victims as damaged for life. While such a statement expresses the severity of abuse's effects, it does not accurately reflect the experience of victims who have healed through treatment.

The ability to overcome sexual abuse varies from one person to the next depending on such factors as personality, life experience, the nature of the assault, the existence and quality of subsequent intervention, and support. On the one hand there is the person who is the victim of sexual abuse and does not perceive the sexual behavior as abuse. A male in his early teens who has "consenting" sex with a woman in her twenties may not recognize any trauma. However, what has occurred between the two is a form of sexual abuse: statutory rape.

At the other extreme is the victim who has been raped or sexually abused and experienced severe trauma. For these individuals, the trauma may lead to long-term emotional dysfunction or even suicide. They live day-in and day-out with the pain and suffering from their abuse.

Still others transcend incredible pain and actually find meaning and growth from traumatic childhood experiences. The research of Dr. Kenneth Pelletier (1994) outlined some of the significant positive outcome of trauma when approached in a thoughtful manner. He wrote:

> "Instead of the experience causing a breakdown, it brought forth a breakthrough to a new and deeper appreciation of themselves and others. A traumatic experience, therefore, is not inherently destructive and may be one means by which a person continues to evolve and come to a more meaningful understanding and appreciation of life itself." [3]

With child abuse in mind, Pelletier goes on to warn: "We can no longer cling to the simplistic model of health that views early life trauma as inherently causing adult mental or physical disorders."[4]

For the sexual abuse victim who experiences trauma, it is difficult to assess the long term outcome with or without therapy. Boyer states:

> "Clinical reports and empirical studies have consistently found that sexual abuse, as well as other forms of maltreatment, may affect children in all areas of development. Victims of sexual abuse, in particular, may be at higher risk for mental health and social functioning problems arising from the powerlessness and stigmatization of the abuse process. The interpersonal problems

[3] Pelletier, Kenneth (1994). Sound mind, sound body. New York: Simon and Schuster. p.44
[4] Ibid. p. 68.

and coping patterns of young women with a history of sexual abuse are reportedly conditioned by long-term negative effects on sexual self-esteem, self-concept, and sexual adjustment"[5.]

Testimony and case studies of victims provide illustrations at both ends of a trauma continuum and in between, portraying the full range of potential human reaction to sexual abuse. Victims of sexual abuse react differently at some levels and very much the same at others. Below is a partial list of some of the more common problems seen in children who have been harmed by sexual abuse.[6]

fear of specific persons	fear of specific places	advanced sexual knowledge
fear of the dark	anxiety	withdrawn behavior
fear of males or females	fear of harm to a family pet	alcohol/drug use & abuse
anger	depression	self-mutilation
loss of appetite	excessive appetite	nightmares
runaway behavior	poor school performance	flashbacks
behavioral problems	sexual promiscuity	sleep disturbances
aggressive behavior	insecurity	behavior regressing to an earlier age
sexual acting out (inappropriate sexual behavior)	fear of being alone	
	irritability	fear of something happening to a close friend or family member
compulsive behaviors, (e.g., excessive bathing)	fear of abandonment	

Adult victims of rape and sexual abuse may show any of the following effects:

sleep disturbances	eating disorders	somaticized emotional pain
fear of specific persons	fear of specific places	anger
fear of being alone	fear of being out of the home (agoraphobia)	fear of males or females
depression		anxiety
insecurity	Feelings of inadequacy	loss of control
suicide ideation	low-self-esteem	compulsive behaviors
withdrawal	sexual dysfunctions	sexual addiction
denial	marital / relationship problems	

[5] Boyer, D. (1996, November/ December). Adolescent pregnancy: The role of sexual abuse. NRCCSA NEWS, 4(6), p. 1.

[6] The presence of any, or all, of the symptoms on these lists does not constitute a definitive finding that sexual abuse has occurred. Many life experiences can bring on these or similar symptoms.

Neither of these lists is exhaustive, and certainly persons experiencing other traumas can have similar symptoms, but they are representative of the more common problems faced by sexual abuse victims.

Also of concern is the potential development of a cycle of sexual abuse in the young victim. Studies of both victims of sexual abuse and sexual abusers have revealed a connection between being sexually abused and becoming sexually abusive. This is not to say that everyone who is sexually abused will become a sexual abuser. A small percentage of victims (variously estimated between 14 and 33%, based on self-reports)[7] appear to react to their sexual abuse by acting out sexually towards others. What can be safely said is of those persons who are sexual abusers, a significant number reveal histories of being sexually abused.

How Sexual Abuse Harms Children

Many books have been written about child sexual abuse with almost everyone detailing ever-expanding checklists of problems arising from this public health problem. Researching them, one succinct summary of effects was very understandable and not overstated. It is referred to as traumagenic dynamics theory.[8]

Developed by David Finkelhor and Angela Brown in 1985, this theory has grown in acceptance over the years and challenges the Post-Traumatic Stress Disorder model in terms of its ability to address traumas specific to the sexual abuse experience. While the authors of traumagenic dynamics theory acknowledge there are many ways in which sexual abuse can manifest itself in problematic ways, they organize the aftermath into four areas of impact. The areas are referred to as traumagenic dynamics and they include traumatic sexualization, betrayal, stigmatization, and powerlessness.

If parents and clinicians can come to an understanding of how each dynamic is caused and how it is expressed behaviorally and emotionally, treatment will logically flow from those observations. In other words, if cause becomes apparent, treatment may be formulated in opposites. For instance, if a child feels powerless from having been sexually assaulted, recovery may come from opposite experiences that give the child a sense of power (empowerment).

Traumatic Sexualization

Traumatic sexualization refers to the ways a perpetrator has influenced a child's sexual development as a result of the sexual abuse. If the sexual assault was

---

[7] Bear, E. (1993). Inpatient treatment for adult survivors of sexual abuse: A summary of data from 22 programs, p. 39. Brandon, VT: Safer Society Press.

[8] Finkelhor, D. (1986). A sourcebook on child sexual abuse. Newbury Park, CA: Sage Publications.

violent, particularly bizarre, frightening, or physically unpleasant, a child's sexuality can be traumatized. Additionally, a child can be harmed in this area when certain parts of their bodies are given distorted importance (fetishized). Twisted, confusing, and immoral sexual messages may have also been conveyed by the perpetrator. Finally, trickery, manipulation, or force may have been linked with sexual acts leaving the child sexually traumatized.

Sexual traumatization may show itself in any of the following ways over the early years, during adolescence, or into adulthood:[9,10]

- Overly curious sexual behaviors
- Re-enactments of abusive acts
- Aggressive sexual behaviors
- Teen prostitution
- Sexual dysfunctions (flashbacks, difficulty in arousal, being non-orgasmic, pain with intercourse, etc.)
- Sexual identity confusion (Am I man enough? Woman enough? Homosexual?)
- Confusing sex with love, care-getting, and arousal sensations
- Sexual fears, phobias, and aversions
- Sexual addiction

Knowing the ways into this morass helps us to understand the ways out. Some of the traumatic sexualization effects may be countered by:

- Providing healthy sex education, that includes affectional and value-based concepts.
- Desensitizing the client to ordinary touch, so that not all touch is fraught with sexual connotations and arousal.
- Building self-esteem through recognition and development of nonsexual competencies.
- Teaching assertiveness skills and decision-making processes.
- Recognizing dangerous, as well as safe, sexual situations.

---

[9] Wyatt, G. E., & Powell, G. J. (1988). Lasting effects of child sexual abuse. Newbury Park, CA: Sage Publications.

[10] Blanchard, G. (1986). Male victims of child sexual abuse: A portent of things to come. Journal of Independent Social Work, 1(1), 19-27.

Betrayal

Having been tricked or manipulated into sex, especially by a trusted and intimate acquaintance or family member, is likely to leave a child feeling deeply betrayed. After being led to believe that the abuser is a good and kind individual, feelings of being misled may be two-fold. First, the victim is disenchanted by the abuser's betrayal of trust and secondly, he/she may feel tricked by the adult who has given reassurances that the abuser is a safe person, someone to be respected and obeyed.

When a child's vulnerability has been manipulated in this way, we have seen a number of reactions unfold in subsequent years:

- Damaged trust (trusting too little or too much)
- Clinging behavior or extreme dependency
- Vulnerability to future abuse
- Social withdrawal
- Aggressive behavior
- Difficulty developing and maintaining intimate relationships
- Depression and anxiety
- Misreading people's character or intentions
- Avoidance of men or women (depending on gender of perpetrator)
- Physical/medical ailments

In response to a violation of trust, parents and clinicians can consider the following treatments:

- Meet commitments and follow through on promises; be prompt.
- Point out manipulation as well as trustworthiness in other people.
- Remind the victim that for every abuser there were many caring people who came forward to help.
- Encourage socializing in safe settings.
- Trust-building experiences.

Stigmatization

When a parent expresses horror and repulsion at what has transpired, children may conclude that they too are horrible or disgusting. If the sexual acts are known to be improper in children's eyes they may feel like bad people for having been involved in such activities, even though they are not at fault or responsible. Often, we have been told that victims feel defiled, unclean, or like damaged goods following a sexual assault. Some victims feel they are to blame for what occurred or that they should have been able to stop it. All of these reactions create stigmas, a personal judgment that something is wrong with them because of their involvement in this experience of abuse.

When one's identity has been harmed, a number of symptomatic behaviors may appear, immediately or many years later. Some examples:

- Low self-esteem
- Self-deprecation
- Self-harm
- Suicide
- Guilt and shame
- Constant apologizing
- Feeling odd or different
- Isolation or withdrawal
- Drug or alcohol abuse
- Other addictions
- Delinquency or criminal behavior

Treatment responses should be geared toward replacing feelings of low self-worth with a better sense of self-esteem. However, being smothered with compliments, praise, or flattery may be counterproductive, especially when the victim feels it is unfounded or less than genuine. Dismissing shameful feelings with comments like "We all know you are a wonderful little girl" or "Now stop that negative thinking" will not be responsive to the core wounds of the victim.

Each individual client should be evaluated and an individualized treatment plan developed and implemented. There are a number of ways that may be helpful. For instance:

- Connect the victim with others in recovery, thereby letting the child know he or she is not all alone, odd, or weird. Victims will be inclined to give other victims the benefit of the doubt and from that, one can develop a sense of worthiness.

- Involve them in activities where mastery, success, and effectiveness can be experienced.

- Encourage self-care and self-pampering. The theory is to "fake it til you make it," to treat yourself well (as if you deserve it) until you are well (and know that you deserve it).

- Talk it through. Put responsibility on the abuser for being in the wrong, being unhealthy, or acting immorally.

Powerlessness

When children are tricked into an abusive situation, they are powerless to stop it. When the abuser is older, bigger, stronger, or in a position of authority, children can also feel powerless. When the assault is violent, children feel powerless. When children are told not to tell or risk being beaten or have another family member harmed, they feel powerless to extricate themselves from the situation. When no one believes the victim, children feel powerless. When the legal or social system fails to protect them, they feel powerless. When other children are subsequently abused by the same abuser, the initial victims feel responsible, guilty, and powerless.

Having no control over one's body, well-being, or life may include any of the following symptoms:

- Anxiety; namely worry about what is about to happen
- Sleep disorders and nightmares
- Fears and phobias
- Hyper-vigilance (sometimes mislabeled as ADHD)
- Disassociation (spacing out, mentally leaving for awhile, entering a trance)
- Depression and learned helplessness
- Becoming an abuser (turning the tables to regain power)
- Becoming aggressive, controlling, and dominant (to compensate for a lowered sense of efficacy)
- Re-enacting the "victim" role in other areas of life
- Tolerating continued or future abuse
- Running away
- Self-mutilation (to feel alive, in control, or to demonstrate emotional pain)
- Identifying with, or becoming attached to, the perpetrator
- Physical manifestations of emotional harm or tension
- Eating disorders
- Dating or marrying another abusive person

To overcome feelings of powerlessness, one must be empowered. Empowering the sexual abuse victim can occur in a number of ways:

- By the presence of supportive parents, caring friends, a sensitive attorney, committed advocates, and counselors who find ways for the victim to be effective and successful
- By participating in a healthy support group
- By mastering a sport or academic task
- By learning assertion skills
- By successfully resolving the legal case (whether by conviction, plea bargain, dismissal, family conferencing, or reconciliation)
- By expressing belief in the child who was abused; validate their reality

Males Are Victims Too

Most people believe that the perpetrator of sexual crimes is a male and that the victim of sexual crimes is usually female. Cable, broadcast, print, and entertainment media usually portray the sexes in these roles and in our choice of using male pronouns for abusers we may contribute to this perception. In fact, while the majority of known sexual abusers are males the number of known female sexual abusers is gradually increasing. This is especially true as it applies to adolescent female sexual abusers. Our colleagues who treat adolescent sexual abusers are reporting an increase in the number of female teens being referred for treatment as sexual abusers. Sexual abuse cases involving women charged as perpetrators are making the national news. In addition, there are now a growing number of books being published on sexual abuse perpetrated by female teens and adults.[11]

Dr. Gene G. Abel's study, referenced earlier, indicated that the most frequently targeted victims among male sex offenders were male children. The study in Appendix A reveals similar findings. Both studies offered participants absolute confidentiality and protection from prosecution for filling out confidential questionnaires or participating in clinical interviews. The ability to disclose additional offenses without the fear of addition prosecution provided abusers with the opportunity to safely disclose the truth about all they had done without fear of negative consequences for their honesty.

From a reporting standpoint, these figures would be in direct opposition to police and FBI reporting statistics concerning sexual crimes. Data indicate the majority of child victims are males. However, reporting statistics from both the

---

[11] The Safer Society Press has published several books that specifically address sexual abuse perpetrated by women (see Chapter 2, footnote 15, or the end pages of this book for a list).

police and child protection agencies suggest that the majority (usually somewhere between 75% and 80%) of child victims of rape and molestation are females. The reason for the discrepancy between the self-report of abusers and the cases reported to agencies is that male victims of sexual assault/abuse are less likely to report these crimes to the authorities.[12]

Adult males seldom see themselves as individuals who could ever be raped. They may not disclose because of fear and shame at the perceived homosexual connotations of being sexually abused by another male. Some males may not disclose sexual abuse by females because it was confusing or because they did not perceive it as abuse. Their peers may have regarded it as a rite of passage denoting manhood, rather than abuse.

In our clinical experience we have worked with men who have literally been raped by women, some involving a weapon. Several studies of sex crimes reveal that an increasing number of female sexual abusers are being reported by male and female children, although female abusers are more likely to abuse male children than female children.[13] Despite the increase in cases involving female sexual abusers, society still grapples with the concept of female teens and adult women being seen as sexual abusers. This difficulty is based upon the traditional roles associated with females, especially in their relationship with children, such as mothers, as caretakers, empathic, protective, nurturing, and loving. All these traditional characteristics and traits are opposite of characteristics associated with abuse.

Males are also less likely to report being victims of sexual abuse because they fear that no one will believe them and that people will make fun of them. Males fear being labeled as vulnerable, weak, or less than a man if they report being abused. If the sexual abuse is not assaultive or committed under threat of violence or harm, the abused males may have other reasons for not reporting such as contracting a sexually transmitted disease.

If the abuser is a male, the male victim may fear disbelief by those to whom he reports, or negative consequences for reporting after being threatened not to tell. In increasing numbers of cases we are seeing perpetrators engaging children in the use of drugs. They also burden the child with information that drug and alcohol use is illegal for children and that they will go to prison too if caught.

Regardless of the gender of the perpetrator, other reasons for males not reporting include threats of harm to themselves, their family members, and/or family pets if they talk. Some fear they will lose some of the freedoms they have and be required to stay around the house and away from friends. Children often hear that sex is "bad" and fear they will be punished for the behavior if

---

[12] For a brief review of factors affecting under reporting of male victims of female abusers, see Allen, C. (1991). Women and men who sexually abuse children: A comparative analysis, pp. 11-20. Brandon, VT: Safer Society Press.

[13] Turner, M. T. & Turner, T. N. (1994) Female adolescent sexual abusers. Brandon, VT: The Safer Society Press.

they tell. Many, if not most, child victims feel that in some way they were responsible for what happened to them, which may also preclude disclosure.

Finally, male children have traditionally been raised differently from female children. Females are often protected while males are encouraged to fight their own battles and not complain. This stereotypic role-modeling bombards children from TV and other forms of media and from their experience observing others, especially males, close to them. While the world around us is changing in some respects, it is our observation that the majority of children are raised in stereotypic male and female roles, and it will remain that way for quite some time. Males hide their emotions more and get stuck in male pride.

Male children are targets of sexual crimes as often as female children. Women may always be the primary targets of adult rape, but male children presently are at equal risk of sexual abuse and molestation. Both males and females, adults and children, can also be the victims of pornography, prostitution,[14] and other sex-for-sale schemes.

Overcoming Sexual Abuse
How Children Heal

A sexual abuse experience is not necessarily devastating to all children. While we have just outlined the traumatizing results abuse can unleash, many children (and adults) walk away from sexual assaults apparently unscathed. How is it that such a disparity in responses can exist? Many studies, along with anecdotal accounts, give us hints of how some children resolve their abuse. Here is what is known:

- A strong sense of self-esteem assists many children to avoid feelings of responsibility, guilt, and stigmatization. Children with a sense of personal worth tend to attribute bad qualities to the perpetrators of sex crimes, not to themselves.

- Having a confidante, especially at home, helps many children ventilate details and emotions and, thereby, understand the experience of abuse. To talk it through, be understood, and not having to shoulder the weight of a secret lifts a burden from child victims.

- Being raised in homes that prepare children for life's inevitable upsets and tragedies can brace children for adversity. Knowing hardships will

---

[14] Male teens are also engaged in prostituting themselves on the streets. Usually their clients are other men. Some authorities suggest that the number of male prostitutes on the streets today is equal to or greater than females.

be interspersed throughout one's life, that help will be available, and positive outcomes are to be expected, is an aid to overcoming abuse.

- When parents do not overreact to the disclosure, it is reassuring for the children. The more parents can respond in an even-tempered way and carry on with daily life in routine ways, the quicker children will rebound from the abuse.

- Good sexual communication at home makes it easier for victims to discuss the assault with minimal discomfort. The more mysterious or taboo the subject of sex is, the greater children's resistance will be to discussing it.

- When a perpetrator accepts responsibility for his/her actions and this is communicated to the victim, recovery will be expedited.

- Choosing the right therapist is a critical decision. Being counseled by a zealot who finds all abuse experiences to be potentially tragic may itself create a tragedy. Look for a counselor who seems balanced in his/her approach to recovery. This is usually someone who is cautious, serious, yet optimistic about the treatment outcome.

- A group experience can empower children by the strength found in numbers. Beware of groups that seem to run forever and to encourage a continuous re-telling of the abuse. This may lock children into a victim identity.

- Parents and therapists must look for and praise any positive attributes their child displayed during or after the abuse. Perhaps the victim quickly spoke out, warned another child, or ran from the perpetrator. These and other strengths should be noted. Let the abuse experience be a reminder of the child's strengths, maybe even an opportunity to discreetly boast about their son or daughter.

As Wayne Muller reminds us in *Legacy of the Heart*,[15] our children need to be reminded they are not broken by abuse. Their suffering does not constitute a mortal wound or a prescription for long-term suffering. Parts of child victims need not be removed, destroyed, torn out, or exorcized. The challenge is both to address and repair what was damaged and to reinforce and reawaken parts of each child that have traditionally been strong, positive, wise, vibrant, and alive.

If children see that our hearts have been hardened toward humanity as a result of the abuse, that will be the legacy they will carry forward following

---

[15] Muller, W. (1992). Legacy of the heart: The spiritual advantages of a parental childhood. New York: Fireside Books.

child sexual molestation. If, on the other hand, they see parents who heal quickly, remain trusting, and exhibit optimism, they will too.

Ritual and Ceremony

Individuals of all ages find rituals that have the potential for healing. Young children are especially suggestible to healing ceremonies. If you are the parent of an abused child who has entered therapy, it may be beneficial to discuss a rite of passage that can ceremonially walk your child out of their trauma.

Think for a moment how we, as adults, have used rituals and ceremonies to heal ourselves. For example, the death of a love one entails wakes, funerals, graveside ceremonies, luncheons, and other healing activities that connect the bereaved family to their community and demonstrate support. Rituals at home can assist children who have been abused. A special time to talk about fears and concerns can help relieve them. Bedtime activities can be soothing and diminish anxiety. A special story, a back rub, soft music, a warm drink, a relaxing bath, or routine safety procedures - locking doors, turning on night lights, saying positive prayers, etc. - can gradually return the victim to a feeling of safety.

Rituals create a mind set that certain predictable things will unfold. Ceremonies provide some of the acknowledgment, validation, and hope a child needs to feel reconnected to his or her community and to believe in a positive outcome.

Monster Therapy

As a result of having been sexually victimized, many children will react by abusing other children in a similar fashion. This behavior must be controlled without causing further harm to the child.

To avoid the further stigmatization of a victim while empowering him/her, many therapists, teachers, and parents have utilized an innovative approach to treatment called monster therapy.[16] Monster therapy is used to help manage anger, control impulsive behavior, build self-esteem, empower the victim, and terminate sexually reactive and abusive behavior.[17]

Frederique Pierre and Sandra Ballester explain in their book, *A Matter Of Control,*[18] that children can be taught that their sexual or aggressive behavior is a monster (they as individuals are not monsters) from whom control must be wrested. Children attempt to gain control over the monster, who is bad, while

---

[16] Ballester, S. & Pierre, F. (1989). A matter of control. Torrance, CA: Monsterworks Publications.

[17] Schopick, M.D., David J. (1995) Safe at last: A handbook for recovery from abuse. Monster Therapy. Burlington, VT: Waterfront Books.

[18] Ballester, S. & Pierre, F. (1989). A matter of control. Torrance, CA: Monsterworks Publications.

they begin to take pride in being someone who conquers monsters. Eventually, when the monster has been managed, some sexualized children go on to help other children afflicted with the same problem which becomes a source of additional self-esteem.

Children are encouraged to see their problem sexual behavior as something outside themselves that gets them into trouble. This monster is hurting them too and must be conquered or controlled. With this conceptualization of the problem, the victim is less inclined to regard him/herself as disturbed. Instead the monster is an opportunity - a challenge - that can garner a sense of self-control and mastery of the problem(s) and pride for the child. It helps them understand that it is the behavior that is bad, not the child who is bad.

Monster behavior is explained as any behavior that gets you into trouble and is just too hard to stop all alone. Together, in a group setting, the therapeutic task is to spot any signs of the monster coming out. The children go out to battle and defeat and control the monster.

Once victims have developed better, stronger impulse control, they can mentor other children in how to control the monster. Being in a teaching role helps children further understand just what is involved in overcoming this problem and further entrenches them in a "new me" identity.

Selecting a Victim's Counselor

Competent, thorough treatment of victims is a form of public-health prevention. A competent therapist using appropriate treatment methods will assist victims of sexual abuse in reducing suffering and the likelihood of engaging in self destructive or other destructive behavior.

There are many reasons to be cautious when entering a counseling relationship.[19] Merely knowing that a therapist has a degree in a related field or perhaps is licensed, accredited, or certified is not necessarily a guarantee of competent, ethical, or sensitive service. Parents of abused children and adults with victim histories need to be wise shoppers. Knowing the language of therapy and relying on good common sense when selecting a therapist will help.

A well educated therapist may not always have good social skills. If the adult or child client can't connect with him/her, perhaps they need to look elsewhere. The relationship with a therapist is the foundation from which a person can risk change and growth. If a person doesn't feel safe in the relationship, or if he/she feels there is something odd about the therapist, the opportunity to bare one's soul about the deepest emotions of the abuse may never occur.

---

[19] Shaufele, N. and Kennedy, D. B. (1998) When you don't know who to call. Brandon, VT: Safer Society Press.

It is also important to note that the client has a responsibility in the therapeutic process as well. Many come to therapy thinking that therapy involves the therapist doing something to the client to make him or her feel better. This is not true. The therapist provides the tools for the client to use in the process of self-improvement. If the client or patient fails to "connect" with the therapist, there is little the therapist will be able to do to assist the client in the therapeutic process.

Many clinicians believe that a safe, respectful, and trusting relationship is far more important than any technique or information a therapist can provide, and it may be especially true when treating both sexual abuse victims and abusers. The therapeutic relationship is the primary change agent. It is the cornerstone upon which growth develops. Without it, all the techniques in the world are of only minimal value. Sexual abuse victims (or their parents) must learn to insist that therapists treat them with dignity, respect, sensitivity, care, and concern. A good therapist is authentic, communicates effectively, has a sense of humor, treats the client as a partner in the therapeutic process, can admit to mistakes and apologize, and is congruent - responding to all persons alike without shame, pretense, or manipulation.

Dineen clearly states how the psychology industry has rapidly grown into a big business with many counselors being reliant on a steady flow of victims to keep their practices afloat.[20] She believes a very circumspect approach to counseling is required to prevent iatrogenic (system induced) abuse. It is Dineen's fear that the field of psychology is too quick to pathologize victim responses to abuse and is disinclined to acknowledge the amazing range of human resiliency that exists.

A professional and ethical victim's psychotherapist will be aware of these caveats and comfortable discussing them with you. The best therapists all have the same therapeutic goal in mind: to get you out of therapy.

Labeling

Therapists should use extreme caution before applying labels to clients, especially victims and perpetrators of sexual abuse. Using restraint, however, is often quite difficult. The American Psychiatric Association publishes the Diagnostic and Statistical Manual of Mental Disorders, Fourth Edition (DSM-IV).[21] It is the diagnostic bible of the counseling business and because insurance companies, including Medicaid, will not reimburse treatment costs

---

[20] Dineen, T. (1996). Manufacturing victims: What the psychology industry is doing to people. Montreal: Robert Davies.

[21] American Psychiatric Association. (1994). Diagnostic and statistical manual of mental disorders (4th ed.). (1994). Washington, D.C.

without clearly-defined diagnoses, virtually no counseling office is without one. Between covers, this compendium currently lists 374 mental disorders, with the numbers growing with each edition. Therapists are trained to evaluate their patients/clients and diagnose them using a standardized diagnostic category. Subsequently, many therapists do not think of patients from a positive mental health perspective that looks for signs of strength and builds upon those qualities. Instead, they diagnose patients and the diagnostic categories or labels, left unexplained to the patient, may result in the patient feeling branded and stigmatized. Labels turn people into nouns. Labeling, as Al Siebert writes, is a child's way of thinking. "It limits understanding. It strips away what is unique about an individual and restricts the mind of the beholder to inaccurate generalizations."[22]

In her book, They Say You're Crazy,[23] Canadian psychologist, Dr. Paula Caplan, considered possible motives of the authors of the DSM -IV. She wrote:

> "Another motive that may impel some or all of the DSM authors is that, if they have never been therapy patients themselves (in most training programs, therapists are not required to undergo therapy) or have never had the most damaging diagnostic labels applied to them, they may simply not stop to think carefully about the effects their decisions will have on millions of patients. This could grow out of mental laziness, fear of being in patients' shoes, or both. In regard to the latter, it can feel dangerous to think too vividly about patients' experiences, because one might discover that even patients branded with labels that make them feel bizarre are not all that different from oneself."

Caplan has insightfully alerted us to the incredible power that labels and labelers hold. She warns that what therapists call a person essentially determines how others will feel about them and how they will treat them. Further, she notes that therapists spend a great deal of their time (and the patient's money) undoing the damage done to the patient's identity and self-respect because of the penchant to label them. There is something fundamentally wrong with a profession, Caplan asserts, that attempts to know people only by their psychiatric classifications and their diagnosed pathology. Dr. Fred Berlin states, "in medicine we label diseases, not the person. These labels should not be misused to stigmatize people. They [labels] can help in identifying illnesses and/or pathology."[24]

---

[22] Siebert, A. (1996). The survivor personality. New York: Perigee Books.

[23] Caplan, P. (1995). They say you're crazy. Reading, MA: Addison-Wesley Publishing Company.

[24] Fred Berlin, M. D. Personal communication July 17, 1997.

There is also a rather innocent tendency to label people by acts that were committed against them. When someone has been victimized, is repeatedly labeled as a "victim" or "survivor," and comes to be known primarily in the context of those experiences, additional damage can be done. Often, these patients are referred to victims' groups for necessary care. Unfortunately for some, the continuous retelling of their trauma fixes them in a victim mold. This insidious labeling process limits one's sense of personal identity, one's freedom, as well as one's capacity to grow beyond their abusive experiences.

Dr. Christopher McCullough, in his book Nobody's Victim,[25] asserts that, "labeling oneself a 'victim' provides temporary relief at the same time it creates a crippling identity." He believes that the helping professionals' tendency to label patients is nothing more than an adult version of name-calling. Classifying people objectifies them, the very process we warn sex abusers to stop when they are involved in therapy. Like Dr. Caplan, McCullough cautions consumers about the big business of treating victims:

> The victim business encourages and supports the concepts of pathology. For example, the DSM-IV purports to define what a 'mental disorder' is - and in fact does exclude from this classification such items as the 'expectable response to a particular event, e.g., the death of a loved one.' However, the manual's effect has been a widespread pathologizing - for reasons pertaining to the dollar end of treatment.

When people are wounded by life's vicissitudes and unfairness, they can be vulnerable to the power of labels. When someone has been assaulted and feels the stigma of that experience, the term disorder screams out loudly. Disordered, abnormal, or mentally ill are all equated with being crazy. Labeling can constitute one more level of abuse heaped onto an already beleaguered patient. It can place his/her whole identity in the realm of damage and sickness.

Therapy and "recovery" keep many patients focused on the past, old hurts, and the negative. In contrast, Wayne Muller encourages a therapeutic approach that finds meaning and growth potential in all types of sexual tragedies. In Legacy of the Heart he notes the unique strengths, profound inner wisdom, remarkable creativity and insight among children who experienced child sexual abuse. He believes that victimization can lead individuals to develop new qualities such as heightened alertness, a discerning awareness of others, improved listening skills, profound empathy, and much more. Seen through his more positive lens, sexual abuse sorrow is more than a disorder, it is in fact a potential spark that can ignite growth and opportunity within those who are prepared to find it.

---

[25] McCullough, C. (1995). Nobody's victim. New York: Clarkson Potter/Publishers.

Similarly, being a "survivor" keeps a person focused on the past. It reminds them that the task of life is to cope and little more. At best they are "getting by" despite the incessant handicaps of their past. It may limit their expectations of life. Instead, the alternate concept of being a "thriver," someone who is robust and living a healthy and positive lifestyle, suggests hope. A thriver makes the most out of every situation. Thrivers are creative, resilient, and certainly not passive. Imagine the power of this label if it was given by an examining psychologist. Imagine as well the difference between being a thriver and someone labeled as suffering with Post-Traumatic Stress Disorder. Yet, to some, even the concept of thriving can place painful demands on a victim.[26]

Problematic Labels and Terminology used on Children and Adults Who Were Sexually Abused

Labels can be harmful to anyone, but especially the stigmatized victim of sexual abuse. While each abused person reacts in a unique way, some common patterns and effects have been recognized. No single diagnosis encompasses or accurately reflects the experience of every abused person, and not every abused person shows all of these effects. Common diagnostic terms and labels used in the treatment and recovery of sexual abuse victims include:

SURVIVOR: An individual who has been damaged by a sexual abuse experience and is attempting to cope with its aftermath. Their ability to find satisfaction in day-to-day living has been handicapped by the abuse.

POST-TRAUMATIC STRESS DISORDER: A syndrome including a variety of symptoms that is triggered by a life-threatening event that the patient is unable to integrate into his/her life. Symptoms of this disorder can include flashbacks, violent nightmares, intrusive thoughts, exaggerated startle responses, phobias, and a tendency toward dissociation.

PSYCHOSEXUAL DISORDER: A failure of the sexual response patterns of the body that leaves the individual inhibited, dysfunctional, or compelled to express him/herself in unconventional, deviant, or perverse ways.

IDENTITY DISORDER OF CHILDHOOD: A damaged or distorted mental outlook adversely affecting one's self-concept, gender orientation, or sexual orientation.

---

[26] Dineen, T. (1996). Manufacturing victims. Montreal: Robert Davies Publishing.

BORDERLINE PERSONALITY DISORDER: Major instability in various areas of life including: interpersonal relationships, behavior, mood, and self-image.

MULTIPLE PERSONALITY DISORDER / DISSOCIATIVE IDENTITY DISORDER: The existence of two or more personalities within the individual with each personality having the capacity to take over full control of the individual's behavior at anytime.

AFFECTIVE DISORDERS: Disturbed moods problematic to the extent that they give rise to sadness, depression, or even suicide.

This medical model focuses on disorders, dysfunctions, problems in living, disturbances, mental illness, impairment, maladjustments, abnormalities, and failures. For some who have experienced sexual abuse, this type of intervention fosters a "damaged goods" identity. The stigmatization that arises from a pathology-based model is often felt and experienced much like the abuse itself. Rather than normalize the rather predictable responses to an assault experience and encourage the patient to draw strength from within, the medical model when not used from a healing perspective may emphasizes brokenness and the need to look for an outside expert who will better know how to respond to the disorders than will the victim. Again, the caution to label only illness and disease, not people exists.

The abused person should not be regarded as sick but instead as a person who is surviving, adapting, or even thriving in instinctive, often very thoughtful and creative ways while needing the help, reassurance, and role-modeling of a reparative relationship (therapist or friend) coming from a perspective outside the abuse. Sexually abused people enter therapy when their coping strategies don't work or interfere with their achievement of the desired life. Many pathological responses are, in fact, logical survival behaviors that are normally expected in situations of severe stress.

In Child Abuse Trauma, nationally known trauma therapist and trainer John Briere offers a very positive alternative to pathology-focused therapies. He describes an abuse-focused psychotherapy that sends an entirely different message. It is an accepting, complimentary, and encouraging message. He writes:

> You have spent much of your life struggling to survive what was done to you as a child. The solutions you've found for the fear, emptiness, and memories you carry represent the best you could do in the face of the abuse you experienced. Although some others, perhaps even you, see your coping behaviors as sick or 'dysfunctional,' your actions have been the reverse: healthy accommodations to a toxic environment. Because you are not sick, therapy is not about a cure -

it is about survival at a new level, about even better survival. Your job is to marshal your courage, to go back to the frightening thoughts and images of your childhood, and to update your experience of yourself and the world. My job, the easier of the two, is to engineer an environment where you can do this important work, and to provide in our sessions the safety and respect that you deserve.[27]

From this perspective patients can "reframe" their previous labels. For instance, multiple personality disorder may be seen as the mind's very creative attempts to find safety and heal itself in an untenable situation, a strategy that the abused person can adapt to everyday life to make it less complex and out of control. Sadness or depression can be regarded as natural responses to unhealthy situations; sexual aversions as a temporary derailment of sexual interest resulting from external linkages of sex and fear, sex and betrayal, and sex/pain. All disorders would better be seen as temporary, painful, yet common responses to the sexual abuse.

The abuse-focused paradigm empowers patients to take charge of their lives. For someone who has experienced the powerlessness of abuse, reclaiming control over one's life and its direction is fundamental to recovery.

While some adults who have been abused have been very damaged, they can do more than simply survive. They can thrive. They are more than a label or a sickness. They are extraordinarily capable people with many gifts yet to be opened. Rather than ask "what's wrong with me?" the victims may be more inclined to surmount the abuse when they ask "what's happened to me?"

Summary

We have described some of the personal costs associated with sexual abuse, but there are others that could not be addressed given the limited scope of this book. The costs can not be solved or resolved by the criminal justice system alone. The "guilty" finding of a perpetrator versus a finding of "innocent" does not heal the victim any more than a guilty verdict heals the victim of a beating or the victim of a drunk driver. Nor does the absence of such a finding render a victim incapable of total recovery and healing.

Sexual abuse is too complex to address solely as a criminal justice issue. If healing among the affected people, including victims, abusers, their families, and the community at large is going to take place, concerned persons must address sexual abuse as a public health issue.

---

[27] Briere, J. N. (1992) Child abuse trauma: theory and treatment of the lasting effects. Newbury Park, CA: Sage Publications.

It is natural and right for those who hear about sexual abuse to want to seek justice, to hold perpetrators responsible and accountable for their actions, and to look for ways to prevent sexual abuse from happening. When people, however, want to punish perpetrators and seek revenge after sexual abuse occurs, it is important to question whether punishment makes society safer. Punishment merely incapacitates some offenders, deters a few, heals no one, and does not prevent sexual abuse. Punishment (versus consequences) is a vindictive re-enactment of abusive behavior. Society becomes caught in the perpetrator's web when it subscribes to the perpetrator's ways of resolving problems.

CHAPTER TEN

Current Strategies for Sexual Abuse Prevention

PART ONE

Levels of Prevention

There are three levels of sexual abuse prevention - primary, secondary and tertiary. Meeting the challenge of sexual abuse prevention requires understanding the problem and the issues that surround it. Educator and therapist, Gail Ryan, states, "Sexual abuse involves a victim and an abuser. Prevention efforts may address the risk of victimization by reducing factors which contribute to vulnerability, or may address the risk of perpetration by reducing factors which contribute to sexually abusive behavior."[1] The goal of primary prevention is to prevent sexual abuse before it occurs. Primary prevention puts responsibility on the would-be abuser not to sexually abuse others. This level of prevention, in its ideal form, stops potential sexual abusers from abusing before they have acted. Primary prevention invites those who believe they have a sexual abuse problem to seek help and treatment, promoting a message of hope and recovery. Primary prevention must also address children developing sexually abusive behaviors. Primary prevention

---

[1] Gail Ryan, Facilitator. National Adolescent Perpetrator Network. The Kempe Center, Denver, Colorado. Personal Communication July 17, 1997.

will only happen with public education and entails cultural healing, self-examination, and growth. It is more than an individual matter, it is a public health matter.

The goal of secondary sexual abuse prevention is to teach people how to avoid becoming a victim. In its most familiar forms, secondary prevention consists of law enforcement and other organizations conducting child sexual abuse prevention and awareness programs in public and private schools, rape awareness, prevention education (by lecture or written pamphlets and brochures), and self-defense classes. Although crime prevention programs and efforts are valuable, secondary prevention programs place the responsibility for sexual abuse prevention on the potential victim. Another form of secondary prevention identifies "at risk" individuals who may be susceptible to become abusive or to be abused and intervenes to reduce that risk.

The goal of tertiary prevention is to stop the abuse from continuing. This may involve treating victims of sexual abuse and teaching them ways to avoid and/or prevent sexual abuse from happening again. Treating sexual abusers and helping them learn ways to not sexually abuse again is another form of tertiary prevention.[2] While treatment is a valuable and worthwhile effort, the problem with this level of prevention is that it occurs after someone has been abused or after the abuser has already caused victimization.

Are we doing enough to prevent sexual abuse and are we moving in the right direction? There is considerable debate surrounding child sexual abuse prevention programs and sexual offender treatment. While these prevention efforts are a necessary part of a comprehensive prevention effort, they are not in and of themselves going to eradicate sexual abuse in our society.

Crime Prevention Programs for Adults

Statistics are often used to generate knowledge and information about important issues. Prevention programs often rely on statistics to generate an interest and the need for these programs and may also be used to demonstrate the outcome of prevention efforts. Below are the most frequently cited national statistics regarding rape.[3]

- 92.2 % of women are sexual assaulted or sexually harassed during their lifetimes.

- One third of women risk being raped during their lifetime.

---

[2] Tertiary prevention with sexual abusers is also a form of primary prevention for victims, if after treatment the sexual offender never commits another sexual offense.

[3] Statics compiled and supplied by the Vermont Network Against Domestic Violence & Sexual Assault, Montpelier, Vermont.

- Every 45 seconds (1,440 times each day), a woman is forcibly raped in the United States of America.

- For every ten rapes that occur only one is reported to police. Fewer than 40% of reported rapes result in charges against the perpetrator and only 3% of the reported and charged cases result in conviction.

- Of all completed rapes of women in the USA, 78% were perpetrated by intimates or acquaintances, including 11% by fathers or stepfathers, 16% by other relatives, and 10% by boyfriends or ex-boyfriends.

- More than 50% of all women react to their fear of rape forgoing activities such as evening entertainment. In contrast 90% of men deny taking any steps to reduce their vulnerability to crime.

- 34-59% of battered women report being sexually assaulted by their partners.

- So many battered women have been infected with HIV by batterers who force them into unprotected sex that the CDC has identified a direct link between battering and the spread of HIV and AIDS among women.

Unrecognized by most people is the extreme amount of sexual abuse and assault that occurs within the American prison systems. Male prisoners are raped daily[4] and few prisoners report being raped because of being identified as a "snitch" in a prison environment. If a male prisoner successfully avoids an assault in confinement he is still not likely to report an attempted attack to prison authorities.

Female prisoners are also subject to rape while in confinement. According to a three-year study by the Women's Rights Project of Human Rights Watch, a New York-based organization that monitors the observance of internationally recognized human rights, male correctional officers in prisons across the United States sexually abuse female inmates with nearly total impunity.[5] However, these women are unlikely to report sexual abuse and sexual assaults to administration, because they believe the authorities will not believe them or that no corrective action will be taken. They also fear retaliation from abusive corrections officers.

---

[4] According to Stop Prisoner Rape of Los Angeles, CA, although studies and estimates vary, between 800 and 1,000 men are raped in American prisons and jails every day, a figure almost as high as that for women raped in the United States each day.

[5] Sex abuse of female inmates is common, rights groups says. (1996, December 16). Criminal Justice Newsletter, 27(4), p. 2.

Determining the effectiveness of sexual abuse prevention programs targeting adult audiences is difficult. Most programs are designed for women and address rape prevention and/or self-defense. The fact that so few rapes are reported makes it difficult to detect the effectiveness of rape prevention education programs. Unreported crimes mar the credibility and reliability of even good-faith estimates.[6] While the effectiveness of rape awareness and prevention programs is uncertain, individual case histories show that self-defense has been useful in thwarting or preventing rapes perpetrated by specific types of rapists. Unfortunately, a potential victim in a crisis situation can only guess what will work in her specific situation.

When a victim discloses that she tried to resist and/or fight off the assailant, it is unlikely during investigation that law enforcement personnel will ask her if she has received rape prevention education. Many people who survive an attempted attack do not report the attempt to law enforcement at all because they see no purpose in reporting an attempted attack that did not result in an assault.

For these reasons, and because so many variables are involved, determining the effectiveness of adult sexual abuse education and prevention programs is difficult. Lacking accurate data, we may never know if adult sexual abuse prevention education has any value other than to help participants feel more confident in a dangerous world.

Child Sexual Abuse Prevention Programs

The following statistics are related to child sexual abuse:

- A study of eight jurisdictions showed over 90% of child sexual abuse cases do not go to trial.[7]

- 91% of prosecutors report prosecuting more child sexual abuse cases than child physical abuse cases.[8]

- The U.S. Department of Health and Human Services reported that more than 140,000 new cases of actual or substantiated child sexual abuse were reported by child protective service agencies in 1994. Of these cases, between 25 and 35 percent of sexually abused children were under the age of seven. The majority, more than 75 percent were abused by someone they knew.[9]

---

[6] Lt. Timothy J. Bombardier, Vermont State Police, Waterbury, Vermont. Personal communication January 23, 1997.

[7] How many cases are prosecuted? (1996). Update, 9(5/6), p. 1-2. National Center for Prosecution of Child Abuse. Alexandria, VA.

[8] Ibid.

[9] United States General Accounting Office. (1996, July 26). Preventing child sexual abuse: Research inconclusive about effectiveness of child education programs. (GAO/GGD-96- 156, p.1). Washington, D.C.: U.S. Government Printing Office.

- National figures indicate that between 30 and 50% of sexual abuse cases are perpetrated by juvenile sexual offenders.[10]

- In Vermont, for example, in 1994 more than 125 children were sexually abused by a child under the age of 14. One third of these abuses, or approximately 40 children, were abused by children under the age of 10. Reported sexual abuse perpetrated by children under 14 years of age has increased 300% within the last ten years.[11]

- In 1991, Social and Rehabilitation Services in Vermont held 135 open cases on children and adolescents whose records contained histories of sexually abusive behaviors against others. Of the 135 cases, 37.8 percent of these children were between the ages of six and twelve and were responsible for 13.2 percent of all child abuse cases substantiated that year.[12]

Child sexual abuse prevention programs and child sexual abuse education efforts have been available for less than two decades. Many pamphlets, booklets, and books have been written for parents and children about avoiding and preventing sexual abuse. Many of these educational efforts teach children about appropriate and inappropriate touch, being assertive, and saying "no" to people who touch or want to touch them in a sexual manner. They encourage children to run away from people who act strangely and tell someone right away if a person tries or succeeds in touching the child in a sexual manner.

Also common are prevention programs directed at children and adolescents conducted in schools that teach participants how to avoid sexual abuse as well as where to report actual or attempted sexual abuse. By 1989, 18 states mandated school-based child sexual abuse prevention programs.[13] The growth of these programs has occurred faster than researchers could evaluate their effectiveness.

Although child sexual abuse prevention education is a valuable aspect of prevention, questions remain pertaining to children's abilities to learn and retain the materials taught to them. The results of research are inconclusive. According to a Government Accounting Office review of the research, "... there was a general consensus among the reviews that there was not as yet any direct evidence that these programs were effective in preventing the occurrence

---

[10] Janice Levins, Executive Director, Safer Society Foundation. (20, September 1996). Presented at the Vermont Bar Association's annual meeting. Killington, Vermont.

[11] Gray, A. & Pithers, W. (in press). Children with sexual behavior problems and their care givers: Demographics, functioning, and clinical patterns. Sexual Abuse: A Journal of Research and Treatment.

[12] Ibid.

[13] United States General Accounting Office. (1996, July 26). Preventing child sexual abuse: Research inconclusive about effectiveness of child education programs. (GAO/GGD-96- 156, p.2). Washington, D.C.: U.S. Government Printing Office.

of child sexual abuse."[14] In addition, researchers remain concerned about whether children with less physical power and knowledge of consequences are capable of resisting sexual abuse attempts by stronger and/or older abusers.

Furthermore, while "... there was general consensus that children could learn concepts about abuse, there was less consensus about whether knowledge was retained over the long term, whether children could learn skills for resisting abuse, and whether children would disclose new instances of abuse after participating in the program."[15] Some research suggests that children retained knowledge and skills from these programs for only three months to a year.

Concern also exists about the potential for negative effects from these education and prevention efforts. Although many children have benefitted from sexual abuse prevention and education programs, some children report (and their parents confirm) negative effects.[16] In fact, "Some critics of education programs have raised concerns that children who participate in these programs may experience increased anxiety or fear that they might be abused, may become oversensitive to appropriate situations involving touch, or may develop negative attitudes toward sexuality."[17] Another negative effect of teaching children prevention strategies may be that children and parents become overly confident and fail to employ other reasonable protection strategies.

Preventing child sexual abuse is critical to the health of our country. Child sexual abuse education and prevention programs are an important component in child sexual abuse prevention. However, these approaches place 100% of the responsibility for personal safety on children who can not be expected to defend themselves from stronger, more sophisticated adolescent and adult abusers. When the burden of self-defense is placed on children, coupled with the difference in size and knowledge, their ability to prevent sexual abuse when the perpetrator is an older/bigger or more ruthless child or an adult is limited. Adults must ultimately retain responsibility for keeping children safe. Although studies regarding the effectiveness of sexual abuse prevention educational programs are inconclusive, we believe that these prevention efforts are still valuable and play a role in sexual abuse prevention. We will need to continue research in this area and evaluate sexual abuse education programs for children, to determine their efficacy.

---

[14] Ibid. p. 3.

[15] Ibid. p. 3.

[16] Finklehor, D. & Dziuba-Leatherman, J. (1995) Victimization prevention programs: A national survey of children's exposure and reactions. Child Abuse and Neglect: The International Journal, 19(2), pp. 129-139.

[17] United States General Accounting Office. 1996, July 26). Preventing child sexual abuse: Research inconclusive about effectiveness of child education programs. (GAO/GGD-96- 156, p.7). Washington, DC. U.S. Government Printing Office.

While significant attention has been directed toward education to teach children to resist and report sexual abuse, much less has addressed the risk of children sexually abusing others during childhood, adolescence, and as adults. The Kempe Center, University of Colorado, began developing training for teachers and caregivers in the mid-1980's to increase understanding of children's sexual behavior and to teach adults to respond to early signs of abusive patterns. Despite availability of such programs in 12 states, this continues to be a neglected aspect in most prevention programs.

Sex Education

Many people do not consider sex education as a tool for preventing sexual abuse of children. It is often viewed as part of an obligatory and less-than-rigorous health curriculum in public and private schools. In some cases sex education is opposed by parents and educators and not included as part of an education curriculum at all. But sex education is a cornerstone for preventing sexual abuse and especially the sexual abuse of children.

Sex education should be taught both at home and as a core subject of school curricula using age-appropriate materials, information, and examples. Children need to learn from an early age that their bodies, especially the sexual parts, are personal and private. Four-year-olds don't need to have information about procreation, but they do need information about how to be safe and to know they can talk to adults about sexual thoughts, feelings, and behaviors.

Many sexual abusers exploit a child's curiosity and lack of knowledge about sexuality. In some cases, sexual abusers use erotic materials and pornography to desensitize, normalize, and entice children to engage in sexual activities. They show explicitly sexual images to children to suggest that this is what other children and adults do. They use trickery, manipulation, bribery, and enticement to lure children into sexual play and use the child's curiosity and need for attention. When children's legitimate questions go unanswered by parents and teachers, molesters may offer information as a means of engaging children in sexual activities.

Sex education should provide children with age appropriate information about anatomy, social customs, sexual feelings and behavior, and reproduction. Children need accurate and honest information to counter the messages and images they are subjected to through television, advertisements, movies, and pornography. That information should never be delivered in a way that associates bodies or sex with shame or fear; those methods have been shown to be ineffective.[18]

---

[18] Kantor, L. (December 1992/January 1993). Scared-chaste? Fear-based education curricula. SIECUS Report, 21(2), p.1.

In addition, sex education should provide children and adolescents with information that might deter them from engaging in sexually abusive acts. Our experience in working with juvenile sexual abusers reveals that many of them do not have adequate information about human sexuality. Some have revealed that they did not know what they were doing was wrong at the time they were sexually abusing others. Over 85% of programs treating child, adolescent, and adult clients who have been sexually abusive, teach sex education as a part of the therapeutic process. Accurate sexual knowledge is often absent in people who engage in sexually abusive acts.[19]

Finally, we believe that the increasing numbers of date rape, acquaintance rape, and marital rape can be reduced by teaching each upcoming generation about healthy human sexual behavior. As a part of a sex education curriculum, young people need to be taught a) myths and misconceptions about rape and child sexual abuse, b) accurate information to counter distorted information in the media regarding healthy sexual behavior, c) the elements of consent, d) the elements of forced sex and sexual harassment, e) the characteristics of unhealthy sexual behavior, f) the characteristics of healthy sexual behavior and attitudes, g) the impact and consequences to victims of sexual abuse and sexual harassment, and h) the consequences for persons who perpetrate sexual abuse and/or sexual harassment. All of this information is basic to a comprehensive program on sex education.

Attachment Programs

Many counselors believe that the roots of criminal behavior and the development of a psychopathic personality is linked to an attachment disorder between the child and his/her parents. Attachment is an affectional bond that normally develops between two individuals that endures over time. The attachment helps children develop a conscience, build self-esteem, trust, and develop empathy for others. Seriously flawed families fail to generate healthy attachments and often produce very disturbed children.[20] To overcome the deficiencies of early life neglect, some treatment programs in British Columbia, Canada, have developed attachment programs with a focus on re-parenting.

This entails intensive care and supervision unlike what most residential facilities provide. Rather than put children in jail or correctional facilities that attempt to punish or consequent residents, attachment programs recreate the family and offer close attention, massive amounts of love and nurturance,

---

[19] Freeman-Longo, R.E., Bird, S.L., Stevenson, W.F., & Fiske, J. A. (1995). 1994 Nationwide survey of treatment programs & models serving abuse-reactive children and adolescent & adult sex offenders. Brandon, VT: Safer Society Press. p.6.

[20] Magid, K. & McKelvey, C. (1989). Highrisk: Children without a conscience. New York: Bantam.

matched with firmness and structure. The children learn that adults can be caring and dependable and they reciprocate in kind. One-on-one care is provided, sometimes for hours on end, to give the child a corrective relationship experience. Importantly, the facility must work closely with parents to transfer the skills, bonding, and trust to them.

It has been found that increasing bonds to families can reduce antisocial behavior including drug abuse and delinquency.[21] Consequently, we must carefully follow the innovative attempts of youth treatment programs that implement attachment principles especially when matched with restorative justice theory - as is now being done in Montana.[22]

PART TWO

Sexual Abuse Victim Treatment

No one is exempt from being the possible victim of sexual abuse. In our clinical practices we have seen both men and women who have sexually abused both male and female children and adults. Children as young as three months and adults in their 80's and 90's have been sexually abused by the clients we have treated. Sexual abusers exploit children and adults who are mentally retarded and/or physically disabled.

After someone is sexually abused, it is important for that person to be evaluated for the need to be involved in treatment. Sometimes, short-term counseling is sufficient, and, depending on the age of the child, a few follow-up sessions as each developmental milestone is reached. In other cases, long-term counseling or residential treatment is indicated. Without evaluation and treatment, the victim of sexual abuse may experience acute and/or chronic problems that decrease the quality of their lives.

Single assaults or repeated abuse and victimization over time can have devastating effects on the victim and his or her prognosis for recovery. This is especially true for child victims of sexual abuse. Children may be affected significantly in their ability to form trusting relationships with others, develop positive self-esteem, empathy, self-confidence, identify and effectively express emotions, and function well in daily life. Fortunately, children can be highly resilient and are likely to respond well to early interventions which offer validation, protection, and reassurance.[23]

The need to treat victims of sexual abuse is seldom questioned. Unlike the treatment of sexual abusers, the treatment of victims of sexual abuse is accepted

---

[21] McCord, J. & Tremblay, R. (1992). Preventing Antisocial Behavior. New York: Guilford Press.

[22] Betz, Fred. June 18, 1997. Personal communication. Fred Betz operates an attachment program at Yellowstone Treatment Center in Billings, Montana, 1-800-726-6755.

[23] Siebert, A. (1996). The Survivor personality. New York: Perigee Book of Practical Psychology Press.

as necessary for victim recovery. Unfortunately, although the sympathy of Americans is usually on the side of the victims, funding for treatment is often the responsibility of the victim and/or the victim's family. Lacking the ability to pay, many victims are placed on waiting lists for clinics and treatment programs that provide reduced-fee, free or very short-term emergency counseling. Many receive no help at all. There are public funds available, however, one example is the Victim's Compensation Programs which provide federal funds to each state.

Research suggests that some sexual abuse victims have also engaged in limited and undetected sexually abusive behavior. A small percentage (less than 15%), of adolescent and adult victims have admitted, during treatment, that they have acted out their anger sexually on another individual.[24] Because some victims have the potential to act out sexually, treatment of sexual abuse victims is an integral part of prevention. Sexual abuse prevention education included as part of the treatment process can help victims learn how to avoid or prevent sexual abuse in the future, as both victims and perpetrators.

There are many reasons to treat victims from a prevention standpoint. In a special report released by the National Institute of Justice (NIJ), researchers Ken Pease and Gloria Laycock wrote, "An individual's past crime victimization is a good predictor of his or her subsequent victimization, often inflicted by the same offender."[25] This is especially true for domestic violence and other crimes where the victim has a close relationship to the abuser such as marital rape and incest.

Understanding this potential for repeat victimization is important to prevention because of the high incidence of repeated sexual abuse by abusers on their victims. Sexual abusers tell victims, "If you tell, I'll go to prison." The victims' feelings of guilt and sense of responsibility for this horrendous outcome for a family member decreases their likelihood of reporting. If society encouraged treatment of abusers and approached sexual abuse as a treatable and preventable public health problem, such threats would likely be less effective in silencing the victims and the abusers would likely be more open to the idea of seeking treatment for their sexual behavior problem. Our work with the families of intrafamilial sexual abuse tells us that in many cases sexual abuse would have been reported much sooner if such threats to the families did not exist.

The previously mentioned GAO report addressed the question of child abuse victims becoming abusive. Although the report was inconclusive regarding the role of sexual victimization in contributing to the development of later offending, all forms of childhood maltreatment are over-represented in both adult and adolescent samples of sexual abusers. In a pilot study conducted at the Kempe Center in Denver, parents whose children has been sexually abused

---

[24] Bear, E. (1993). Inpatient treatment for adult survivors of sexual abuse, p. 39. Brandon, VT: Safer Society Press.

[25] Stopping repeat victimizations called key to crime prevention. (1997, January 2). Criminal Justice Newsletter, 28(1), p. 4.

reported that the risk of their child becoming a child molester was one of their greatest fears.[26] Gail Ryan states, "By providing these parents, as well as therapists who treat sexually abused children, education regarding the dynamic process of victims becoming victimizers, The Kempe Center's Perpetration Prevention Project proposes interventions to reduce sexual risk. This constitutes a secondary level of prevention with an 'at risk' population which may begin to decrease the prevalence of sexual abuse for the next generation."[27]

Sexual Offender Treatment Programs

In 1993 there were 142,520 arrests for forcible rape and other sexual offenses in the United States. If between one in seven and one in ten sexual assaults are reported as some estimates suggest, the number of arrests could be multiplied by seven to ten in order to better determine the number of sexual assaults being committed in the United States each year. In addition, the Federal Government estimates that there are approximately 234,000 identified sexual abusers under supervision by corrections departments throughout the United States.[28]

Different forms of sexual offender treatment have been in existence in the United States since the 1940's. In 1978, Edward Brecher identified 22 programs in America treating sexual offenders.[29] By 1994, the Safer Society Program & Press had identified more than 1,700 programs treating children, adolescents, and adults with sexual behavior problems.[30]

People often ask us if there is a "cure" for sexual abusers. People define cure differently and we do not want to debate the definition of cure. However, when people ask about cures for sexual abusers, they generally mean a treatment that renders the person safe and no longer at risk to engage in sexually abusive behavior. What we can say today is that hundreds of thousands of individuals have participated in specialized treatment programs and have gone on to lead productive lives and have not been rearrested. The quality of their lives has improved and it appears they are avoiding further sexually abusive behaviors; a testament to the success of some treatment programs.

---

[26] Gail Ryan, Facilitator. National Adolescent Perpetrator Network. Kempe Center, Denver, CO. Personal communication July 21, 1997.

[27] Ibid.

[28] Laurie Robinson, Assistant Attorney General. (24, November , 1996) Opening Remarks and Welcome. A National Summit: Promoting Public Safety Through the Effective Management of Sex Offenders in the Community. Washington, D.C.

[29] Brecher, E. M. (1978). Treatment programs for sex offenders: Prescriptive package. U.S. Department of Justice. Superintendent of Documents stock number 027-000-00591-8. Government Printing Office. Washington, DC: U.S. Government Printing Office.

[30] Freeman-Longo, R.E., Bird, S.L., Stevenson, W.F., & Fiske, J. A. (1995). 1994 Nationwide survey of treatment programs & models serving abuse-reactive children and adolescent & adult sex offenders, Brandon, VT: Safer Society Press. p.6.

Most of the information and knowledge regarding sexual abuse etiology, sexual abuser treatment, and related information has been gathered from sexual offender treatment programs. These contributions and the potential for us to learn much more about these issues must be kept in mind as another reason to continue and expand future funding of treatment and research efforts.

There are three general types of treatment approaches with sexual abusers:[31]

- the medical, organic, biological, or physical approach includes surgical castration, hormonal/pharmacological treatment, and psychosurgery,

- the psychotherapeutic approach which includes individual, group, and familial counseling, and

- the cognitive-behavioral approach which covers a variety of cognitive and skills training methods as well as behavior control techniques.

Researchers have conducted many outcome studies that look at the efficacy of sexual offender treatment, primarily as measured by recidivism, or the number of offenders who are arrested for another crime after they are released from prison, community supervision, or treatment. In numerous reviews "there was no consensus among the reviews about what treatment works to reduce the recidivism of sexual offenders. Use of the cognitive-behavioral model was most often reported to be promising, particularly with child molesters and exhibitionists.[32] However, because of the methodological limitations inherent in the studies, a quantitative estimate of the impact of cognitive-behavioral treatment on recidivism was not attempted in these reviews."[33]

According to the United States General Accounting Office, the recidivism studies conducted in the past have had several problems."First was the absence of comparison groups. This made it difficult to judge whether recidivism results were attributable to the treatment, to the method used for selecting certain types of offenders for treatment, or to other factors unrelated to treatment that could affect recidivism. Another major methodological problem identified in the reviews was inconsistent and inadequate follow-up periods."[34] Among the research reviews were other concerns such as some studies being so flawed that no firm conclusions could be drawn.

---

[31] United States General Accounting Office. (1996, June 21). Sex offender treatment: Research results inconclusive about what works to reduce recidivism. (GAO/GGD-96-137., p. 2) Washington DC: U. S. Government Printing Office.

[32] Hanson, R. K. (1997) How to know what works with sexual offenders. Sexual Abuse: A Journal of Research and Treatment. 9(2), pp.129-145.

[33] United States General Accounting Office. (1996, June 21). Sex offender treatment: Research results inconclusive about what works to reduce recidivism. (GAO/GGD-96-137., p. 2) Washington DC: U.S. Government Printing Office.

The lack of conclusive scientific data regarding sexual offender recidivism is not reason enough to discontinue treatment efforts, especially given the depth and breadth of information we have derived from them. Even if we do not know enough to draw firm conclusions, it does seem likely that at least some abusers are helped to avoid further offenses as a result of what they get from treatment. "Even for offenders who are rearrested," notes Gail Ryan, "some research such as the study from California's research project suggests that treatment efforts may delay additional offenses so that the number of subsequent offenses may be less."[35] The GAO report goes on to say, "most reviewers, [of these studies] even those who were quite positive about the promise of sex offender treatment programs, felt that more work was needed before firm conclusions could be reached." They cited the methodological limitations of studies as the major obstacle to drawing firm conclusions about treatment effectiveness.[36]

One problem of the GAO report is its failure to look at the most recent studies. The report primarily focused on a group of publications that did not include advances in the field of sexual abuser treatment during the past decade. During the past ten years, a number of studies regarding sex offender treatment and recidivism have been conducted and published. They are very encouraging and some show comprehensive treatment of pedophilia and other types of sexual abuse has a 90% or better success rate.[37, 38, 39, 40] Rapists are a more difficult clientele and the success rates vary between 75-85% success, according to one expert,[41] and over 90% by others.[42]

---

[34] Ibid. p.4

[35] Gail Ryan, Facilitator. National Adolescent Perpetrator Network. Kempe Center, Denver, CO. Personal communication July 21, 1997.

[36] United States General Accounting Office. (1996, June 21). Sex offender treatment: Research results inconclusive about what works to reduce recidivism. (GAO/GGD-96-137., p. 7) Washington DC: U.S. Government Printing Office.

[37] Olsen , S. S. (1997) Cognitive-behavioral treatment for sex offenders: a look at recidivism. Oregon Adolescent Sex Offender Treatment Network Newsletter, p. 1. Eugene, OR.

[38] Lotke, E. Sex offenders: does treatment work? 1996, May, 21(5), pp.1-3. Corrections Compendium.: Lincoln, NE: CEGA Publishing.

[39] Marshall, W.L. & Pithers, W.D. (1994) A reconsideration of treatment outcome with sex offenders. Criminal Justice And Behavior, 21(1) pp.10-27. American Association for Correctional Psychology.

[40] Nagayama-Hall, G. C. (1995) Sexual offender recidivism revisited: a meta-analysis of recent treatment studies. Journal of Counseling and Clinical Psychology. 63(5) pp. 802-809. American Psychology Association, Inc.

[41] McGrath, R. J., Hoke, S. E., & Vojtisek, J. E. (1997) Cognitive-behavioral treatment of sex offenders: a treatment comparison and long-term follow-up study. Unpublished manuscript.

[42] Berlin, F., Hunt, W., Malin, H., Dyer, A., Lehne, G., & Dean, S. (1991). A five-year plus follow-up survey of criminal recidivism within a treated cohort of 406 pedophiles, 111 exhibitionists and 109 sexual aggressives: issues and outcomes. American Journal of Forensic Psychiatry, 12(3). Baltimore, Maryland. pp. 5-28.

Finally, if sex offender treatment is going to continue to be a valuable prevention effort and information source, then the appropriate funding must be forthcoming from government, scientific, and public health foundation sources. The field of sex offender treatment continues to provide current information regarding sexual abuse, its etiology, and prevention strategies. Both treatment and research regarding sexual abuse must be funded if we are to increase our knowledge, explore new treatment possibilities, and evaluate efficacy.

How Sex Offender Treatment Works

Treatment works! That good news has been with us for some time, but despite the GAO's cautious review, in the last few years research studies have demonstrated strong enough evidence to convince even skeptics that treatment works better than no treatment[43, 44] Johns Hopkins University has reviewed treatment programs from around the world and discovered that even some of the most worrisome sexual predators, pedophiles and adult rapists, respond very well to rehabilitative efforts.[45] Now that research supports comprehensive treatment as effective tertiary (and primary) prevention, there is no longer a reason not to spread this news, educate the public, and begin formulating rational public policy based on the findings. As responsible citizens and members of the media seeking to combat a serious public health problem, we must use this information to secure treatment for both sexual abusers and victims, knowing that not all sex abusers should be, or will be, behind bars until their deaths. And when they are returned to public life, our best hope is that they will be restored to a healthier state by the effective methods now available.

So what works? Many treatment providers will assert that their program is effective. Success is being seen all around us. And based on our experience as clinicians and trainers, the primary key to success is the ability of therapists to make a vital personal connection with each and every sex abuser being treated - even the most diabolical, brutal, and uncooperative of them.

All the science, technology, medicines, and techniques are of limited value unless applied within a solid and respectful therapeutic relationship. Treatment providers have learned to put aside personal and political prejudices that have

[43] McGrath, R. J. (Winter 1995) Sex offender treatment: does it work? Perspectives 9(1) pp. 24-26. American Probation and Parole Association.

[44] Sex offender treatment program: initial recidivism study - executive summary. 1996, August 15. Alaska Department of Corrections Offender Programs and Alaska Justice Statistical Analysis Unit Justice Center :University of Alaska. Justice Center Home Page: Microsoft Internet Explorer 12/7/96.

[45] Berlin, F., Hunt, W., Malin, H., Dyer, A., Lehne, G., & Dean, S. (1991). A five-year plus follow-up survey of criminal recidivism within a treated cohort of 406 pedophiles, 111 exhibitionists and 109 sexual aggressives: issues and outcome. American Journal of Forensic Psychiatry, 12(3), pp.5-28.

stymied success in times past. It is now clear that therapists who approach sex abusers with hateful, punitive, and vindictive attitudes perpetuate abusive attitudes in their clients rather than modeling how the client can learn to relate on a mutually respectful basis. Hate breeds more hate. Respectful firmness, however, is usually received well by abusers.[46]

If treatment is to be effective, relationships must be built between therapists and abusers that foster openness, disclosure, honesty, and change. As with all human beings, sex abusers need to believe they will be treated with dignity and professionalism before they will let their guard down and risk being vulnerable.

Unfortunately, some clinicians have been too comfortable assigning responsibility for treatment failures exclusively to the repeat abuser. Sometimes, when therapeutic boundaries break down, the clinician carries society's attitudes of vengeance into the counseling session. At times abusers have been shamed, brow-beaten, threatened with punishments for minor mistakes, and treated condescendingly by therapists. Then, when the abuser refuses to cooperate in a hostile environment and shows no willingness to cooperate with counseling, blame is laid at his feet. At the urging of punitive therapists and hard-line corrections personnel, society saw that the abuser was totally in the wrong and the therapist could do no wrong. Many therapists are not held accountable for their unprofessionalism and the part they play in the abuser's failure to become engaged in treatment.

It's a frightening truth that, setting aside their sexually abusive behavior, male sex abusers are often strikingly normal American men. They resemble most non-abusers in terms of their beliefs and emotional condition. Knowing this, we can anticipate that many of them will respond to methods and means that would work with most any of us. Like other men, they are looking for ways to grow and improve themselves. Like other men, they need manly ways to extricate themselves from the humiliation of their crimes. Like others, they often don't know where to turn for help. Like us, they need a trusted companion to guide them safely through the change process. The responsibility to meet those needs rests with a therapeutic community that is brave enough to challenge today's political climate of hate, look beyond all the emotionalism, and strive to connect with each sex abuser who comes their way. In doing so, society can be better protected.

Qualities of a Good Sex Abuser Therapist

To make the essential connection with a sex abuser, many personality traits and ethical guidelines must be present. They complement a good education, an understanding of treatment techniques and tools, and the credentials to practice.

---

[46] Blanchard, G. (1995). The difficult connection. Brandon, VT: Safer Society Press.

One of the qualities of an effective therapist is authenticity, the ability to be real, genuine, and spontaneous. Sex abusers, while being disingenuous during their assaultive periods, expect their therapists to be otherwise. To be authentic, the therapist must be quite comfortable with himself/herself and comfortable in the company of all kinds of people, sexual abusers included.

Another quality is that of congruence. The therapist must practice what is being preached, act in the fashion that they teach, and be the same type of person from patient to patient and colleague to patient. They must model the qualities expected in a recovering abuser.

Vulnerability is what we expect from patients but often clinicians are unwilling to risk it themselves. Many therapists have been trained to see professionalism as requiring an image that never shows cracks in their armor. But judicious expressions of vulnerability let abusers know we are real, we are as human as they are. With that realization they are more inclined to invest their energy in the treatment process. Being vulnerable doesn't have to mean only showing weakness. It can be a sign of courage, wholeness, and honesty.

Equality in the counseling arena is not total or complete. Certainly the abuser must not be entrusted with many of the therapist's power and controls. Yet, when an abuser is approached as a partner in the therapy process, when he is encouraged to brainstorm with the therapist and help develop a treatment plan, equality is felt and change takes place.

Humor works with all types of clients. Many therapists have tried, however, to keep this healing tool out of our sessions with sex abusers to avoid being accused of being light on crime or insensitive to victims. Still, humor has its place from time-to-time. It provides tension relief in the somber sessions with sexual abusers. It enables therapists to confront some individuals more effectively. It allows the client to receive therapist suggestions more readily. It also works to build relationships, the cornerstone to effective therapy. A good and healthy therapist will have a good and healthy sense of humor that everyone finds engaging.

Warmth doesn't have to be earned to be a part of the counseling environment. Abusers can't learn what they have never seen nor experienced. As with parenting, this warmth must be matched with authority and firmness. Goodness begets goodness just as cruelty generates more cruelty. It is a part of professionalism.

Effective therapists are not afraid to moralize with their patients and they do so in the most dignified way. Rather than shame an abuser, or look down on him, they vigorously search for and reinforce any patient value or spark of morality that can be ignited in the counseling setting. They challenge an abuser's negative thinking and behaving. Always, the confrontations are done with care and respect.

Any therapist who claims to know the cure for sex offending should be avoided. There is no cure with many serious mental health problems and sexual abuse is no different. There is only the hope of better control through eternal vigilance. But further, that type of conceit, that arrogance, is something we never want to pass along to a recovering sexual abuser. A substantial degree of humility translates to a substantial degree of mental health and a lowered risk of continuing to abuse.

The therapist who is technique-focused to the extent that rapport is rarely felt will be limited in ability and treatment success. When technique becomes paramount, all is lost.[47] It is the humanness that is brought into counseling, more than any mechanical approach, that spawns growth. On the other side of the coin, beware of the therapist who can't (or won't) administer an objective assessment test, always refuses to use biofeedback measurements, or never is open to drug treatments that can augment counseling.

How Can We Know A Sex Offender Is Safer?

Sexual abuse is not just about sex, just like alcoholism isn't just about thirst. Knowing all the factors that gave rise to an abuse cycle can help determine the way out. Parents, spouses, older children of abusers, friends, clergy and others can look for signs indicating movement toward recovery. Here are a few:

- The abuser accepts full responsibility. No longer does he say "the booze made me do it." No longer does he say "She dressed provocatively." Instead the abuser says, and believes, that he accepts total responsibility for where he was, what he thought, and what he did.

- The abuser acts differently. He doesn't promise he will never do it again. An abuser in recovery recognizes that words are an inadequate substitute for action. He also is humble and educated enough to acknowledge that he is always at risk to return to a former way of life. Consequently, his everyday behaviors and his entire lifestyle, rather than just words, reflect this change away from power-seeking, manipulation, and control.

- The abuser is less selfish and self-absorbed. He shows more concern and empathy for others. He may volunteer time helping others. Other clients may receive his help and support. Perhaps he has joined a community service group.

---

[47] Yalom, I. (1980). Existential psychotherapy. New York: Basic Books.

- The abuser stays in touch with other recovering men. Never does the recovering abuser get so smug or self-confident that he claims never to need the support of other men. Humility is ever-present.

- The abuser knows his high risk situations. Before traveling too far down the road toward reoffending, he self-corrects and employs the knowledge and interventions he has learned in therapy. His insights quickly are translated into a corrective action plan.

- The abuser doesn't use sex or alcohol abusively. Neither sex nor alcohol is used in a pain-relieving manner. Alcohol, if used at all, is always enjoyed in moderation.

- The abuser's thinking is no longer distorted. Rationalizations, minimization, projecting flaws onto others, attributing inappropriate motives to others, objectification, arrogance, and other unhealthy thought processes have been replaced with a solid reality orientation. He is less confused and much more honest.

- The abuser may be more spiritual. Attending religious services is one thing, being purposefully and caringly involved in the family of man is quite another. When he shows sensitivity for others, he feels like he fits in, and adheres to the values he resurrected in therapy. There is reason for optimism.

- The abuser's time is well spent. Along with a purpose in life, he now has direction. He is busy with a new life he enjoys. Rarely does he complain of boredom. His job is satisfying. Idle time has diminished and is not spent cruising for victims or frequenting old haunts.

- The abuser's self-esteem has improved. He no longer berates himself or needs to berate others. The good in others is frequently noted. Less time is spent apologizing. Confidence is up. He is at peace with himself.

- The abuser's sex life is more serene. From once being an intensity junkie in search of partners, orgasms, and conquests, he has learned to enjoy a quieter and more satisfying sex life. Intensity has been replaced with intimacy.

- The abuser is more assertive, but less aggressive. He knows what he wants, knows how to ask for it, but doesn't trample over other people en route to his goals. Arguing and fighting have diminished.

- The abuser's need to control is reduced. He is far less driven to have people and circumstances comply with his demands. Compromise is a part of his life. Feelings of frustration are less frequent.

- The abuser's anger has diminished. Now the ability is there to express a wider range of emotions than just anger. He can identify and appropriately ventilate the emotions that previously led to angry outbursts (e.g., fear, insecurity, helplessness, shame, frustration, sadness, etc.).

- The abuser's social skills have improved. He's not afraid to go out and meet new people. Listening skills are better. Relationships are less competitive. People are less threatening. He trusts more. Loneliness has diminished.

- The abuser handles family problems with greater ease. Not everything is a crisis. Not everything needs to be fixed now. All family members have a vote in resolving conflicts. He seeks consensus.

- The abuser is less jealous. His level of personal insecurity has lessened. Partners are no longer watched, stalked, or falsely accused. He isn't as threatened by other men.

- The abuser has reassessed old friends. Partners in crime no longer come by. Drinking buddies respect his new lifestyle and he avoids them as necessary. Relationships with old lovers have been terminated. Dangerous people and environments are avoided.

- The abuser's anxiety is diminished. Once high-strung, today he knows how to calm himself without assaulting, drinking, or pursuing high voltage excitement. He can enjoy the moment.

- The abuser is no longer depressed and forlorn. There is a more positive quality about him.

- The abuser isn't afraid to return to counseling. No longer does he need to deny problems or solve them completely on his own. Counseling is not seen as a threat to his identity, but as a resource to be tapped when needed. Occasionally, he will return to an abuse group meeting for a "booster" session.

- The abuser has addressed his own victimization. He has integrated abuse experiences into his life and now is at peace with himself. He is no longer burdened with a shame-based identity.

- The abuser understands his cycle and uses interventions. He has learned to identify when he has the urge to act out and uses the skills, coping responses and interventions he learned in treatment.

- The abuser demonstrates empathy. He is able to identify and express his feelings as well as identify with the feelings of others.

- The abuser consistently thinks about the impact of his actions on himself and others. He does not act impulsively.

Many sexual abusers are understandably eager to put their crime behind them and move on. Once counseling has been terminated, it can be difficult to go back. Some men believe that returning to therapy represents failure. Quite the opposite is true. The healthy man recognizes there will repeatedly be crises and setbacks throughout his life. He knows that mental health is not about the absence of crises in his life. It is about the ability to recognize them early and respond in a quick and efficient manner.

Community members and support people of recovering abusers, who form an important link in the public health model, shouldn't wait for glaring signals. Expressing loving concern early in a firm and respectful way assures a recovering abuser that his happiness is important to the community's safety. Knowing he is happy is one of the best assurances that he will not abuse. After all, happy men are much less likely to be sexual abusers.

• CHAPTER ELEVEN •

Prevention for the 21st Century

"Medicine is healing of all sorts for the body, mind and spirit utilizing science whenever possible and including epidemiology and the sciences of prevention ... Public health must take a major role in prevention of child maltreatment."
- David L. Chadwick, M.D.[1]

The Financial Costs and Use of Community Resources

In the late 1980's and early 1990's three separate studies were conducted to look at the costs to society for a single case of child sexual abuse. A Vermont study conducted in 1987 suggests that every time one child is sexually abused and the abuser is apprehended, prosecuted and convicted it costs taxpayers between $138,000 and $152,000. The costs include all related investigation and court costs, as well as five years of incarceration without treatment for the abuser, two years of parole supervision, and two years of treatment for the victim.[2] A 1989 Massachusetts study found similar costs and

---

[1] Chadwick, D.L. (1997, May 14). The health care system and child maltreatment from 1972 to the present: what next? [Keynote address] The 25th Annual Child Abuse and Neglect Symposium at Keystone, Co. Sponsored by the Kempe Center, Denver CO.

[2] Pithers, W. (1992). Estimated cost savings of sex offender treatment in Vermont in 1987. Recidivism packet Brandon, VT: The Safer Society Press.

estimated the cost of each case of child sexual abuse at approximately $183,000.[3] This study included the same investigation and court costs as well as seven years of incarceration for the abuser, five years of parole supervision, and just one year of treatment for the victim.

In Canada, a third and similar study was conducted in 1992 by William Marshall, a leading authority on sexual abusers and a member of the faculty of the Department of Psychology at Queen's University in Ontario. Marshall determined that the costs of investigation, prosecution, and incarceration, etc., for each child sexual abuse case would cost approximately $200,000 Canadian.[4] Without prevention, sexual abuse will continue to take its financial toll on America. In today's economy, these costs would be even higher.

The costs of sexual abuse in America are high, and particularly those of criminal sexual abuse. These costs are difficult to calculate, however, the funds spent prosecuting a single case of child sexual abuse could have far-reaching positive effects on reducing sexual abuse in communities if applied to sexual abuse prevention strategies and restorative justice models. The prosecution of sexual abuse crimes and long term incarceration bare tremendous costs that become the burden of the taxpayer.[5]

Legislation focused on sexual predators, chemical castration, public notification, building prisons, prosecuting sexual crimes with maximum penalties, and treating perpetrators and victims of sexual abuse are all very costly. For example, more than 2.5 million children were abused (including physical, sexual, and other forms of abuse) in the United States in 1990.[6] Preventing problems is generally more cost effective than treating them. Child abuse is no different. The state of Michigan, for example, spends approximately $823 million annually dealing with child abuse. In contrast, Michigan estimates the costs of prevention programming at $43 million annually.[7] As researcher Robert Caldwell notes:

> "The case for prevention is persuasive. Not only is it the humane approach, it is the financially responsible approach. Programs designed to prevent child maltreatment serve society in several

---

[3] Prentky, R. & Burgess, A.W. (1990, January), Rehabilitation of child molesters: A cost-benefit analysis. American Journal of Orthopsychiatry, 60(1), pp. 108-117.

[4] Marshall, W. L. (1992). The social value of treatment for sexual offenders. Proceedings of the Canadian Sex Research Forum. The Canadian Journal of Human Sexuality, 1(3), pp.109- 114.

[5] Freeman-Longo, R. E., & Knopp, F. H. (1992). State-of-the art sex offender treatment: outcome and issues. Annals of Sex Research, 5(3), pp. 142-160.

[6] Daro, D., & McCurdy, K. (1991). Current trends in child abuse reporting and fatalities: The results of the 1990 annual fifty state survey. [Working paper #808]. Chicago: National Committee for Prevention of Child Abuse.

[7] Caldwell, R. A. The costs of child abuse vs. child abuse prevention: Michigan's experience. June 12, 1992. Found on the Internet. January 23, 1997. Http://pilot.msu.edu/user/caldwel9/costs.html.

ways: they build stronger, healthier children; they reduce the burdens on state services such as education, law enforcement, corrections, and mental health; and they free money to be spent on more life-enhancing projects. An ounce of prevention truly is worth a pound of cure."

Unfortunately, most prevention programming is a result of a shoestring budget of patchwork funding from pro bono work, private foundations, government grants, and individual donations. In fact, in the 1980's, the Coca Cola Corporation spent more money on advertising Coke® than the federal government spent on public awareness campaigns to educate the American public about child abuse and neglect.[8] America needs more prevention programs in order to reduce the sexual abuse problem and prevention programs must become a mainstream effort. Early intervention coupled with early parent education results in decreased incidents of child abuse.[9] As Dr. Richard Krugman, Dean of the School of Medicine at the University of Colorado and Editor of the international journal *Child Abuse & Neglect* writes, "Problems that are not openly discussed cannot be solved."[10] Dr. Krugman continues:

A public health approach to this problem would state that untreatable, uncontrollable chronic sex offenders are a public health menace and nuisance. It is not their fault - they have a problem we do not know how to control. Thus, they need to be quarantined - not in prisons, but in public health hospitals where they can be cared for and studied. Unless we develop new research approaches to this population, we will never make progress.

Lest anyone think that the public health approach has no place in dealing with abuse and neglect issues, I will leave you with a speculative question: suppose it is genetic? There is no room here to explore this issue, other than to say that the finding of a single gene responsible for nurturance in mice is enormously interesting and should stimulate a great deal more research on the neuroscience and genetics of abusive and neglectful behavior.

What if funding for child abuse research even came close to that appropriated for research on muscular dystrophy, juvenile diabetes,

---

[8] Donnelly, A.C. (1997, May 14). Public Education about Child Abuse and Neglect from 1972-1997: Educating Ourselves and the Future. Keynote Address. The 25th Annual Child Abuse and Neglect Symposium, Keystone, CO. Sponsored by the Kempe Center, Denver CO.

[9] Ibid.

[10] Krugman, R. D. (1997, Spring). Three wishes for the future of child protection. The APSAC Advisor, 10(1), pp. 2-3. The APSAC Advisor is the official newsletter of the American Professional Society on the Abuse of Children.

and other diseases that have 1% its incidence! Thirty-five years from now, we might have made substantially more progress toward true prevention of child abuse and neglect than we have made to date. Would that it be so![11]

In his keynote at the Governor's Prevention Conference in Burlington, Vermont, Con Hogan, Vermont Agency of Human Services Secretary, reported that the State of Vermont had saved hundreds of thousands of dollars through prevention programs of all kinds, including sexual abuse prevention, Success by Six, drunk driving education, and others.[12]

The Challenge for the Future

We have discussed the need for America to change current thinking and attitudes regarding sexual abuse if we are serious about preventing the criminal sexual abuse problem. Part of that change requires society to focus on prevention rather than exclusively on punishment. As James A. Mercy and his colleagues note, "The history of public health has shown repeatedly that the search for prevention policies and programs pays off."[13]

There are several ways to significantly reduce the incidence of sexual abuse for future generations if society is ready to accept the challenges and responsibilities associated with prevention efforts. First, we must challenge America's tunnel vision regarding sexual abuse. The unfortunate reality is that sexual abuse will not go away unless we change many of our beliefs and attitudes. Mercy, et al., write, "Recent experience with public health information and education campaigns for reducing smoking and cardiovascular disease and preventing acquired immunodeficiency syndrome (AIDS) suggest that similar efforts can be important parts of the public health approach to preventing violence."[14] Public education will help challenge our current thinking about sexual abuse.

Second, everyone must get involved. People are no longer ignoring the facts regarding sexual abuse. If people arm themselves with accurate information regarding the causes of sexual abuse, the extent of the problem, and what we are currently doing to prevent it from occurring in the future, they will be better equipped to decide what public policies will work best in their communities. Donnelly notes, "The public wants to do something about child abuse and neglect. Today Americans are more self-reliant and no longer

---

[11] Ibid.

[12] Hogan, C. "Economic of Prevention"[Keynote address] Governor's Conference on Prevention. Burlington, Vermont. (1997, May 13).

[13] Mercy, J. A., Rosenberg, M. L., Powell, K. E., Broome, C. V., and Roper, W. L. (1993, Winter). Public health policy for preventing violence. Health Affairs.

[14] Ibid.

expecting government to solve the problem. The public is willing to play an active role in prevention. The problem the public faces is not knowing what to do and how to get involved, therefore, they are very pessimistic about their ability to help and make a difference."[15]

In this regard, Donnelly recommends six things that need to be done over the next 10-25 years to reduce child abuse and neglect:[16]

1. Develop more resources in public awareness and education.

2. Public education and prevention efforts need to be repetitive, not short-term or time-limited. There is always a new generation to educate.

3. Efforts at education and prevention must be far more mainstream, not just public service announcements. We must think, "Is this good for kids?"

4. The public must be engaged on multiple levels. They need to know how they can a) help their neighborhood, b) help their community, and c) help the community next door.

5. Professionals need to be the lightning rods to engage the public.

6. The key messages for society must focus on prevention in the early years of life, the use of early intervention, and be aimed at effective parenting.

Third, a restorative justice model should be strongly considered for replacing the current and ineffective criminal justice model regarding sexual abuse prevention. Restorative justice is not being soft on criminals, nor is it a substitute for punishing sexual offenders who commit heinous crimes. According to Fran Henry, President of STOP IT NOW!, "Restorative justice means you hold someone accountable and you hold out something [positive] …you cannot do one without the other."[17]

Fourth, we believe that there must be a concentrated effort by politicians and policy makers to focus on primary prevention efforts to reduce sexual abuse. Primary prevention means stopping the abuse before it occurs. Primary prevention is holding the potential abuser responsible for stopping any abuse before it starts and holding the abuser accountable for his or her actions so it doesn't happen again. Primary prevention takes the responsibility for preventing sexual abuse off the shoulders of potential victims and puts it where it belongs, with the abuser.

---

[15] Donnelly, A.C. (1997, May 14). Public Education about Child Abuse and Neglect from 1972-1997: Educating Ourselves and the Future. Keynote Address. The 25th Annual Child Abuse and Neglect Symposium, Keystone, CO. Sponsored by the Kempe Center, Denver CO.

[16] Ibid.

[17] Keeler, S. Group: child abuse can be stopped. The Burlington Free Press. Friday, January 17, 1997. p. 3B.

Sexual Abuse Prevention

Because of its widespread occurrence and estimated frequency, the sexual abuse epidemic places everyone in the position of being a potential victim. However, a common attitude and response to sexual abuse has been "It is not my problem," or "It won't happen to me." Many women who are raped have told themselves before the assault, "It will never happen to me, I don't go to bars at night." The mother of a child whom the father has abused would never predict this tragedy would befall her family. The spouse of a sexual addict is horrified at the reality of his or her partner. None of us is immune. These are attitudes that foster denial, breed apathy, and threaten prevention efforts. Regardless of attitude or opinion, any national problem that has reached epidemic proportions is everyone's problem. It may be someone else's problem today but that does not preclude any of us from being affected by sexual abuse, in some capacity, tomorrow.

The most successful campaigns dealing with public health issues have focused on public education, through extensive use of the media and providing avenues for getting help to the persons with the identified problem. As Mercy, et al.,[18] note:

> Public health has now become much more sophisticated in the use of marketing techniques to bring about change. We know that we need to formulate precise objectives, identify target audiences, carefully develop culturally competent messages, and then measure the impact of these marketing efforts on the outcomes of interest.

> In developing strategies, society can directly apply the five public-health violence-prevention goals identified by Mercy and colleagues to sexual abuse prevention efforts. The five goals include:

> First, [violence-prevention public health campaigns] must make people aware of the magnitude and characteristics of the problem of violence today. Second, they must give hope to individuals and communities, informing them that there are things that work and things that people and communities can do to prevent violence. Third, they must mobilize individuals, organizations, and communities to act. Fourth, they must provide information about what works and how to conduct effective programs. And fifth, they must be designed so that we can measure their effectiveness and use that information to constantly improve them.[19]

---

[18] Mercy, J. A., Rosenberg, M. L., Powell, K. E., Broome, C. V., and Roper, W. L. (1993, Winter). Public health policy for preventing violence. Health Affairs.

[19] Ibid.

Media and Prevention Increasing Individual Awareness

As Mercy and his colleagues point out, the first goal for violence prevention is to make people aware of the magnitude and characteristics of the problem. Throughout this book, we have attempted to do that. One of the most powerful tools for educating the public is the use of the electronic and written media. This is especially true of the electronic media. The news can be invaluable as a vehicle to educate the public about social issues and specifically about sexual abuse. With proper and factual information, the media can help dispel myths about sexual abuse and encourage people to become active in prevention efforts within their communities.

Unfortunately, the media can be a double-edged sword. It can help prevention efforts by educating the public with factual information to help mobilize prevention efforts, and it can continue to instill fear in the public and contribute to promoting and reinforcing sexual abuse and sexual violence. The media can contribute to promoting no-cost or low-cost public health campaigns and informative, well-researched documentaries and news stories about sexual abuse prevention and treatment. On the other hand, the media can be problematic, as we discussed in Chapter Eight.

The media can play a major role in sexual abuse prevention with well designed public service announcements aimed at public education and targeting potential and actual abusers with primary prevention campaigns. These news specials, documentaries, educational messages, and public service announcements must be repeated frequently.

Communities Can Reduce Sexual Abuse

The second goal in preventing violence is giving people and communities hope. While we do not want to mislead people into believing that all sexual abuse can be eradicated, we believe that reducing the amount of sexual abuse that occurs in our country is entirely possible, especially criminal sexual abuse. The best methods for accomplishing this task are through public education and primary prevention efforts.

How can we give you hope that sexual abuse can be reduced in your community? We believe that by reading this book you have taken the first step. People develop hope when they have information and facts available to them. If you personally research other public health education programs and campaigns for drunk driving, HIV/AIDS, and smoking, you will find that they have been very successful. There is every reason to believe that a similar campaign for sexual abuse can be effective in reducing criminal sexual abuse.

Mobilizing To Act

Most efforts to deal with social and other problems take form and substance when a few people who are movers and shakers become involved and get others to stand behind a particular cause. The next step is to get involved. Everyone must take action, volunteer, write letters, etc., to engage others in their neighborhoods and communities. Each person must play a role in encouraging others to address the sexual abuse problem. Individuals, organizations, foundations, and social service agencies are all potential resources for educating the public and dissemination of information. In Vermont, for example, public pressure and citizen involvement have all but eliminated nude dancing establishments and adult bookstores in the state.

Educating the Public About Prevention Programs

As a nation we have the means and ability to educate Americans about human sexuality and sexual abuse. We cannot let occasional setbacks discourage us from moving forward in advocating appropriate sexual education and abuse prevention.[20] Public education efforts must a) teach about the problem, b) address the various measures to correct the problem, and c) engage the public to participate in public education and awareness programs.

Measuring the Effectiveness of Prevention

It is often difficult to evaluate prevention programs. All efforts at public education and prevention need to be evaluated in terms of their effectiveness, as well as for necessary revisions and updates. Some areas for evaluation of the efficacy of these education and preventions programs may include a) a decrease in the number of sexual abuse cases being prosecuted (plea bargaining included), b) a decrease in the number of reported cases. When advocacy and prevention programs are started, initially one may see an increase in reporting as the new resource is made available before a decrease is reported that results from the prevention effort. The difficulty lies in evaluating something that has not happened and therefore is not reported, c) a decrease in the number of individuals being convicted and incarcerated in the correctional system, and d) a decrease in the number of legislative efforts directed targeting sexual abuse. When prevention efforts are truly working the steady increase in sexual abuse cases we have experienced in the past 25 years will reverse direction and continue to decrease over several years.

---

[20] Often there are political costs of open communication, for example the removal of Surgeon General Joycelyn Elders for openly discussing education about masturbation in schools.

PREVENTION FOR TOMORROW

A National Campaign

It astonishes us that until STOP IT NOW! began in 1995, there has never been a national campaign to stop sexual abuse. We have never seen, heard, or read public service announcements appealing to potential sexual abusers to seek help for their problem before they sexually abuse. Sexual abuse is a silent epidemic that is no different from other problems and potential epidemics in our country. Violence in America, child abuse, domestic violence, drug abuse, HIV/AIDS, drunk driving, and second-hand cigarette smoke have all been the focus of national prevention campaigns that have used public service announcements on television, radio, and in the written media. As recently as 1997, updates on the second-hand cigarette smoke issue have appeared in the media.[21]

We believe that sexual abuse prevention requires a national campaign to acknowledge sexual abuse as a public health problem. If society expects people who are prone to act out sexually to get help for their problem and stop their behavior, then society must offer the opportunity for sexual abusers and persons at risk for sexually abusing to step forward and get help. All of the other prevention campaigns have provided hope and the opportunity for treatment, even when there is not a cure for the particular problem. To prevent sexual abuse from becoming a more widespread epidemic, we must provide potential and active abusers the same opportunities for hope and recovery and decrease their demonization. This can happen by addressing sexual abuse as a public health issue.

Changing Public Attitudes Through Education

Public education is the cornerstone of any major problem that requires resolution. This is especially true about sexual abuse. People's values and attitudes are formed by what they know about a particular issue. Those values and attitudes are subject to change when people acquire new information. Personal beliefs, attitudes, and values affect opinions which, in turn, determine the action individuals are likely to take. Prevention campaigns require each of us to look at ourselves, as well as addressing the problems of others.

Most people have not taken the time to take a personal inventory regarding their personal beliefs and values regarding human sexuality. Our personal beliefs, attitudes, and values, however, shape our behavior regarding sexual abuse and the abuse of human sexuality in general. Therefore, Americans must educate themselves about sexual abuse and other abuses of human sexuality, if

---

[21] Second hand smoke. (1997, May 20). Rutland [VT] Daily Herald, p. 1.

they are going to commit themselves to prevention efforts. Many people oppose sex education in the schools and actively speak out against it, yet some of the same people do not speak out against the violence and explicit sex in the media that has a great deal of potential to shape the sexual beliefs and attitudes of our younger generation. Many do not publicly object to the many problems and abuses we have addressed in this book. These are not mutually exclusive areas if one is going to address preventing sexual abuse.

Since sexual abuse is perpetuated, in part, because people who sexually abuse do not understand what is healthy human sexuality and what is abusive sexual behavior, we must educate them. Clinical experience tells us that there would be less sexual abuse perpetrated by children and adolescents if they knew that it was hurtful and wrong. Many abusers have had no formal sex education and their beliefs, attitudes, and knowledge are based upon inaccurate information and distortions.

Prevention begins with knowledge which helps to change public attitudes and correct distortions. The increasing prevalence of sexual harassment in America is a clear example of the need to change values, attitudes, and beliefs. Many people do not consider sexual language, the use of sexual terms to curse and swear, sexual innuendos, and sexual jokes as harassing or threatening to others. It is a norm that can be addressed by early education and teaching children and adolescents about healthy sexuality and the appropriate versus inappropriate use of sexual boundaries, sexual language, sexual gestures, and sexual behavior. If current harassers faced uniform disapproval, much the same way cigarette smokers do, they may be influenced to change their behavior.

We also believe that many people who invest in the sex-for-sale industries might invest less, or not invest at all, if they knew the industries contributed to sustaining sexual abuse. The fact that money is exchanged for these products or services reflects the way consumers think about their actions. Many of society's ills are the product of a materialistic culture that places high value on money and power.

The consumers of pornography, prostitution, 900 phone sex numbers, and other sex-for-sale industries should be warned about the potential personal, financial, and psychological damages they may experience as a result of indulging. Imagine if all adult-oriented materials and services of a sexual nature had a warning similar to alcohol and cigarettes that read:

> Warning: The use of these materials may result in psychological distress, financial problems, contribute to sexual addiction, and may exploit the actors and models.

Or for prostitution, nude dancing, adult entertainment and services:

> Warning: Engaging in these activities or services may result in psychological distress, financial problems, marital or relationship problems, or contribute to sexual addiction for both the consumer and/or the service providers.

Unfortunately, much of what Americans know about sexual abuse and criminal sexual behavior, comes from sensationalized television talk shows and abbreviated news casts. Inaccurate figures, statistics, and statements appear in magazines, news articles, and television broadcasts and cable services.[22] Very little information that Americans receive about sexual abuse and criminal sexual behavior comes from the professional literature and scientific journals.

As we mentioned in Chapter Four, research indicates a link between child sexual abuse and teen pregnancy. These data suggest the need for education as a means of prevention. For example, as Butler and Burton write:

> In a Pennsylvania study consisting of interviews with 41 young women, who had all been teenage mothers, twenty-two (54%) of the young women revealed they experienced at least one sexually abusive incident by age 18, but only one had talked with a counselor about the experience. In six cases, the victim had told no one. A paramount challenge for practitioners, then, is to develop safe contexts for victims to talk about their experiences and to find sensitive methods to aid the recovery process.[23]

Since victims are not likely to report these incidents, the best prevention for sexual abuse-related teenage pregnancy may be education of those males likely to engage in sexual relations and/or abuse of teenage females.

Prevention efforts should also be directed at young males as potential perpetrators. Many colleges have developed successful programs dealing with acquaintance and date rape and educating young men regarding their obligations to female friends and partners. These programs should be adapted for middle schools and high schools.[24]

---

[22] Most of the people interviewed on television talk shows, in magazines, and in news articles are not scientists and researchers. Instead, many interviewees are citizens, victims of crime, and activists. These interviewees often cite information and statistics that are outdated or non-scientific, or they cite only those aspects of the research that support their opinions. Often, production time or print space does not allow a comprehensive review of the relevant research. After reading, watching, and listening to hundreds of articles and shows, we are concerned that responsible research, credible statistics, and factual data regarding sexual abuse are not being cited by the media on a routine basis. Too many reporters do not even call credible scientific resources to get a reality check on the figures they are citing: are they current, credible, within a reasonable range supported by responsible research?

[23] Butler, J. R. & Burton, L. M. (1995, November/December). Research results suggesting link between child sexual abuse and early pregnancy provide new considerations for practitioners. NRCCSA News, 4(6), p. 4.

[24] Ibid.

We must educate ourselves about the issues of sexual abuse and sexual violence, their origins, and measures we can take to get at the roots of the problem, if we are going to commit ourselves to preventing it.

Prevention Through the Life Span

Prevention of both victimization and perpetration must begin at birth and continue across the life span. Research has identified a constellation of developmental and experiential factors which seem to contribute to the risk that a child might be vulnerable to be sexually abused or might become abusive. Parent education, advice, and support efforts which have been developed to prevent physical abuse, neglect, and violence in the home can easily incorporate sexual abuse victimization and perpetration prevention goals. It has been hypothesized that the three most common characteristics of all abusers are 1) the lack of empathy, 2) a distorted sense of responsibility and control, and 3) low self-esteem. All of these deficits originate in the individual's earliest experiences in the first few months of life. Home health visitors and pediatric healthcare providers must be educated and encouraged to foster empathic development in the care of infants and toddlers.[25]

Early Identification

We have known for some time that there is a cycle of abuse regarding child abuse. There are growing numbers of children identified because they are acting out sexually abusing other children. Research has developed methods to help professionals, teachers, and others identify children who may have been sexually abused. Research in this area has also given us the ability to detect, often through direct observation, children who are beginning to act out sexually. Curriculum for training teachers and caregivers to understand and respond specifically to children's sexual behaviors have been available from the Kempe Center's Perpetration Prevention Project since 1988.[26]

Being physically ill is considered as a deviation from the norm. Being mentally ill is also a deviation from the norm. If someone has a behavioral problem that deviates from acceptable responsible behavior, they need to be treated to eliminate the behavioral problem rendering them behaviorally healthy.

---

[25] Ryan, G. & Lane, S. (1997) Juvenile Sexual Offending: Causes, Consequences, and Corrections. San Francisco, CA: Jossey Bass.

[26] Implementing the Kempe Center's curriculum, from 1991 to 1994, The Safer Society Program in Vermont offered training to teachers, bus drivers, and school aides on identifying, appropriately naming, and firmly and respectfully confronting potentially abusive behaviors in elementary school children. The training was called "Primary Perpetration Prevention" and included a proposal for tracking children exhibiting such behaviors throughout their school careers by means of an entry in their medical records. Similar efforts are underway in numerous other states as well.

By identifying early signs of abusive attitudes, behaviors, and/or sexual confusion in childhood, we can use goal oriented interventions (and therapy, as indicated) to interrupt the development of sexually abusive behavior. As with other health problems, professionals and others can use early identification for purposes of prevention. To begin such measures will require parent, teacher, and professional education, and a willingness among school administrators and state governments to use the technology and methods available to us. Gail Ryan observes, "Parents and school boards [and some religious groups] have sometimes been resistant to sex education (and even, in some instances, to sexual abuse prevention programs)."[27] She goes on to say, "However, parents and teachers do recognize their responsibility to validate and correct children's behavior. The problem has been that adults have not been well educated to understand sexual behaviors in the context of child development. Training on this topic has been welcomed and must be made widely available."

By shifting the way we think about sexual misbehavior to proactively reduce the risks of sexual victimization and perpetration, rather than focusing on punishment and the criminal aspects, the public's health and the child's sexuality can be protected. Less shame and stigma are attached to being ill than to being labeled criminal. People are more likely to step forward when they are not afraid of being attacked, shamed, ridiculed, or ostracized.

Early identification of sexual abuse victims and children who are "at risk" to act out in sexually abusive ways is a classic example of secondary prevention. By identifying children who need specialized therapy and/or education, the potential for sexually abusive behavior to be corrected or avoided stops the cycle of abuse.

Human Relations Training

In addition to teaching sex education to each generation, parents and both public and private school systems should develop a mandatory curriculum on human relations. Human relations is an important aspect of interpersonal communication, as well as a cornerstone of social functioning. Recent studies looking at outcome of adolescent sexual abuser treatment suggest that the success of these programs is in part attributed to enhancing self-esteem, social skills abilities, interpersonal skills, and self confidence among adolescent sexual abusers in treatment.[28]

---

[27] Gail Ryan, Facilitator. National Adolescent Perpetrator Network. Kempe Center, Denver CO. Personal communication July 21, 1997.

[28] Prentky, R., & Harris, B. Risk Assessment with juvenile sex offenders [workshop]. (1997, April 14). National Adolescent Perpetrator Conference Cherry Hill, N.J.

Healthy sexual relationships are based upon the ability of two persons to effectively communicate their likes, dislikes, desires, and needs in regard to the sexual experience. In addition, young persons who are prone to be taken advantage of sexually, abused sexually, or sexually harassed will be less likely to have these experiences if they can appropriately assert themselves and stand up for their rights. Human relations training can teach our future generations how to stand up for themselves, and be assertive (rather than aggressive or passive-aggressive) in obtaining what they need or want from others, including the right to have control of their body and their behavior.

The Pre-Sentence Alternative Program

The criminal justice system's lack of meaningful response to juvenile sex offending motivated one community in Vermont to act. Through a local collaboration between a law enforcement officer, a treatment provider, a state's attorney, a social service director, and a diversion director the Pre-Sentence Alternative Program (PSAP) was created.[29] This program allows citizens to participate in preventing future victims of child sexual abuse. Through early intervention PSAP holds the sexual abuser legally accountable and mandates specialized treatment.

Although PSAP evolved from the diversion model, a voluntary program for first-time offenders, its components are much more extensive. The incentive behind the program is that it offers the abuser the freedom to admit responsibility and get the treatment needed without earning a conviction record. Through treatment PSAP offers emotional restitution to victims, gives abusers the tools needed to understand and manage their abusive behavior, and keeps the community safe. Results are promising as PSAP has not had one reoffense from the clients that have successfully completed the treatment program.

The process works by pulling a cross-section of people from a community to meet and talk with the offender and help break the secrecy surrounding sexual abusing. Abusers meet with a review board consisting of community volunteers trained in understanding the complexity of sexual abuse. The review board works with abusers to change destructive behaviors and offer support for positive changes. The abuser knows he or she is going to be held accountable for past and present behavior. This accountability includes a consistent and truthful approach requiring a strict adherence to the rules of the program.

Initially a state's attorney will refer juveniles who have been charged with sexual assault or lewd and lascivious conduct to the program. The referral decision is made by following PSAP criteria:

---

[29] The Pre-Sentence Alternative Program, PO Box 761, Rutland, VT 05702, phone: (802) 775-7495.

- the perpetrator must have no prior convictions for sexual abuse,

- there was no use of excessive physical aggression in the current case, and

- the victim must agree to let the perpetrator use the alternative program rather than going to court.

All juveniles referred to PSAP must admit responsibility for the offense, either orally at a juvenile merit hearing or in writing if charged as an adult. The admission of guilt will be used to prosecute if the case is returned to court at a later date but will not be used against the abuser if not accepted into the program through no fault of his own. All juveniles must undergo a comprehensive psychosexual evaluation in order to determine appropriateness for outpatient community-based treatment.

All referred clients must be represented by a lawyer for the explanation of their legal rights. Abusers must accept certain limits to therapeutic confidentiality and give permission for information to be shared between the review board and their treatment provider. A parent or guardian of the abuser must agree to be involved in the treatment process. This involvement usually entails attendance at a monthly support group. The purpose is to open the channels of communication and offer education about sexual abuse issues.

The review board's decision to accept or reject the referral is based on the treatment provider's assessment of the abuser's risk to re-offend and amenability to outpatient treatment (amenability is willingness to cooperate, complete assignments and abide by program rules). It is crucial that victims and their families have input into the referral decision and the review board process. They are given an opportunity to share concerns and information with the review board.

Once accepted, the review board decides on contract conditions that must be met in order to complete this program. Common contract conditions include compliance with treatment recommendations, absolutely no baby-sitting (to reduce access to vulnerable children), no drugs or alcohol, not to be in the presence of anyone two or less years senior or two or more years junior without a responsible adult physically present. The abuser must also contribute to the victim's treatment fund in an amount determined by the review board.

The review board decides the frequency of meetings with the offender. At each meeting the board has reviewed and is prepared to discuss the progress reports from the therapist, family, and school. Abusers are asked about their progress, homework assignments for their group therapy, and any problems that may have occurred. Any contract violations may be cause for having their case returned to court for prosecution. Any new offense will result in immediate dismissal and return of the case to court for prosecution.

The therapist, the abuser's group, and the review board determine when an abuser has successfully completed the program. If treatment goals and restitution requirements are met, the case is returned to the state's attorney and the charge is dismissed without prejudice. This gives the attorney the right to re-file the original charge should the juvenile engage in further sexually abusive behavior within the statutes of limitations.

The PSAP is able to use community resources to hold a juvenile offender accountable:

- for breaking the silence surrounding sexual offending behaviors by involving the community,

- for restoring the victim and prevent future victims,

- to the family, therapy group, and treatment provider who offer support for the offender, and

- to the legal system which helps avoid denial and minimizing, while offering a cost-effective, meaningful alternative to the tradition criminal justice system.

The average case duration is 3.5 years. Abusers pay for their own treatment costs. The PSAP legally mandates treatment, holds the abuser accountable, and gives the abuser the opportunity to avoid criminal conviction.[30]

STOP IT NOW!

STOP IT NOW! is a national nonprofit organization established to introduce a new approach to prevent the sexual abuse of children.[31] What makes this organization so unique in its mission is to make child sexual abuse a recognized public health issue. Through public education, research, and policy changes, the organization is shifting people's attitudes and behaviors much as organizations have done around other public health issues such as drinking and driving, HIV/AIDS, and smoking.

STOP IT NOW! has founded its work on three premises:

First, that child sexual abuse can be prevented, and that the powerful tools of public health can change society's attitudes and actions regarding this issue.

Second, that adults need to take the burden of prevention off children's shoulders and put it where it belongs, with adults. Because most abused children are dependent on their abusers, putting children on the front line or prevention will not stop the abuse. The next step is to hold abusers directly accountable by encouraging them to stop, report the abuse, and get treatment.

The third guiding premise runs contrary to the current popular belief that abusers cannot change. Studies show that 89 percent of sexual abusers who

---

[30] The PSAP was founded and developed by Jan Levins the present Executive Director of the Safer Society Foundation, Inc.

[31] STOP IT NOW!; PO Box 495; Haydenville, Massachusetts. 01039 (413) 268-3096.

molest children can and will stop their harmful behavior if a) they are reached effectively, b) they complete a mental health treatment program for sexual abusers, and c) they maintain the necessary support to keep from abusing again.

Of particular interest is STOP IT NOW!'s public education pilot program called STOP IT NOW! VERMONT. Since 1992 STOP IT NOW! and a coalition of organizations and individuals throughout Vermont, have been working together to make STOP IT NOW! VERMONT a reality. STOP IT NOW! VERMONT is testing whether the tools of public health, which have been used so effectively to reduce serious social problems like drinking and driving, can be used to successfully prevent the sexual abuse of children. The program is testing whether abusers and potential abusers can be reached through a public health campaign, and whether the abuser or potential abuser will hold him or herself accountable to get into treatment to end abusive behaviors.

STOP IT NOW! VERMONT: A Model.

STOP IT NOW! VERMONT was launched as a pilot media and outreach campaign targeting abusers and potential abusers, adults who may know an abuser, and the parents of sexually abusing youth. Through news items, advertisements, public service announcements, brochures, workshops and conferences STOP IT NOW! VERMONT challenges each of these target audiences to confront the behaviors and take action. Through these media tools, STOP IT NOW! VERMONT brings a human face to this difficult issue. Media events have offered opportunities for survivors and recovering sexual abusers to speak together so that others can learn about the cycle of abuse and how to stop it. Other events give parents of sexually abusing youth the chance to talk with professionals about what resources are needed to prevent the sexual abuse.

The media and outreach program is designed to increase the public's awareness of the frequency and trauma of child sexual abuse. But the campaign is also designed to motivate each of the target audiences to action. The goals of the campaign are:

- to challenge abusers to stop their abuse immediately and seek treatment;

- to empower family, peers, and friends to confront abusing behaviors;

- to educate parents on the differences between healthy sexual development and sexual abuse and provide information about where to seek help; and

- to create a social climate that will not tolerate the sexual abuse of children and to build public knowledge about what to do when the warning signs of an abuser are visible.

One of the innovations of STOP IT NOW! VERMONT is a helpline for abusers, potential abusers, and people who may know an abuser to call for confidential information and help. (1-888-PREVENT.) The program does not provide amnesty, but gives information on treatment as well as a protocol to follow for turning themselves into the legal system and receiving treatment. Through the toll-free number, STOP IT NOW! VERMONT provides information about:

- resources for abusers who want to stop sexual abuse;

- information for people who may know an abuser and how to confront specific behaviors;

- information for any adult who cares about a child regarding the difference between healthy sexual development and sexually abusing behaviors;

- steps of the legal system for sexually abusing adults, adolescents, or children to take responsibility for their crimes;

- how to get effective treatment and the value of treatment for sexual abusers; and

- referrals to therapist and/or attorneys.

In addition, STOP IT NOW!, seeks to educate the public about sexual abuse, open avenues for the public to begin to talk about sexual abuse, and engages in outreach to further educate and assist individuals, organizations, and agencies about sexual abuse prevention and treatment.

In the first two years of the pilot program, nearly two thirds of the calls are people who identified themselves as abusers or people who may know an abuser (typically the caller knows both victim and abuser). As of the writing of this book, the full evaluation has not been complete. Anecdotally, the organization knows of at least a half-dozen abusers who have responded to the public messages and taken responsibility for their crimes and turned themselves into the legal system. Until now, no program has tried to reach this audience, nor tracked the number of abusers who will come forward. Initial results support the idea of opening doors adults and juveniles to take responsibility for their sexually abusing behaviors.

Abusers who call the helpline and turn themselves in to authorities are taking a monumental step in stopping the sexual abuse of children. But STOP IT NOW! VERMONT goes farther. STOP IT NOW! VERMONT is attempting to create an exception in society that it is valuable for friends and family to talk about child sexual abuse and confront behaviors that make them or others uncomfortable. To help with this part of the campaign, STOP IT NOW! VERMONT offers brochures and other materials that describe how to talk about sexual behaviors, list the warning signs of an abuser, and explain what to do if someone recognizes child sexual abuse.

Thanks to this innovative pilot effort, adults in Vermont have been learning how to intervene when they encounter child sexual abuse, abusers have called a helpline, and a few have come forward to turn themselves into the legal system for treatment. As more and more interventions are made before abuse occurs, STOP IT NOW! VERMONT promises to become one of the nation's glowing example of primary prevention.

Transformative Justice

While many Americans are quick to point out how ineffective our criminal justice system is, most turn to that same system for solutions with every increase in crime. More laws, more jails, and longer sentences is the never-ending solution. What is needed are some creative alternatives, some fresh new ideas.

One doesn't have to look far to find innovations in the delivery of justice. To our immediate north, Canadians, often led by their Aboriginal Peoples, have developed a variety of intervention strategies with sexual abusers. Many of their treatment and prevention strategies are summarized in *Satisfying Justice,* a publication of the Church Council on Justice and Corrections in Ottawa.[32]

Canadians, along with Australians and New Zealanders, make reference to restorative justice, transformative justice, and satisfying justice. All are quite similar and argue in support of greater victim and community involvement. Just as important is a diminished emphasis on adversarial court proceedings that increase tensions and do little to heal victims or abusers. Reconciliation and restitution are important components of most of these programs. Mediation is encouraged. Punishment is seen as a measure of despair that has little to do with justice and even less to do with healing the injured parties. Punishment is viewed as the deliberate infliction of pain, something abusers do but not something in which a community should become involved. Whenever reasonably possible, it is the desire of community justice teams to keep offenders in the community where "reintegrative" shame can be experienced. Abusers are expected to face the pain and humiliation brought on by their crimes and not have incarceration serve as an escape.

Citizens are re-empowered when the courts allow them the initiative for alternative sentencing. This becomes a labor-intensive process in which citizens must meet victims and abusers and participate in sentencing,

---

[32] Church Council on Justice and Corrections, (1996). Satisfying Justice. Ottawa, Ontario: Phoenix Creative Services. Copies can be obtained from Correctional Service of Canada at 1-800-665-8948 or fax orders to (613) 545-8247.

treatment, and probationary responsibilities. Psychologists and probation officers are often excluded from the process. By increasing community involvement it is much more difficult to pass the buck, leaving responsibility for the eradication of crime on the shoulders of law enforcement or the courts, groups all too easy to chastise for their ineffectiveness.

At a smaller level, some communities (especially in New Zealand and Canada) participate in family group conferencing. This approach to crime tends to bring smaller numbers of people together than do community-based programs. Usually the victim, the perpetrator, and their families come together to mediate solutions outside the courtroom. The goal is to connect or re-connect the abusers to family and community. Abusers may thereby feel more guilt, but at the same time, are less alienated. Always, as with any form of innovative justice programming, the ultimate goal is the restoration of social bonds and the reintegration of each affected person back into the community.

Other components of the new justice programs usually include:

- consensus decision-making

- emphasis on restitution

- avoiding the stigmatization of victims and offenders that happens when they are labeled by criminal justice and mental health systems (e.g., sex criminal, personality disordered)

- community graduation ceremonies for abusers who have successfully completed treatment (to celebrate their growth, healing, and re-integration).

In alternative programs of this kind, judges still retain ultimate authority. Yet, once they have explored a new justice program and have experienced the sweet taste of success, most happily abdicate much of their authority to the community as do prosecuting and defense attorneys[33] Money is saved, healing occurs, and perhaps most importantly, a sense of community is rekindled.

These are truly revolutionary approaches to justice. Yet, most have their origins in ancient aboriginal traditions that are being revisited and reworked to address the crimes of today. The solutions for the future have been right behind us where we are least inclined to look. It is time for us to investigate the solutions that other nations have developed. They offer us great hope.

---

[33] Ross, R. (1996). Returning to The Teachings: Exploring Aboriginal Justice. Toronto: Penguin Books.

Restorative Justice in the 21st Century

When our only tools for fighting crime are laws and prisons, we can expect they will be used to excess. This became apparent in March 1997 when the *Criminal Justice Newsletter* reported that one of every 20 Americans will serve time in prison during his or her lifetime.[34] When local jails or juvenile correctional facilities are added to the formula, it causes us to ask the question, "Will anyone, except parolees, be free to administer the prisons?" Clearly, we must search for new models that address crime in a more humane and effective fashion.

From a criminological perspective, there are few reasons to believe that the punishment model for addressing crime has made a significant difference in changing crime in America. If this were the case, we would be building fewer prisons, not more. We continue to hear stories about the revolving doors of America's prison system, but we have not heard the success story of imprisoning criminals. Many researchers attribute the recent decline in some violent crimes as a reflection of the aging of the baby-boomer population, not to tougher laws and criminal sanctions.

Many enlightened thinkers and criminal justice professionals have begun to turn to a model of criminal justice known as restorative justice. Restorative justice is a set of values recognizing the poor track record of prisons and tougher laws as a proven failure of the criminal justice system to turn around the crime wave in America. It takes into account the research and data being collected in America regarding the etiology of crime and then proposes realistic solutions, not emotional reactions to crime to alter its course.

The restorative justice model seeks to redefine crime and punishment and counters the retributive model we have been following for many years. It considers crime as an injury to the victim and the community, not primarily to the state. Restorative justice considers imprisonment as punishment with no restorative value to the victim of crime or the criminal.[35] As of 1995, the Edna McConnell Clark Foundation reported that "5 million people in the United States are under supervision of the criminal justice system, 1.5 million in prisons or jails, the rest on probation or parole."[36] The cost to build one prison bed and keep it filled with one prisoner for thirty years (the length of an average life sentence) is $665,000.[37]

---

[34] 1 out of 20 persons expected to serve prison time (1997, March 18). Criminal Justice Newsletter, p. 2.

[35] We recognize there will always be some sexual abusers who will need incarceration for the purpose of protecting the public even though restorative value may not be present.

[36] The Edna McConnell Clark Foundation. (1995). Seeking justice: Crime and punishment in America.. New York: Author. The Edna McConnell Clark Foundation's address is 250 Park Avenue, New York, NY 10017.

[37] Ibid.

Restorative justice seeks to heal victims and abusers while holding the abuser responsible for his or her actions and accountable to others. Communities become involved and the abuser is confronted with the fact that his or her behavior impacts the victim(s) and the community. Therefore, the abuser is encouraged to make restitution to the victim(s) and the greater community. Examples of restorative justice efforts include:

- Victim-offender mediation sessions: This process is less likely with stranger-to-stranger sexual abusers and is more common in cases that involve sexual abuse between family members, friends, and acquaintances.

- Victim restitution: This is a common approach used with sexual abusers, the abuser may be held responsible for paying the costs of his or her own treatment and that of the victim(s). Lacking these financial resources, the abuser may be required to participate in other activities such as community service and treatment efforts that somehow benefit the recovery of the victim (for example, letters of apology in which the abuser acknowledges his responsibility for his behavior and absolves the victim of responsibility or blame).

- Reconciliation and settlement: This method is not as likely to be used with many sexual abusers, although in those cases involving sexual abuse of family members, or victims known to the abuser, it may be more feasible.

- Victim input on conditions of probation and parole for the abuser: In this instance, the victims may strongly request or require that the abuser is mandated to participate in treatment.

- Community services that involve educating others about the wrongs of one's actions such as victim impact panels.

Assessment and treatment of sexual abusers is a component of a restorative justice model. Once a sexual abuser has pled guilty or has been found guilty of committing a sexual offense, and before sentencing, a comprehensive specialized psychosexual assessment should be performed by an experienced clinician who specializes in sexual abuser assessment and treatment. Sentencing of the convicted sexual abuser should take place after the evaluation so that risk, dangerousness, and amenability to treatment can be considered.

Differences between Restorative Justice and Retributive Justice

Retributive justice differs from restorative justice in that victims and the larger community play only a peripheral role, if they are included at all. The crime is against the state and the victim has limited input into the entire process. The crime is depersonalized, which does little to enhance the criminal's understanding of the impact of his criminal behavior on others. Restorative justice involves the victims and the community directly in the criminal justice process. The criminal is more likely to understand that the impact of his actions extend far beyond the victim of his crime.

• Retributive justice holds the criminal accountable to the state.	• Restorative justice holds the criminal accountable to the victim and to the community.
• Retributive justice maintains the crime is an act against the state.	• Restorative justice maintains that the crime is against the person and the community.
• Retributive justice endorses the criminal being held accountable and that accountability equals suffering and punishment. More punishment is considered more accountability to the crime.	• Restorative justice maintains that the criminal being accountable is the criminal taking responsibility for his actions by repairing the harm and achieving appropriate reparation.
• Retributive justice defines the offender by his deficits.	• Restorative justice defines the offender by his behavior.
• With retributive justice the efficacy of punishment is evaluated in two ways: 1) the threat of punishment deters crime, and 2) punishment changes behavior.	• Restorative justice pursues the efficacy of the system and is not punishment. It seeks to: 1) have the offender to be responsible for his behavior and 2) to repair the harm done to the victim and society.
• Retributive justice considers crime an individual choice.	• Restorative justice considers crime a product of both individual and social dimensions, and the community seeks to support the victims of crime.
• Retributive justice holds the criminal justice system responsible for controlling crime.	• Restorative justice seeks to prevent crime within the community.

Our desire to punish must be overcome if we are to overcome crime. Punishment all too often is a cloak for our desire to seek vengeance, in essence a desire to be criminal to criminals. It is a reflection of how the crime mentality has enveloped us. We are beginning to think like criminals. Karl Menninger, perhaps one of the most eminent criminologists of this century, advised us on this issue many years ago. It is time to revisit his theories and reconsider them.

With regard to punishment, Menninger wrote:

> Being against punishment is not a sentimental conviction. It is a logical conclusion drawn from scientific experience. It is also a professional principle; we doctors try to relieve pain, not cause it.[38]

The contemporary spirit of vengeance was with us over 30 years ago when Menninger also wrote:

> And just so long as the spirit of vengeance has the slightest vestige of respectability, so long as it pervades the public mind and infuses its evil upon the statute books of law, we will make no headway toward the control of crime.[39]

Beyond the ethics and morality of our decision making, there is the pragmatic perspective toward crime prevention. If we can take the time to examine how abusers think, we can begin to find our way out of this morass and we will end up aligned with the thinking of Menninger. For instance, knowing as we now do that shame is a propellant of crime, it makes no sense for judges to use public shaming media events to combat crime. Consequences work but humiliation does not. As James Gilligan warns:

> Nothing stimulates crime as powerfully and as effectively as punishment does (since punishment stimulates shame and diminishes guilt, and shame stimulates violence, especially when it is not inhibited by guilt).[40]

Additionally, most all addictionologists will agree that shame is probably the most powerful catalyst in a sexual addiction cycle. Why then, should we increase a sexual abuser's shame in our effort to contain his/her behavior? It is an approach that makes no sense and dangerously escalates assaultiveness.

Sexual abuse is wrong, but the unique logic behind it makes a twisted sort of sense. In other words, it becomes difficult for some individuals to understand healthy sexual behavior and the appropriate boundaries that maintain it when the messages and public images they are faced with often encourage abusive sexuality. Once understood, sexual abuse can be greatly reduced. It requires, however, a willingness to expend large amounts of time reaching out to both victims and abusers in an attempt to comprehend their experiences. It requires the public to understand and become involved in preventing sexual abuse. Understanding requires much more effort than punishment.

---

[38] Menninger, K. (1966). The crime of punishment, p. 204. New York: The Viking Press.

[39] Ibid., p. 218.

[40] Gilligan, J. (1996). Violence: Our deadly epidemic and its causes, p. 187. New York: Grosset/Putnam.

Summary

Given the scope and limits of this book, we have attempted to provide an overview of the sexual abuse problem in America and address it from a public health perspective. Its brevity in addressing certain issues kept our focus and task reasonable. Future editions of this book will continue to address these issues and make additional recommendations on how we may begin to prevent sexual abuse.

Few people disagree with the statistics that suggest criminal sexual abuse has reached epidemic proportions in our country; however, there is much disagreement and debate about the most effective ways to address this serious social problem and how we can best prevent it in the future.

We encourage you to look at the past 25 years and decide for yourself whether our current methods and strategies of creating tougher laws and punishing sexual abusers are resulting in a decrease in criminal sexual abuse. If your answer to this question is "no," please join your community in rethinking future directions and in supporting credible primary prevention of sexual abuse.

Punishment is not prevention. We believe the criminal justice system must play a role in sexual abuse prevention and treatment and that it must hold criminal sexual abusers accountable for their behavior. We do not believe that all sexual abusers should be handled the same manner because not all sexual abusers are the same. Some sexual abusers must be incarcerated because they pose a clear and immediate danger to others. But society and the criminal justice system should handle those low risk sexual abusers by using the restorative justice model.

There are several things individuals can do to involve themselves in sexual abuse prevention. Participating in public education prevention efforts such as developing or distributing educational materials is one way almost anyone can get involved. Organizing communities to prevent sex-for-sale businesses operating in neighborhoods and communities is another. Writing to television producers and major television networks about the nature of materials and sexual content of materials aired on television can begin to move networks and television programming in a different direction. Another is boycotting companies that promote products through sexualizing children and others. There are many opportunities for each of us to get involved.

We have reviewed the current strategies for preventing sexual abuse and briefly described promising new concepts and ideas that focus on primary prevention. These are but a few examples of how society can move in a more responsible direction regarding sexual abuse prevention. To reduce sexual abuse in America, citizens must work on preventing it from occurring. Prevention requires public education. We believe this is best accomplished by heeding the advice of the CDC, the AMA, the WHA, and the APA, who are now calling for violence and sexual violence to be addressed as a public health issue. Using a public health model holds tremendous promise today for reducing sexual abuse in America tomorrow. Prevention is not punishing a behavior after it occurs. Prevention is stopping the problem before it occurs.

All Truth Goes Through Three Stages,
First, it is ridiculed,
Second, it is violently opposed, and
Third, it is accepted as self-evident.
- Schopenhauer

The Hollow Water Experiment in Justice

A recent trip to a remote aboriginal village in Manitoba, Canada opened our eyes to new possibilities in the treatment of sexual abuse. In the dead of winter in 1997, the Hollow Water band of Ojibway Indians opened their doors, their lives, and their secrets for our examination. Here, far to the north of Winnipeg, we witnessed a unique method of addressing problems of sexual violence methods approved and supported by Crown (prosecuting) attorneys and several judges from across Canada. A method that stands in stark contrast to the legal and psychological systems widely accepted as the norm across Canada and the United States.

Like most cultures on the North American continent, the Ojibway have witnessed a rapid rise in interpersonal violence, usually accompanied by significant chemical abuse. Typically, Caucasian prosecutors, defense attorneys, judges, and psychologists intervened with conventional theories regarding the causes and treatment of these disorders. When the sexual violence continued unabated, aboriginal peoples went in search of new/old, traditional solutions for methods of healing that best resonated with their ancient beliefs.

With concerned amusement, the Hollow Water people watched the white mans' criminal justice system fail to apply justice to most victims and offenders. Instead of justice, they saw punishment being inflicted. Instead of healing, bitterness was created. Instead of cooperation, an adversarial process occurred. The Ojibway, among other first nation peoples, took it upon themselves to rethink the entire legal system beginning in 1984. By the early 1990's, a new model was in place that promised more familiar and perhaps even more effective strategies for healing. Rather than concentrating on the punishment of abusers, the new model focused on righting wrongs, restoring fractured interpersonal relationships, and returning social harmony to the entire community.

The Hollow Water people recognized that sexual abuse had an impact on the entire community, not just victims, perpetrators, and their families. A ripple effect of discomfort was spread throughout the community following each disclosure of abuse. Consequently, it was inadequate to provide support only to those most directly involved. The entire band was now going to be offered care to restore the harmony that was lost through abuse. This new/old approach would come to be referred to as the "justice as healing" project or as "sacred justice."

There are many features of this program which are nothing short of revolutionary. It dramatically contrasts with Western law's emphasis on the criminal act itself, the criminal as the exclusively responsible party, the desire for punishment and vengeance, lengthy periods of incarceration, fines, court orders, and the denial of treatment to denying abusers. Sacred justice believes that with every incident of abuse, there is community dysfunction at its root, which needs treatment. Abusers are encouraged to stay in the community and feel the shame arising from their acts. Jail is discouraged. Reconciliation is attempted in most situations.

Similarly, psychological intervention is handled uniquely. The Ojibway language, with its emphasis on verbs instead of nouns, is not accustomed to labeling people. In fact, the psychological practice of finding pathology in a diagnostic manual is thought to limit an individual's chance for growth, to "freeze" them at their present level of functioning. Rather than tend to the criminal act and how it can lead to a diagnostic label, aboriginals see relationships as the central diagnostic factor. The abuser has not arrived at this point of dysfunction but is an emerging being. He/she is on a path, moving-towards or about-to-emerge into a more healed existence.

Aboriginal healers believe such serious disorders are symptomatic of a serious rift in one's relationship to his/her fellow band members. Rather than send that person away to an isolated penitentiary, their answer is to infuse massive amounts of community support to restore their relationships to a healthy balance. While we seek to remove this lesion from our world, the Ojibway believe they must embrace this brother or sister and eliminate the abuser's feelings of alienation and disconnection. To Americans, a sex offender is beyond repair and must be caged far from victims and community. In

Hollow Water, a first-time violent criminal walks the streets and reports to fellow citizens who serve as probation officers.

The Ojibway believe antisocial acts demonstrate that people are no longer in healthy and supportive relationships with family, friends, and community. In the non-Native American community, committing a crime seems to mean that the individual is a bad person and therefore must be punished. In the Objiway view, the threat of incarceration prevents abusers from coming forward and taking responsibility for the hurt they are causing. It reinforces silence and secrecy, and therefore promotes rather than breaks the cycle of violence. The Native Canadian communities view a wrongdoing as a misbehavior or an area of ignorance that requires teaching, or an illness that requires healing.

Other differences in these two systems are quickly evident by glancing at the following table:

WESTERN LAW	TRADITIONAL LAW
1] Focus on criminal acts	1] Acts do not occupy center stage. Focus on restoration of relationships.
2] Seek punishment and vengeance.	2] Seek to teach, reconnect, and support.
3] Incarcerate before and after trial.	3] Stay in community, face the people, and avoid isolation.
	4] Reparation or amends.
4] Fine.	5] Team of trained peers and facilitators share power with the judge in a circle.
5] Judges hear the case from bench.	6] Acknowledge denial as part of offending.Focus on dynamics.
6] Push for admission of guilt.	
7] Label the abuser (criminally or psychologically)	7] Great care not to label. Labels minimize potential for change and are disrespectful.
8] Deny treatment to abuser while incarcerated.	8] Treat the community in every instance. If abuser is incarcerated, treat while in custody.
9] Pre-court motions and plea bargaining.	9] Pre-circle breakfast, smudging, sweats, prayers, and gifts.
10] Push to adjudicate in court with attorneys	10] Avoid court whenever possible. Court is unsafe environment that does not contribute to healing.
11] Western law made up of "thou shalt nots"	11] Teach what one should do; duties and obligations to one's community.
12] System intervenes after problems have developed.	12] Focus is on prevention.
13] Legal system is hierarchical.	13] Sacred justice system is circular and shares responsibility.
14] Psychological treatment (if any treatment is provided)	14] Spiritual treatment.

It is an expressed goal of the community healing team to avoid court for as long as possible while abusers gradually assume responsibility for their crimes. Unlike our legal system that pushes for immediate disclosure and refuses treatment to deniers, Ojibway healers recognize denial as a normal and expected part of brokenness that, if approached carefully, will diminish over time. Once responsibility is assumed by the abuser, court is scheduled.

Even the courtroom experience does not resemble the Western legal system. Judges at Hollow Water (and neighboring communities) do not sit on an elevated platform and rule from above. They join in a circle with the victim, the perpetrator, their respective families, and community members. All are equals who share in the process of shaping a court order. Anyone can speak at a sentencing circle with the goal of community consensus before them. The judge will formulate an order based on what has been said over a time period that can extend up to 14 hours.

A community notice of the sentencing hearing can draw as many as 250 of the region's 600 people to the band (community) hall. A guiding set of rules governs everyone's conduct at this highly emotional time. Everyone, perpetrator included, must be treated with kindness, dignity, and respect. Prior to sentencing, a sweat lodge ceremony is held for the perpetrator(s) and victim(s) to reflect and pray on their behavior. The band hall and courtroom are smudged with the smoke of sweet grass to invite the Creator's presence and form a sacred environment. A community breakfast is served to bring people together and promote good will.

In this environment of reverence, it is rare for a community member to ever recommend incarceration, even when faced with some of the most violent sex criminals. The Ojibway believe "Incarceration actually works against the healing process, because an already unbalanced person is moved further out of balance."[40] Furthermore, they contend jail is a place where abusers are likely to become more defiant, more self-centered, short-sighted, and untrusting. Additionally, because inmates have so many daily decisions made for them, their capacity for responsible decision making is diminished while incarcerated.

Sentences may entail individual healing by a specially trained paraprofessional from outside traditional counseling circles. Group therapy run by aboriginal paraprofessionals is an integral part of healing with male and female sexual abusers participating in the same groups. Reconciliation meetings and restitution are commonly instituted. Restitution might entail donating fish or game to the elderly or less fortunate. It may involve construction work or direct care to someone in crisis. In all things, however, a restoration of human relations and an increase in interpersonal contact is sought.

Once on the path to recovery, referred to as the healing path, one is joined by other community members who are on a similar journey. Little demarcation is made between the healers and those being healed, as everyone in Ojibway culture is thought to be in the constant process of unfolding into a healthier person. As Crown prosecutor Rupert Ross has written:

---

[40] Ibid.

Aboriginal healing processes constantly stress values like respect, sharing, humility, and so forth. It has to do with an understanding that the Healing Path is not something that 'sick' people need, totally 'healthy' people supervise, and the rest of us can largely ignore. It is a path we must all walk on. We all have healing contributions to make to others along the path, and others have healing contributions to make to us.[41]

An increased awareness of our interconnectedness with each other is necessary to buy into this system. To address only the isolated acts of solitary individuals is to miss the big picture and in all likelihood escalates the problem of sexual abuse. The fact that abusers visibly remain in the community reminds each Hollow Water resident of the ongoing need to address problems of sexual exploitation. Because the community is encouraged to participate so closely in the sacred justice system, sexual abuse is not a secret and is not inclined to be regarded as an exclusive problem belonging to just those persons committing the acts. With each crime the community renews its commitment to healing and growth, this serves to activate a prevention program that cultivates a more healthy culture that is designed to reduce future occurrences of abuse. These methods of community involvement far surpass the present-day efforts of "Megan's Law" community notification efforts.

The Hollow Water program has been in existence for only a few years. Consequently, there are no longitudinal research results that can attest to its success. For now we are left with anecdotal accounts of the healing project's effect on individuals and the community. Our personal observation of a limited number of recovering men and women gives us encouragement. It may be the United States, like Canada, will have to re-examine its criminal justice system and the psychology industry. We may find the common sense and community participation seen in remote aboriginal tribes may have revolutionary application in our own treatment system. Nothing short of dramatic change in our current system will begin to heal the communities that spawn sexual abuse. That change will require an open mind and a look to the past if the future is to be seen clearly.

We are delighted that you have chosen to read this book. After reading it, we encourage you to do your part, whatever that means for you, to help fight the problem of sexual abuse. It may be as simple as passing this book on to a friend. If each of us makes a personal effort to stop sexual abuse, we will have come a little closer to creating a safer society.

---

[41] Ibid.

If you have information about the sexual abuse problem or ideas and information regarding new and innovative prevention strategies, we would very much like to hear from you. You can mail your ideas or information to: Robert E. Freeman-Longo and Geral Blanchard; Sexual Abuse In America, PO Box 340, Brandon, Vermont 05733 or fax it to Sexual Abuse In America (802) 247-4233.

TABLE 1 - OFFENDER DEMOGRAPHICS

SAMPLE - Child Molesters (C.M.) =30 Rapists (R) = 23 Total N = 53

ITEM	C.M.	R	N
Age at time of first offense	15	18	16
Age at time of first arrest	28	23	26
Age at time of first conviction	28	24	26
Age at time of first incarceration	29	24	27
Age at time of present treatment	34	30	32
Number of prior arrests for sex offenses	1.5	1.9	1.7
Number of prior sex offense convictions	1.6	1.7	1.7
Number of prior incarcerations	0.4	0.7	0.5
Total number of arrests for sex offenses	45.0	43.0	88.0
Total number of convictions for sex offenses	49.0	40.0	89.0

TABLE 2 - OFFENSE DATA

OFFENDER TYPE	#RAPE	#C.M.	#EXH	#VOY	#OBP	#FROT	TOTAL	N
Child Molesters	213	5891	2193	9314	404	2652	20,667	30
Rapists	178	319	757	3341	152	343	5,090	23
TOTALS	391	6210	2950	12655	556	2995	25,757	53

CRIME	# CRIMES	# VICTIMS	% VICTIMS
Rape	391	330	01.90%
Child Molestation	6210	8700	5.00%
Exhibitionism	2950	2150	12.36%
Voyeurism	12,655	10557	60.70%
Obscene Phone Calls	556	540	03.11%
Frottage	2995	2945	16.93%
TOTALS	25757	17392	100.00%

FREEMAN-LONGO, 1985

TABLE 3 - CHILD MOLESTATION VICTIM DATA

CHILD MOLESTERS
Victim (female)

Age	0-5	6-12	13-17	N
	61	221	48	330

Victim (male)

Age	0-5	6-12	13-17	N
	26	443	48	517

RAPISTS
Victim (female)

Age	0-5	6-12	13-17	N
	2	8	7	17

Victim (male)

Age	0-5	6-12	13-17	N
	0	6	0	6

Female Child Victims - 347 = 40%
Male Child Victims - 523 = 60%
FREEMAN-LONGO, 1985

TABLE 4 - RAPE VICTIM DATA

CHILD MOLESTERS
Victim (female)

Age	0-5	6-12	13-17	18-30	31-50	51+	N
	3	28	4	7	2	0	84

Victim (male)

Age	0-5	6-12	13-17	18-30	31-50	51+	N
	3	84	7	1	0	0	95

RAPISTS
Victim (female)

Age	0-5	6-12	13-17	18-30	31-50	51+	N
	1	8	27	79	11	0	126

Victim (male)

Age	0-5	6-12	13-17	18-30	31-50	51+	N
	0	0	5	20	0	0	25

FREEMAN-LONGO, 1985

• APPENDIX B •

WHAT CONSTITUTES AN ETHICAL VS. UNETHICAL THERAPEUTIC RELATIONSHIP

Signs of an Ethical Therapist:

1. The therapist politely spells out the professional parameters of the counseling experience (e.g., no social relations, no romantic encounters, etc.).

2 The therapist allows clients to work at their own pace as well as on the issues that they believe have direct bearing on their situations. The client's ideas are incorporated into the counseling plan.

3. The therapist does not attempt to make clients unnecessarily dependent on him/her. The goal of therapy is frequently communicated: To not need therapy.

4. Clients are not badgered to share unnecessarily explicit details about their lives or sexuality.

5. The therapist's intentions are always clear, logical, and understandable.

6. The therapist is warm, caring, and supportive but always in a professional way. Clients sense he/she respects their need not to be touched, to receive reassuring contact, or to be given space.

7. His/her interactions with other patients are consistent and quite similar - always warm, but consistently professional.

8. Clients are challenged and confronted from time to time. Disagreements are acknowledged. Clients are pushed when necessary. In other words, the client's growth is always paramount. The therapist's image and needs do not need the client's attention. The client remains the priority.

9. The client is treated as an equal. The therapist doesn't position herself/himself on a pedestal. The client and therapist are professional partners working together on an important task.

10. The therapist requests supervision and/or consultation as a routine part of therapy. Therapy is not done in total isolation.

Signs of an Unethical Therapist:[42,43]

1. He/she tells the client what he or she needs (e.g., a hug, a home visit, more sex, etc.).

2. He/she shows favoritism to a particular client (e.g., permission to call his/her home after hours, reduced fees, rides home, etc.) much like an incestuous father might build feelings of obligation or indebtedness in his child.

3. Sessions routinely run long even when the client doesn't feel and hasn't expressed a special need for the time.

4. The therapist discloses very personal information to clients about his/her life, sexuality, or relationships.

5. The therapist positions him/herself as something of a guru, a maverick, or as someone who has exclusive access to "the cure."

6. The client feels obligated to return for check-ups long after termination seemed merited. The client begins to feel like he or she is taking care of the therapist's needs - much like children in incestuous situations often feel.

7. The therapist seems depressed and unfulfilled.

8. All therapeutic issues seem to take on sexual importance; non-sexual issues are quickly dismissed.

9. The therapist wants to get to know the client within the community - as a friend, luncheon date, or as a recreational partner.

10. The therapist touches the client in a way that feels confusing, sexual, or inappropriate.

[42] Blanchard, G. (1991). The role of sexual addiction in the sexual exploitation of patients by male psychiatrists. American Journal of Preventive Psychiatry & Neurology, 3(1), 24-27.

[43] Peterson, M. (1992). At personal risk. New York: W. W. Norton & Company.

About the Authors

Robert E. Freeman-Longo, MRC, LPC, CCJS

ROBERT E. FREEMAN-LONGO, is Director/Publisher of the Safer Society Press, a nonprofit press and project of the Safer Society Foundation, Inc. He is an international consultant in the field of sexual abuser assessment, treatment, and program development, and is founder and first President of the Association for the Treatment of Sexual Abusers.

Rob was the director of the Sex Offender Correctional Treatment Program, Mental Health Division, Oregon State Hospital, Salem, Oregon from April 1983 through August 1989. He was formerly the Director of the Sex Offender Unit, North Florida Evaluation and Treatment Center; Gainesville, Florida and consultant to the sex offender programs for the State of Florida. He currently spends one day per week treating adolescent sexual abusers.

Rob has trained professionals in law enforcement, mental health, protective service agencies, victim advocate programs, and the judicial system internationally. He is a consultant and trainer for the National Institute of Corrections and has helped develop sexual abuser treatment programs throughout the United States, and in Australia, Canada, and New Zealand.

In addition, Rob has published more than thirty articles and chapters in the field of sexual abuse treatment, and pioneered the Safer Society Press sexual abuser workbook series. He is the coauthor of the books *Who Am I And Why*

Am I In Treatment?, Why Did I Do It Again?, How Can I Stop?, Empathy & Compassionate Action, Men & Anger: Understanding and Managing Your Anger for a Much Better Life, and has coauthored the Safer Society's biennial Nationwide Surveys of Sex Offender Treatment Programs & Models since 1992. He is also co-presenter on the Safer Society Press videos *Relapse Prevention For Sex Offenders* and *A Structured Approach To Preventing Relapse: A Guide For Sex Offenders.*

Rob serves as the media representative for The Association for the Treatment of Sexual Abusers, the public relations person for the Safer Society Foundation, and is a media commentator on sexual abuse prevention and treatment. Rob and the director and staff of the Safer Society Foundation, Inc. have worked extensively with the media to help educate the public about the sexual abuse problem and sex offender treatment. He has appeared on numerous television news magazines and radio and television talk shows, and served as technical consultant to the ABC-TV movie *The Face of Rage,* and the HBO documentary *Rapists: Can They Be Stopped?* based upon the program he directed in Oregon.

Rob has specialized in the sexual abuse field and has worked with victims, and with juvenile and adult sex abusers in residential hospital, prison, and community-based settings since 1976.

Geral T. Blanchard, M.A.

GERAL BLANCHARD is a private consultant and program development specialist in the field of interpersonal violence. For over 25 years he counseled both victims and perpetrators of sexual violence.

Geral was the first person to conduct research on the prevalence of sexual addiction among sexual abuser populations. He was also the first person in the United States to teach college courses on incest and incest treatment.

Geral has also taught internationally on the subjects of sexual abuse and child protection for the American Association for Protecting Children of Denver, Colorado and at the Institute for Behavioral Medicine of Golden Valley, Minnesota.

Additionally, Geral has developed treatment programs for perpetrators and victims of domestic violence. He has assisted in the development of sexual abuse treatment programs for victims and perpetrators throughout the United States, as well as in Canada and Sweden. He is a regular consultant at the Wyoming State Penitentiary in Rawlins and currently is cooperating in creation of an innovative sexual abuser treatment program at that facility.

Many of his professional publications on interpersonal violence have appeared in psychiatric, social work, human sexuality, pastoral psychology, child protection, and group work journals. Geral has published five treatment manuals and two previous books on sexual abuse entitled *Sex Offender Treatment: A Psychoeducational Model* and *The Difficult Connection: The Therapeutic Relationship in Sex Offender Treatment.*

Geral has appeared on both regional and national radio and television programs sharing his optimism regarding the successful treatment of sexual abuse victims and perpetrators. He served as a technical consultant for the Arnold Shapiro television production, *Scared Silent,* and has been contributor to Redbook magazine on the subject of child sexual abuse.

Geral now resides in the Big Horn Mountains of Wyoming and maintains an office in nearby Sheridan.

Act Now to Prevent Child Sexual Abuse!

The Safer Society Foundation, Inc., is a nonprofit national organization committed to sexual abuse prevention and treatment. The Safer Society has been working in the area of sexual abuse prevention and treatment since 1976. Two dollars ($2.00) from the sale of each copy of SEXUAL ABUSE IN AMERICA is directly applied to child sexual abuse prevention.

Your donation, no mater how great or how small, will be directly applied toward the Safer Society Foundation's efforts at preventing child sexual abuse.

If you are interested in making a personal donation to The Safer Society Foundation, Inc., for preventing child sexual abuse or for the many other areas of our work, please make a copy of the next page, fill it out, and mail it with your donation to: The Safer Society Foundation, Inc.; PO Box 340; Brandon, Vermont 05733-0340.

I am interested in supporting efforts to prevent child sexual abuse. Please accept my enclosed tax deductible donation in the amount of $ to further the Safer Society Foundation's efforts to prevent child sexual abuse.

Name

Address

City

State

Zip

Day time phone:

Evening Phone:

Please apply my contribution toward:

Please make checks payable to Safer Society Foundation Child Abuse Fund; PO Box 340; Brandon, Vermont 05733-0340.

You can also make a donation on your credit card. In addition to the information above, please fill out the following. The Safer Society Foundation accepts Visa or MasterCard.

☐   Visa

☐   MasterCard

Account #

Expiration date:

Your name as it appears on your card:

Signature

Safer Society Publications

Tell It Like It Is: A Resource for Youth In Treatment by Alice Tallmadge and Galyn Foster (1998). $15.00.

When You Don't Know Who To Call: A Consumer's Guide to Selecting Mental Health Care by Nancy Schaufele, M.S.W., and Donna B. Kennedy (1998). $15.00

Back on Track: Boys Dealing with Sexual Abuse by Leslie Bailey Wright and Mindy Loiselle (1997). $14. A workbook for boys ages 10 and up. Foreword by David Calof.

Assessing Sexual Abuse: A Resource Guide for Practitioners edited by Robert Prentky and Stacey Bird Edmunds (1997). $20.

Impact: Working with Sexual Abusers edited by Stacey Bird Edmunds (1997). $15.

Supervision of the Sex Offender by Georgia Cumming and Maureen Buell (1997). $25. Practical manual for probation/parole officers, court and treatment personnel, police, families and others.

STOP! Just for Kids: For Kids with Sexual Touching Problems Adapted by Terri Allred and Gerald Burns from original writings of children in a treatment program (1997) $15.

Shining Through: Pulling It Together After Sexual Abuse (Second Edition) by Mindy Loiselle & Leslie Bailey Wright (1997). $14. A workbook for girls ages 10 and up. Revised edition includes sections on sexuality, self-esteem, and body image.

A Primer on the Complexities of Traumatic Memories of Childhood Sexual Abuse: A Psychobiological Approach by Fay Honey Knopp & Anna Rose Benson (1997) $25.

The Last Secret: Daughters Sexually Abused by Mothers by Bobbie Rosencrans (1997). $20.

37 to One: Living as an Integrated Multiple by Phoenix J. Hocking (1996). $12.

The Brother / Sister Hurt: Recognizing the Effects of Sibling Abuse by Vernon Wiehe, Ph.D. (1996) $10.

Men & Anger: Understanding and Managing Your Anger for a Much Better Life by Murray Cullen & Rob Freeman-Longo. Revised and updated, new self-esteem chapter. (1996). $15.

When Children Abuse: Group Treatment Strategies for Children with Impulse Control Problems by Carolyn Cunningham and Kee MacFarlane. (1996). $28.

Empathy and Compassionate Action: Issues & Exercises: A Workbook for Clients in Treatment by Robert Freeman-Longo, Laren Bays, & Euan Bear (1996). Fourth workbook in a series of four for adult sex offenders. $12.

Adult Sex Offender Assessment Packet by Mark Carich & Donya Adkerson (1995). $8.

The Difficult Connection: The Therapeutic Relationship in Sex Offender Treatment by Geral T. Blanchard (1995). $10.

From Trauma to Understanding: A Guide for Parents of Children with Sexual Behavior Problems by William D. Pithers, Alison S. Gray, Carolyn Cunningham, & Sandy Lane (1993). $5.

Adolescent Sexual Offender Assessment Packet by Alison Stickrod Gray & Randy Wallace (1992). $8.

The Relapse Prevention Workbook for Youth in Treatment by Charlene Steen (1993). $15.

Pathways: A Guided Workbook for Youth Beginning Treatment by Timothy J. Kahn (Revised Edition 1997). $15.

Pathways Guide for Parents of Youth Beginning Treatment by Timothy J. Kahn (Revised Edition 1997). $8.

Man-to-Man, When Your Partner Says NO: Pressured Sex & Date Rape by Scott Allen Johnson (1992). $6.50.

When Your Wife Says No: Forced Sex in Marriage by Fay Honey Knopp (1994). $7.

Female Adolescent Sexual Abusers: An Exploratory Study of Mother-Daughter Dynamics with Implications for Treatment by Marcia T. Turner & Tracey N. Turner (1994). $18.

Who Am I & Why Am I in Treatment? A Guided Workbook for Clients in Evaluation and Beginning Treatment by Robert Freeman-Longo & Laren Bays (1988; 8th printing, 1997). $12. First workbook in a series of four for adult sex offenders. Also available in Spanish.

Why Did I Do It Again? Understanding My Cycle of Problem Behaviors by Laren Bays & Robert Freeman-Longo (1989; 6th printing, 1995). Second in the series. $12.

How Can I Stop? Breaking My Deviant Cycle by Laren Bays, Robert Freeman-Longo, & Diane Hildebran (1990; 5th printing, 1995). Third in the series. $12.

Adults Molested As Children: A Survivor's Manual for Women & Men by Euan Bear with Peter Dimock (1988; 4th printing). $12.95.

Family Fallout: A Handbook for Families of Adult Sexual Abuse Survivors by Dorothy Beaulieu Landry, M.ED.. (1991). $12.95.

Embodying Healing: Integrating Bodywork and Psychotherapy in Recovery from Childhood Sexual Abuse by Robert J. Timms, Ph.D., and Patrick Connors, CMT. (1992). $15.00.

The Safer Society Press is part of The Safer Society Foundation, Inc., a 501(c)3 nonprofit agency dedicated to the prevention and treatment of sexual abuse. We publish additional books, audiocassetttes, and training videos related to sexual abuse prevention and treatment. For a catalog of our complete listings, please check the box on the order form (next page).

Order Form

SHIPPING ADDRESS:

Date: _____

☐ *Please send a catalog.*

Name and/or Agency _____

Street Address _____

City _____ State _____ Zip_____

Billing Address (if different from shipping address):

Address_____

City _____ State _____ Zip_____

Daytime Phone (_____)_____

Purchase Order # _____

Visa or MasterCard # _____ Exp. Date _____

Qty	Title	Unit Price	Total Cost

Sub Total	
VT residents add sales tax	
Shipping (see below)	
TOTAL	

Make checks payable to:
Safer Society Press

US FUNDS ONLY.

*All prices subject to change
without notice.*

Mail to:
Safer Society Press
PO Box 340
Brandon, VT 05733-0340
(802) 247-3132

Shipping:
1- 9 items add $5 for shipping & handling.
10 or more, add 8% for shipping & handling.

Rush Orders:
add $10.00 and call for actual shipping charges.

Bulk order discounts available.

Phone orders accepted with VISA/MasterCard.